craigslist®
4
Everyone

Jenna Lloyd
Sherry Kinkoph Gunter

Que

800 East 96th Street,
Indianapolis, Indiana 46240 USA

craigslist 4 Everyone

Copyright © 2009 by Que Publishing

ISBN-13: 978-0-7897-3828-8
ISBN-10: 0-7897-3828-7

Library of Congress Cataloging-in-Publication Data

Lloyd, Jenna.

  Craigslist 4 everyone / Jenna Lloyd.

    p. cm.

  Includes index. 39282347   12/08
  ISBN 978-0-7897-3828-8

  1. Craigslist.com (Firm) 2. Internet advertising. 3. Internet marketing. 4. Online social networks. I. Title. II. Title: Craigslist for everyone.

  HF6146.I58L66 2009

  658.8'72—dc22

             2008040862

Printed in the United States of America

First Printing: October 2008

Trademarks

Warning and Disclaimer

Bulk Sales

Que Publishing offers excellent discounts on this book when ordered in quantity for bulk purchases or special sales. For more information, please contact

    U.S. Corporate and Government Sales

    1-800-382-3419

    corpsales@pearsontechgroup.com

For sales outside the United States, please contact

    International Sales

    international@pearson.com

Associate Publisher
Greg Wiegand

Acquisitions Editor
Michelle Newcomb

Development Editor
Robin Drake

Managing Editor
Patrick Kanouse

Senior Project Editor
Tonya Simpson

Copy Editor
Chuck Hutchinson

Indexer
Ken Johnson

Proofreader
Kathy Ruiz

Technical Editor
Vince Averello

Publishing Coordinator
Cindy Teeters

Book Designer
Anne Jones

Compositor
Bronkella Publishing

Contents at a Glance

Foreword

Introduction

Part I: craigslist 101

1   Putting craigslist on the Map 7

2   Welcome to the Neighborhood 17

3   Safety First 43

Part II: Posting on craigslist

4   All About the Listings 61

5   Successful Listing Strategies 77

6   Listing in the Community 91

7   Listing in the Housing Section 113

8   Listing in For Sale 139

9   Listing in Services 159

10   Listing in Jobs and Gigs 187

11   Listing in Resumes 207

12   Listing in Personals 225

Part III: The Other Side of craigslist

13   Responding to Listings 245

14   Keeping Busy with Listings 253

15   Win-Win Results in Listings 277

Index 301

Table of Contents

Foreword xii

Introduction 1
   How This Book Is Organized 2
   Conventions Used in This Book 3
      Capitalization and Special Formatting 3
      Web Page Addresses 3
      Special Elements 4
   Let Me Know What You Think 4

I   CRAIGSLIST 101 5

1   Putting craigslist on the Map 7
   A Simple Idea 7
   The Best of Intentions 8
   Looking into the Future 11
   Who Is Craig Newmark? 12
      Craig's Vision 12
      Change of Focus 13
      Nerd Values 13
      David and Goliath 14
      One to Watch 14
   Craigslist Foundation: "Helping People Help" 15
   From Here… 16

2   Welcome to the Neighborhood 17
   Navigating the Home Page 19
      Finding Your Way Home 19
   Joining the Community 20
      Creating a Craigslist Account 20
   Getting Around Town 24
      Exploring Your Neighborhood 25
      For Inquiring Minds 27
      Getting Involved 30
   The Town Square 31
      Giving Yourself a Handle 33
      Getting Involved 35
      Dressing Up Your Posts 39
      Staking Your Claim 40

Roadside Assistance 41

Follow the Rules 42

From Here... 42

3   Safety First **43**

Internet Safety 43

Secure Your Computer 43

Protect Your Information 45

Spot Scammers Before They Spot You 48

Out-of-Area Buyer 49

Overpayment Scam 53

Nigerian 4-1-9 Scam 53

Safe and Pleasant Transactions 54

Safe and Sound Online Dating 55

From Here... 58

II   POSTING ON CRAIGSLIST **59**

4   All About the Listings **61**

Anatomy of a Listing 62

Playing By the Rules 64

The Posting Process 65

Getting Creative 73

The craigslist Police 74

Editing and Deleting Posts 76

From Here... 76

5   Successful Listing Strategies **77**

Example of an Unsuccessful Listing 78

Steps for Creating a Successful Listing 78

Step 1: Educate Yourself 79

Step 2: Set Your Goal(s) 80

Step 3: Take Pictures 81

Step 4: Write a Listing That Addresses Your Goal(s) 85

Strategies in Action 88

From Here... 89

6   Listing in the Community **91**

Get Out There: Activities 92

Get Together: Events, Classes, and Groups 93

Events 95

Classes 95

Groups 96

Find What's Missing: Lost+Found 98
Express Yourself: Artists and Musicians 100
Take Care of Baby: Childcare 102
What's Happening: Local News, Politics, and General 104
Live Green: Rideshares 105
Get the Help You Need: Volunteers 107
Pets: A Controversial Issue 108
From Here… 112

7 Listing in the Housing Section **113**

Selling Solo 114
Move That Property in Real Estate for Sale 115
    An Agent's Best Friend 115
    What Do You Have to Offer? 116
    What's Going on Next Door? 120
    Map Out Your Information 121
Talk the Talk 121
    Focus on Your Target 127
    Leave Them Wanting More 128
    Put It on Paper 131
    A Flashing Neon Sign 132
    A Picture Is Worth… 133
Filling a Vacancy 133
Office/Commercial Property 135
    Know Your Business 135
    Location, Location, Location 136
    Getting It "Write" 136
Parking/Storage Rental 137
From Here… 137

8 Listing in For Sale **139**

Looking Through the For Sale Categories 140
Planning Your Ad 143
Writing Great Ads 146
    Writing a Great Posting Title 147
    Writing a Great Posting Description 148
    Tips for Category-Specific Listings 150
Ad Posting Basics 153
Responding to Contacts 156
Advertising No-No's 157
From Here… 158

9   Listing in Services **159**

Phone Verification 160
Planning Your Marketing 164
Don't Keep Reinventing the Wheel 166
Before You Do Anything Else 167
Put On Your Advertising Exec Hat 167
Ready to Write! 168
Offering Free Content 168
Automotive Services 169
Beauty Services 170
Computer Services 171
Creative Services 172
Erotic Services 174
Event Services 174
Financial Services 175
Household Services 176
Labor and Moving Services 177
Legal Services 178
Lessons and Training 179
Real Estate Services 180
Skilled Trade Services 180
Small Business Ads 181
Therapeutic Services 182
Travel and Vacation Services 183
Writing, Editing, and Translating Services 184
From Here... 185

10   Listing in Jobs and Gigs **187**

Comparing Online Job Resources 187
Looking Through Job Categories 188
Writing a Successful Job Listing 193
Listing Basics 193
Beyond Basics 195
Posting a Job Listing 197
Posting Gigs 203
Responding to Applicants 205
From Here... 206

11   Listing in Resumes **207**

Knowledge Is Power 208
Your Most Important Sale 208
Dealing with Job Search Jitters 209

What to Look For 210
Where to Look 211
What to Do with the Information 213
Your Features and Benefits 214
It's All in the Numbers 215
Define Your Marketing Strategy 216
Create a Killer Resume 216
From the Top 220
Getting It All Down 221
From Here... 224

12 Listing in Personals **225**

Deciphering the Code 227
What Do You Really Want? 230
Nine Secrets for Successful Online Relationships 232
Igniting Sparks 236
Thinking Long-Term 237
Thinking Short-Term 237
Strictly Platonic: Making New Friends 238
Missed Connections: Finding Someone Who Caught
Your Eye 239
Rants and Raves: Expressing Yourself 240
Put It in Writing 241
From Here... 242

III THE OTHER SIDE OF CRAIGSLIST **243**

13 Responding to Listings **245**

Locating What You Want 245
How to Reply 251
From Here... 252

14 Keeping Busy with Listings **253**

Enriching Your Life with the Community 253
Activities 255
Artists 256
Childcare 257
General 258
Groups 259
Pets 260

Events 261

Lost and Found 262

Musicians 263

Local News 263

Politics 264

Rideshare 264

Volunteers 265

Classes 266

Catapult Your Career in Jobs and Gigs 266

Job Search Tips 267

Perusing the Job Listings 268

Perusing the Gigs 270

Responding to Job Listings 271

Fill Your Social Calendar with the Personals 272

Warning: Enter at Your Own Risk 272

Personals Categories: Something for Everyone 275

From Here… 276

15 Win-Win Results in Listings **277**

Find Your New Abode in Housing 278

Looking for Houses or Apartments to Rent 280

Finding Rooms or Roommates 281

Seeking Sublets or Temporary Spots 282

Housing Wanted 283

Swapping Houses 284

Finding Vacation Rentals 285

Searching for Storage Space 287

Looking for Commercial Space 287

Real Estate for Sale 289

Let's Make a Deal in Merchandise 291

Get It Done with Services 295

Fill That Job Opening in Resumes 299

From Here… 300

Index **301**

About the Author

Jenna Lloyd is a leading authority on online marketing and an expert in multichannel retailing. As head of Applied Force Marketing (www.appliedforcemarketing.com), she works hands-on with small and large businesses to create and implement powerful marketing strategies that quickly increase her clients' sales and profits.

Ms. Lloyd also works as a freelance business writer and editor. In addition to writing highly effective marketing and advertising copy, Ms. Lloyd has been the technical editor of several books for Que Publishing. She has used craigslist successfully in her business and personal life since 2001 and includes it as a part of a comprehensive marketing strategy for all of her clients.

Dedication

The book is dedicated to Alec, Ian, Ana, John, and Glen—the greatest family and cheerleading squad any person could ask for.

Acknowledgments

First and foremost, I want to thank my amazing editor, Michelle Newcomb. There are no words to describe my appreciation for Michelle's talent, support, patience, and belief in me, all well above and beyond the call of duty.

Many thanks to author Michael Miller, who introduced me to the world of publishing and to Michelle. Thanks to development editor Robin Drake and technical editor Vince Averello, who helped me gain clarity when things got fuzzy, and to the wonderfully supportive team at Que, including Vince Mayfield, Tonya Simpson, and Chuck Hutchinson. Also, thanks to Jeff Zeak, Dr. Harlan Kilstein, Mike Morgan, Anthony Coyne, Leah Carson, and Jay Simcic for their positive influences on me and this book. Thank you to Alec Williamson for providing the photographs used in this book.

And a special thanks to Craig Newmark for providing feedback on the outline and chapters in this book.

We Want to Hear from You!

As the reader of this book, *you* are our most important critic and commentator. We value your opinion and want to know what we're doing right, what we could do better, what areas you'd like to see us publish in, and any other words of wisdom you're willing to pass our way.

As an associate publisher for Que Publishing, I welcome your comments. You can email or write me directly to let me know what you did or didn't like about this book—as well as what we can do to make our books better.

Please note that I cannot help you with technical problems related to the topic of this book. We do have a User Services group, however, where I will forward specific technical questions related to the book.

When you write, please be sure to include this book's title and author as well as your name, email address, and phone number. I will carefully review your comments and share them with the author and editors who worked on the book.

Email: feedback@quepublishing.com

Mail: Greg Wiegand
Associate Publisher
Que Publishing
800 East 96th Street
Indianapolis, IN 46240 USA

Reader Services

Visit our website and register this book at informit.com/register for convenient access to any updates, downloads, or errata that might be available for this book.

Foreword

I started craigslist as a service to share information with my friends and neighbors. Now craigslist is a platform where over 50 million people, living in some 550 cities located in over 50 countries, help each other get through the day. Our focus is on everyday needs like getting a job or place to live, connecting with other people, or maybe selling or finding new stuff.

From one perspective, we're like a flea market, which is as much about community as it is about commerce. craigslist is a marketplace in the ancient sense—"chaotic, sometimes unruly, and vividly human" writes Penelope Green of the *New York Times*. "craigslist is about us, not them," wrote David Weinberger, regarding community perception.

Our community and company have built a culture of trust, where the usual trustworthiness of people effectively works. That trust derives from a near-universal shared value—the notion that you should treat people like you want to be treated. Sure, that's a platitude, but we transform it by putting everyday practice into a real way of doing business. Like any community, there are some bad people out there, so be careful, but those are a tiny fraction of humanity, and the overwhelming majority of well-intentioned people help detect and counteract the bad guys.

craigslist is a serious business that offers a serious community service. We're not altruistic, noble, or pious, we just follow through with our values. As a business, we feel that we do well by doing good for our members. We follow through on shared values, each and every day. That means that much of our decision-making is driven by community needs, not our personal needs and desires.

We hope this book helps you gain a better understanding of how to get the most of these values within your own craigslist community, no matter where you live. And in that vein, we ask for your help to keep us following through on our commitment to our community values. We welcome your participation and feedback as one of the craigslist community members.

Have fun!

—Craig Newmark
craig@craigslist.org

Introduction

In an online world crammed with flash, hype, and fly-by-night, Craig Newmark has grown a single good intention into one of the top 50 most visited websites in the world! With more than 40 million users to craigslist a month, a lot is happening there. And this book will help you to make the most of all of it.

You won't find a better site to buy, sell, or advertise on than craigslist. Think about it: Where else can you sell a $5 kids' toy, a $15,000 car, or a $500,000 house without paying to list or handing over a chunk of change from the selling price? Find a date, find a friend, or find your lost dog without spending a dime. Market your business, join a class, or land your dream job without ever leaving the site. And those are only a few of the many possibilities.

Think of craigslist as the online gathering place for your offline activities—a way for you to connect with other people in your area. Whatever you want to accomplish, craigslist can help you do it. And this book shows you how you can become a part of the craigslist community.

Whether you're in need of something, hoping to get rid of something, or wanting to promote something, the opportunities for you on craigslist are very exciting. Following the steps and strategies covered in this book gives you a big advantage over the typical craigslist community user.

Craig and staff have never saddled the website with lengthy rules and restrictions, which is one reason why so many users put little thought and planning into creating successful listings. In this book, you'll learn how to create attention-grabbing listings, what information to include, and how to write ads that get attention and motivate people to act.

You'll learn not only how to list, but also how to find what you want—and get it. And you'll learn how to protect yourself, your computer, and your personal information when online and when using craigslist.

How This Book Is Organized

This book is organized into three main parts, as follows:

- Part I, "craigslist 101," covers how craigslist went from a simple idea to a collection of more than 500 communities. You'll gain insights on Craig Newmark, craigslist's fascinating founder and customer service rep. These chapters also cover creating an account and navigating around the site. And you'll learn everything you need to know to keep your computer, your information, and yourself safe when using craigslist.

- Part II, "Posting on craigslist," starts by showing you the steps to follow to post a listing on craigslist. You'll also learn marketing strategies to design successful listings that set your advertisements apart from the pack. These chapters cover the individual craigslist sections and categories, showing you exactly how to create successful listings and take advantage of all their features.

- Part III, "The Other Side of craigslist," lays out the steps for responding to craigslist postings. You'll learn what to look for— and look out for—when searching listings in each category.

Together, the 15 chapters in this book show you the ins and outs of craigslist and online marketing so that you'll be able to create stand-out listings that grab attention or quickly find whatever you need. Before long, you'll be telling your friends about all the successful deals you've made using craigslist.

Conventions Used in This Book

I've tried to make this book entertaining and easy to read. It shouldn't require any coaching, but you might find it helpful to know how specific types of information are presented.

Capitalization and Special Formatting

craigslist doesn't follow standard rules of capitalization. Craig purposely chose not to capitalize the craigslist name or any titles used on the site, and I've followed his lead in this book.

Because many of the craigslist section names, category names, and so on are ordinary words, I've used a special format for onscreen items to help distinguish them from regular text. For example, when you read about the **community** section, the special formatting of the word *community* indicates that you'll be able to click that word on the craigslist screen—in this case, to go to the main community page. For simplicity, this book uses that special formatting for any craigslist screen item you can click or select, including menu items, buttons, and links.

Web Page Addresses

There are many web addresses in this book, including sites that offer valuable information to help you make better use of craigslist. If the site requires the World Wide Web (www) designation to be typed, I've included it in the web page address; otherwise, I've left it out. For example, you could type either of the following to get to the web page for this book:

www.craigslist4everyone.com

craigslist4everyone.com

Technically, either address should start with http:// (as in http://www.craigslist4everyone.com). Because Internet Explorer, Firefox, and most other web browsers automatically insert this part of the address, however, you don't have to type it—and I haven't included it in any of the addresses in this book.

Special Elements

You'll also come across a few special elements in this book that provide additional information to supplement the main text. These elements are designed to make your learning faster, easier, and more efficient.

 An Info note includes useful information that will help you to better understand or make better use of the text you're reading.

 A Warning highlights information about a potentially dangerous situation. I don't use it lightly, so pay special attention when you come across this type of item.

Tip 4U A Tip is a helpful piece of information—a little trick, actually—that helps you increase the odds of success on craigslist.

Let Me Know What You Think

I enjoy hearing from readers. If you have a question, a story to share, or something you just have to set me straight about, feel free to email me at c4e@craigslist4everyone.com. I read every email message personally and respond to as many as time permits.

If you want to learn more about what's happening on craigslist, take advantage of some free offers, and find out about any updates to this book, check out the website at www.craigslist4everyone.com.

craigslist 101

1 Putting craigslist on the Map 7

2 Welcome to the Neighborhood 17

3 Safety First 43

Putting craigslist on the Map

In early 1995, the Internet was still in its infancy. Although many technophiles and academics were regularly using electronic bulletin boards and newsgroups, Internet access for the home was just beginning to catch on. With the advent of the World Wide Web, however, people were beginning to share information in new ways. It was in this new cyberspace that a San Francisco–based software engineer named Craig Newmark observed people helping each other online—the beginning of online networking and virtual communities. Newmark liked what he saw and wanted to contribute in his own way.

A Simple Idea

Newmark thought that people in the Bay Area information technology community would appreciate being notified about various local events. He created a simple email newsletter that he sent to friends—and anyone else who requested it. Tech-savvy multimedia people responded, and interest quickly grew through word of mouth. As the number of recipients of his newsletter increased, Newmark soon needed a list server to handle the requests, with an electronic database for subscribers. As a name for the list, he had settled on "sf-events," but some of his friends wisely suggested "craigslist" instead—keeping the name personal and unpretentious.

Info 4U Part of keeping the list name unpretentious is the lower-case letter at the beginning of the name: It's "craigslist," not "Craigslist."

Realizing that it was possible to use a software program to turn email into web pages, Newmark wrote the code, and the craigslist.org web-site was born. Early on, Newmark handled most of the postings him-self, but the site quickly increased in popularity, and soon people were listing all types of information, including job openings and apartment rentals.

Community response to the idea of helping others and bringing peo-ple together using the Internet had taken the site far beyond anything Newmark had imagined. It wasn't long before craigslist became well known as a free online classifieds site serving the San Francisco area.

The initial craigslist design was minimalist, and remains so to this day—a straightforward, categorized layout, free of all the attention-grabbing animated clutter too often found on corporate websites (see Figure 1.1). Despite being approached in 1997 to put banner ads on the site, Newmark decided to keep craigslist commercial-free.

The Best of Intentions

By 1998, Newmark was running craigslist out of his home as a hobby, while still believing that his true calling was programming. He enlisted volunteers to help keep up with the site's explosive popular-ity, but it wasn't enough. Realizing that craigslist needed a more for-mal structure, in April of 1999 Newmark devoted himself to running craigslist full time. Within 12 months, craigslist had nine full-time employees, including CEO Jim Buckmaster, who originally came on board as lead programmer and chief technical officer.

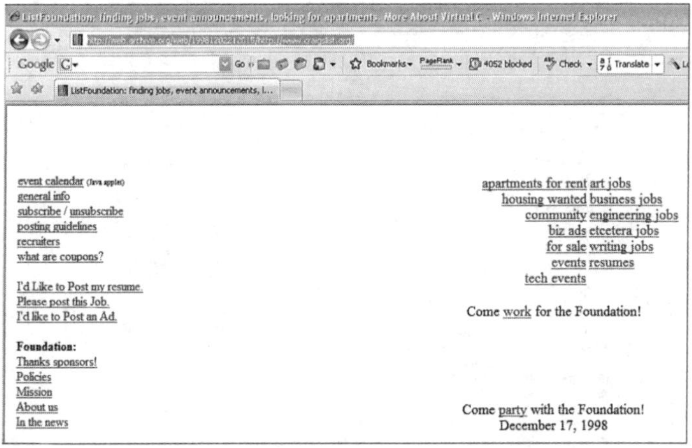

Figure 1.1
craigslist's home page circa late 1996, initially hosted at www.cnewmark.com.

craigslist's growth has always been based on Craig Newmark's strong belief in providing outstanding customer service and meeting people's needs, while remaining cost-free to more than 99% of its users. Categories, features, and policies are added or modified largely in response to user requests. When craigslist incorporated in 1999 as a private for-profit company, fees were imposed on San Francisco job ads to cover expenses. However, this change was made only after the proposal was announced on the website and craigslist visitors were able to post public responses to the idea.

Expanding Newmark's vision beyond San Francisco, in 2000 Buckmaster added craigslist communities for Boston; Chicago; Los Angeles; New York; Portland, Oregon; San Diego; Seattle; Washington, D.C.; and Sacramento. Although the formats are identical, to keep the focus local, each community is separate. Posting the same ad in more than one community is prohibited. Continued expansion in 2001 led to Vancouver, British Columbia, Canada, being the first craigslist community outside the United States. Rapid expansion has continued. As of July 2008, craigslist has more than 560 sites, representing all 50 states and more than 50 countries (see Figure 1.2).

Figure 1.2
craigslist's current home page.

Because craigslist mainly consists of user-generated and user-moderated content, merely duplicating the format for each community might not appear to be a particularly great accomplishment. However, take into consideration the fact that as of August 2008 craigslist has 40 million unique users each month, self-publishing more than 30 million listings, and you might begin to see the complexity of it all. The site receives 10 billion (that's *billion*, not *million*) page views each month and is ranked #28 in Top English Websites by Alexa, a website information company. With 25 full-time employees, craigslist provides an astonishing amount of data management, technical resources, and customer service.

As with any business, craigslist has experienced challenges and growing pains along the way, but, unlike many companies, craigslist has remained true to Newmark's original vision. Although still privately owned, craigslist announced in 2004 that eBay had acquired 25% equity in the company from a former craigslist employee.

Despite industry speculation of craigslist's looming commercialization, until recently all parties continued to coexist peacefully, and craigslist had remained largely unaffected by the change. In a surprise move in April 2008, eBay filed a lawsuit against craigslist, accusing the board of directors of actions that diluted the value of eBay's holdings. As of this writing, craigslist has yet to respond, but Jim Buckmaster's take on the suit can be found at blog.craigslist.org/category/legal/.

As a privately held corporation, craigslist is not required to disclose its revenues or executives' salaries, but some industry analysts have estimated craigslist's 2005 revenues to be as high as $25 million, and those figures have only increased since then—not bad for a company that isn't trying to make money!

Looking into the Future

It isn't easy to project the future of a company whose founder describes it as a "happy accident," who chuckles at the mention of a business plan, and who proudly states that nearly all the company's advances have been based on user requests.

Newmark has indicated that craigslist will continue to expand into other cities and countries according to consumer demand. Although communities in non-English–speaking countries were first added in 2004, a handful of sites were recently made available in multiple languages. Newmark has said that craigslist will continue working to meet the need for widespread multilanguage support but is not ready to execute a full-scale implementation yet.

A good portion of craigslist's technical resources will probably be directed at meeting the ever-increasing needs of a high-traffic website. Speed, reliability, and security must be maintained to keep the sites running smoothly, all while evaluating and integrating advancements in Internet technology.

craigslist probably will need to make at least some design changes to support the increasing numbers of mobile web users accessing the Internet via cell phones and handheld computers. The craigslist home page is where most changes would take place, if the intention is to maintain the current overall format.

One of the biggest challenges that craigslist will continue to confront is the battle against spammers, scammers, and users who conduct illegal activities. craigslist has always devoted resources to these issues, but since cyber-criminals are quick to develop new methods, the war rages on.

Who Is Craig Newmark?

It might seem obvious that Craig Newmark's greatest accomplishment is his unparalleled success at creating a simple, noncommercial online community designed to bring people together. However, that's really just the tip of the iceberg for this mild-mannered computer whiz.

Born in 1952 in Morristown, New Jersey, Craig Newmark is quick to admit that while growing up he was the epitome of a nerd. Complete with taped-together, black-rimmed glasses and a pocket protector, he was clearly destined for big things in the field of computers. After graduating from Morristown High School, he attended Case Western Reserve University, where he earned both bachelor's and master's degrees in computer science.

After college, Newmark moved to Boca Raton, Florida, to work as a senior associate programmer with IBM. His career with IBM spanned 17 years, relocating him to Detroit and Pittsburgh along the way. He left IBM in 1993 to join Charles Schwab, where he worked in systems security architecture for the San Francisco headquarters, promoting his belief in the Internet as the wave of the future for businesses.

Craig's Vision

It was during his time at Charles Schwab that Newmark took that fateful first step and started emailing the event notices that would grow into craigslist.

Becoming proficient in Java programming when it was first introduced, Newmark left Schwab in 1995 to pursue more lucrative contract work. For the next three years, he focused on his programming career, evangelizing the Internet wherever he went. He still viewed craigslist as a goodwill gesture, running it out of his home with the help of volunteers.

Change of Focus

When craigslist's popularity snowballed in 1999, Newmark gave up his programming career and devoted himself full time to craigslist. With the need to cover company salaries, Newmark incorporated craigslist as a for-profit company—but one that was never profit-driven.

Within months, Newmark realized that he wasn't the best choice to run the day-to-day operations and promoted Jim Buckmaster to CEO—a promotion that included a stake in the company. Buckmaster excelled at running craigslist as a lean, customer-focused website, and Newmark happily assumed his roles as spokesperson and customer service representative, largely devoted to fighting fraud on craigslist. craigslist's formal public relations are handled by Susan MacTavish Best.

The job of customer service rep is one that Newmark takes seriously, regularly putting in 50-hour weeks, often working remotely from his favorite San Francisco coffee house, Café Reverie, or typing away on his laptop between public appearances.

A media darling with a laidback manner and a dry sense of humor, Newmark frequently appears in interviews in print and electronic publications.

Nerd Values

While the success of craigslist might have brought fame, Craig Newmark's self-described "nerd values" help feed a growing curiosity about the man who likes to be thought of as a customer service rep rather than as craigslist's founder, and prefers public transportation over a fancy car. Newmark's philosophy is simple: Make a decent living, provide for your future, and then do what you can to change the world.

Newmark achieved icon status with craigslist users—and endured ridicule from the corporate world—for his steadfast refusal to commercialize the site and reap untold fortunes from advertising and information-harvesting. CEO Buckmaster shares Newmark's vision of craigslist as a public service organization, both balking at the idea of driving profits for profit's sake.

Despite his newfound celebrity, Craig Newmark has remained unaffected, keeping his email address (craig@craigslist.org) posted in several places on the Internet, and responding to email himself—usually rather quickly, too! He also writes a blog (cnewmark.com), where his writings often cover events and organizations promoting social change.

David and Goliath

According to some news media executives, Craig Newmark may one day be known as the man who single-handedly slew the newspaper industry. Long dependent on classified advertising dollars to help generate the steep profits that many shareholders demand, newspaper executives were quick to accuse craigslist of spiriting away millions of dollars in classified ad revenues—according to some estimates, up to $50 million in San Francisco alone.

Newmark downplays that effect of craigslist, suggesting that websites such as Monster.com and AutoTrader.com have a greater negative impact on newspaper revenues, and is quick to point out that a high percentage of craigslist postings never would have been placed in fee-based print classifieds.

Newmark's most persuasive argument is that to thrive, the newspaper industry needs to change its mission. Having experienced a steady drop in circulation since the 1960s—when television became a normal part of everyday American life—and an aging reader base, conglomerates in the newspaper industry should see themselves as community service organizations, focused on bringing truth to the world, rather than making profit their driving force.

One to Watch

Based on his comments in public appearances and interviews that Craig Newmark has given in recent years, it's apparent that he now has bigger things in mind when helping others. Most telling are his uncensored blog entries, often promoting ventures dedicated to advancing world peace, promoting new journalism business models, or outing political misconduct.

Newmark regularly writes about—and is an international board member of—One Voice (onevoicemovement.org), a powerful grass-roots movement with the goal of ending the Israeli-Palestinian conflict by uniting the overwhelming majority of inhabitants who desire a peaceful two-state coexistence in the Middle East. Not one to take himself too seriously, on the other hand, Newmark has also funded the "Craig Newmark Memorial Latrine" at the Hisham ben Abdil Malek boys' school in the city of Jericho.

In his desire to support journalism, Newmark has also invested $28,000 in NewAssignment.net, a nonprofit site founded by Jay Rosen, a journalism teacher at New York University. The hope is to create a new and better business model by networking journalists with the public for investigative reporting projects. Newmark believes that this collaboration can create new jobs and increase the integrity of investigative journalism.

In September 2008, Newmark attended the Global Creative Leadership Summit (CreativeLeadershipSummit.org), a conference held to address the challenges of globalization. He participated in discussions on the globalization of Islam, and how the Internet will affect our political processes and the way in which businesses are run.

Given his increasing involvement in social activism, Newmark is often asked if he intends to enter the political arena. Although he indicates an interest in better understanding the political process and expresses frustration with the state of politics, Newmark insists that he has no political aspirations.

Craigslist Foundation: "Helping People Help"

Created in 2000 by Craig Newmark and several others, the Craigslist Foundation (CraigslistFoundation.org) promotes social entrepreneurship. At first providing small grants and free web hosting, the foundation later launched the Nonprofit Venture Forum, a small-scale event that introduced grassroots organizations to potential donors.

 Unlike craigslist itself, the foundation spells the name with an initial cap: "Craigslist Foundation."

Hoping to create a more effective business model, Craigslist Foundation hired Darian Heyman as executive director. Heyman reinvented the organization as an educational and networking resource for nonprofits worldwide. While craigslist's motto is "Doing well by doing good," the foundation's motto is "Helping people help."

On October 23, 2004, Craigslist Foundation held its first-ever Nonprofit Boot Camp, intended to empower the next generation of nonprofit leaders. With more than 500 attendees, the conference was wildly successfully. Craigslist Foundation now holds annual Nonprofit Boot Camps in San Francisco and New York City, with more cities in the planning stages.

Each boot camp is a high-energy, one-day experience organized in collaboration with more than 150 nonprofit support organizations, teaching attendees how to start and run a successful organization. Registration cost for the day is currently only $50. More than 2,000 people attended the 2007 San Francisco gathering. An online version of the Nonprofit Boot Camp is also available on the Craigslist Foundation website. Craigslist Foundation is positioning itself as the craigslist for the social entrepreneur.

From Here...

With a simple idea, the best of intentions, and tireless determination, Craig Newmark has enacted positive change around the world. Thanks to his efforts, readers of this book can make the best possible use of the original idea—craigslist—to buy, sell, swap, and otherwise improve their own lives and those of others who share in the community.

Welcome to the Neighborhood

Because craigslist was originally created to connect the folks in San Francisco, until recently its home page was the Bay Area site. With virtual communities in all 50 states and more than 560 cities worldwide, however, on your first visit you'll find yourself on the sites page (www.craigslist.org/about/sites.html), which has links to all the community home pages (see Figure 2.1). On the craigslist sites page, click the location nearest you. If you then choose a state or country, you'll be able to select from a list of communities in that region. Later in this chapter you'll learn how to set the default to your own hometown when you open an account.

At first glance, the craigslist home page might look as though it includes everything but the kitchen sink. However, if you take a minute to get familiar with the layout, you'll feel right at home (see Figure 2.2). With users' needs and speed in mind, this home page is simply a site map—with direct links to all the listing sections, common tasks, and many of the virtual communities that comprise craigslist.org.

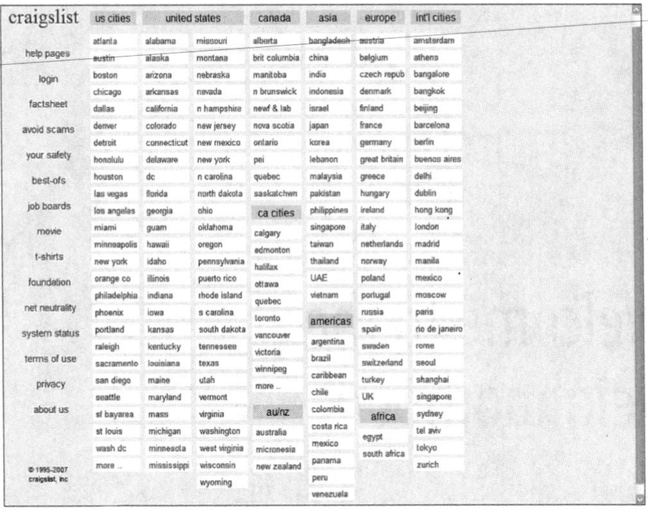

Figure 2.1
On your first visit, you'll start out at the sites page.

Figure 2.2
The craigslist home page.

Navigating the Home Page

The craigslist home page is made up of three sections: the navigation column on the left, a community menu on the right, and category links in the center. This straightforward layout allows you to reach any page in any craigslist community with only a click or two.

Finding Your Way Home

The three columns of community links on the right side of the home page make it easy to reach any craigslist site. On the craigslist home page, the first column is a partial list of U.S. cities at the top, followed by Canadian and international cities. All 50 states; Washington, D.C.; Puerto Rico; and Guam are displayed in the middle column. A complete list of countries makes up the third column. Choosing any city link takes you directly to that community's home page. In most cases, clicking a state, province, or country takes you to a directory of craigslist sites within that area.

You can also click the craigslist logo at the upper-left corner of the home page to reach the craigslist sites page.

The craigslist home page is essentially identical for each site. No matter which community you're visiting, you can easily identify your location by checking the title bar across the top of the page, which displays the community name (see Figure 2.3). Larger cities such as San Francisco, Los Angeles, and New York also have subdivisions to help you focus your efforts. On the home page, links to these areas are displayed in the title bar to the right of the community name.

Info 4U The community name also appears in your browser's title bar.

Tip 4U Notice the tiny superscripted letter *w* next to the community name in the craigslist home page's title bar? It's a link to the community's Wikipedia (wikipedia.org) entry. Wikipedia is a free, user-generated, online encyclopedia.

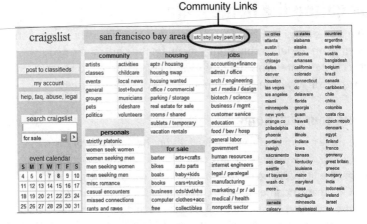

Figure 2.3
Journey to other craigslist communities by using links on the home page.

Joining the Community

Being the free spirits they are, craigslist's management doesn't require anyone to have an account to use the site, but having an account makes things easier and faster. The only information you provide is an email address. While craigslist is devoted to fighting spammers, I strongly recommend *not* using your primary email address. Chapter 3, "Safety First," explains why and offers some easy alternatives.

Creating a Craigslist Account

To create a new craigslist account, follow these instructions:

1. Click the **my account** link on the left side of the home page.

2. When the Account Log In page appears (see Figure 2.4), select the **Click here to sign up** link located directly below the login box.

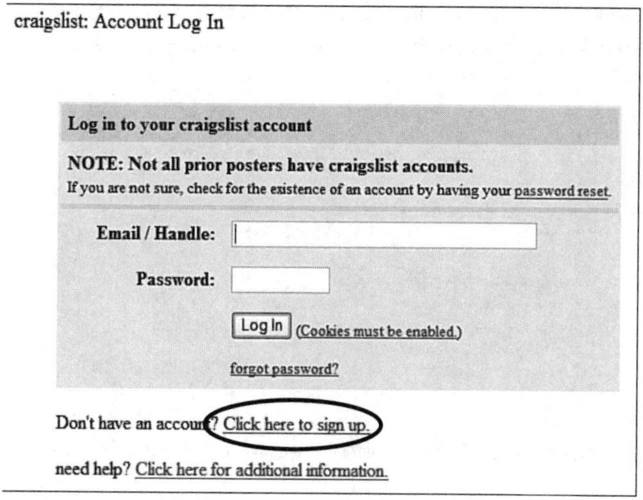

Figure 2.4
The craigslist Account Log In page.

3. When the account signup page appears (see Figure 2.5), enter your email address. Then type the verification word into the box and click the **create account** button.

A confirmation page will appear, indicating that a link to activate your account was sent to the email address you entered.

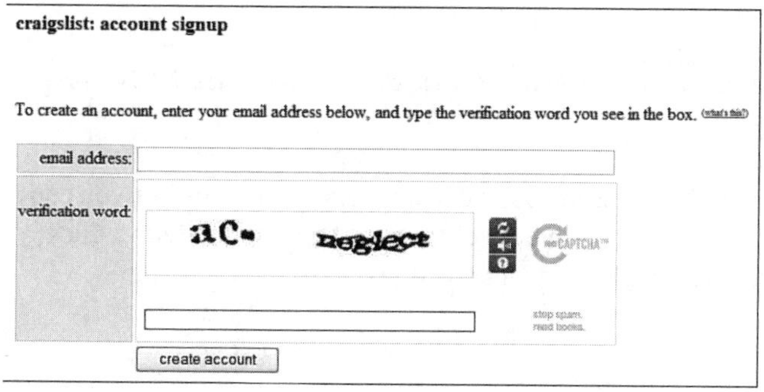

Figure 2.5
The craigslist account signup page.

4. When you receive the confirmation email message (see Figure 2.6), click the link to continue the account creation process.

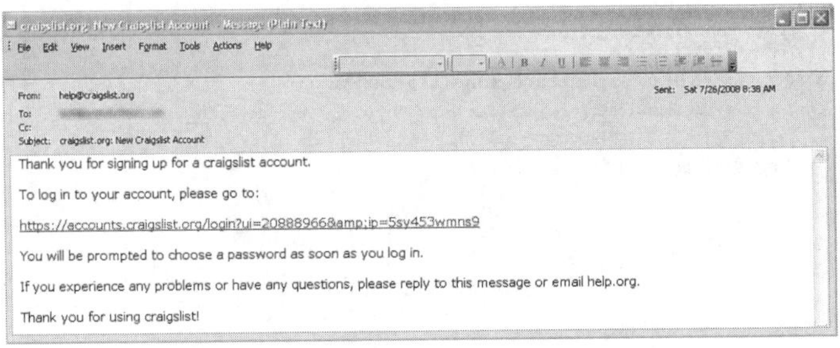

Figure 2.6
Respond to the New Account email message to confirm that you want to create a craigslist account.

5. The choose new password page opens in a new window, as shown in Figure 2.7. Enter the same password in both boxes, click the **Submit Password and Log In** button, and log in.

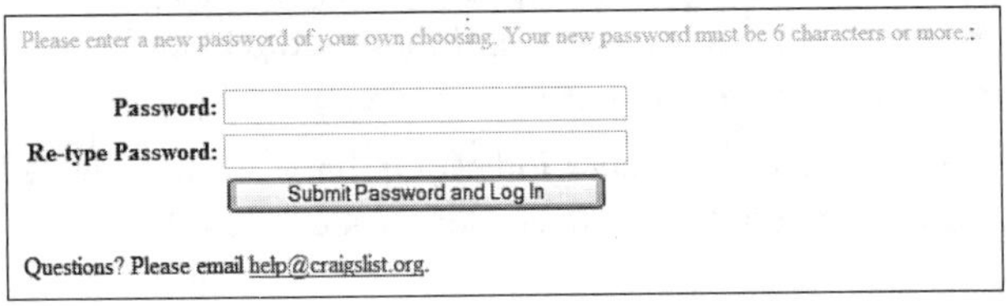

Figure 2.7
Choose a new password on this screen. Tips for creating effective passwords are included in Chapter 3.

6. When the terms of use screen appears (see Figure 2.8), you can use the scrollbar on the right to read through the terms. Click the **I ACCEPT** button when you're done.

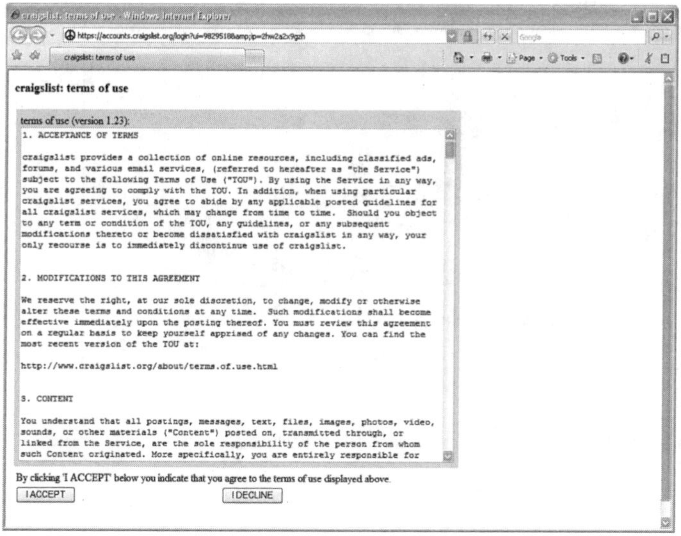

Figure 2.8
You'll learn more about the craigslist terms of use later in this chapter.

7. When the craigslist account page appears (see Figure 2.9), click the **settings** link to customize your account settings.

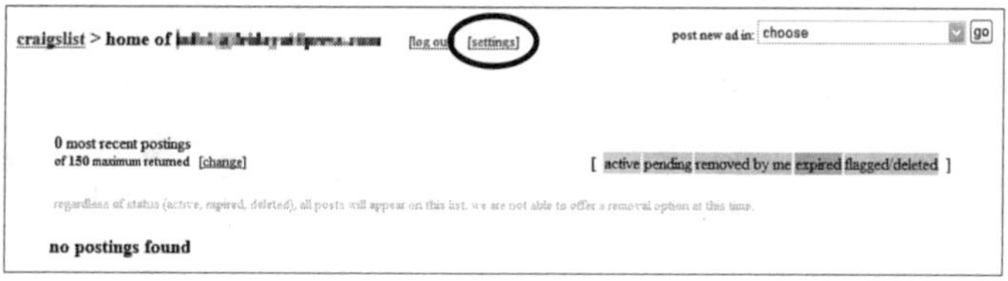

Figure 2.9
On your craigslist account page, you can post and manage your listings.

8. When the settings page appears (see Figure 2.10), pull down the community list and select your default site. You can also change other details, such as your email address, password, and the number of postings displayed on your Account page.

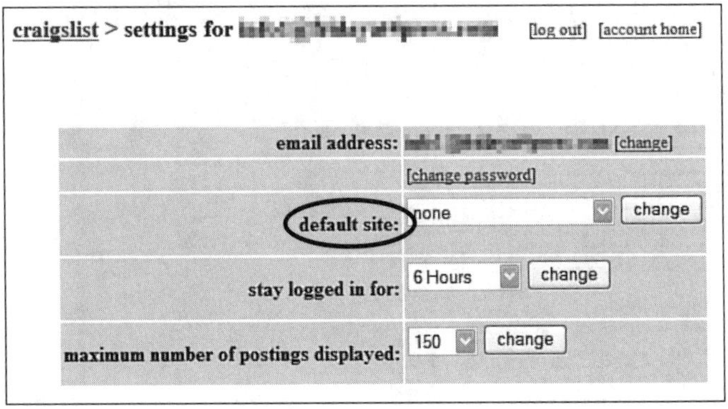

Figure 2.10
On the account settings page, specify your preferred default craigslist site.

Getting Around Town

From your craigslist community, you can use the left-hand navigation column to access the classifieds, learn more about craigslist, or find out what's happening in your neck of the woods. craigslist's easy-to-use layout puts the most common tasks in the upper-left corner of the home page (see Figure 2.11).

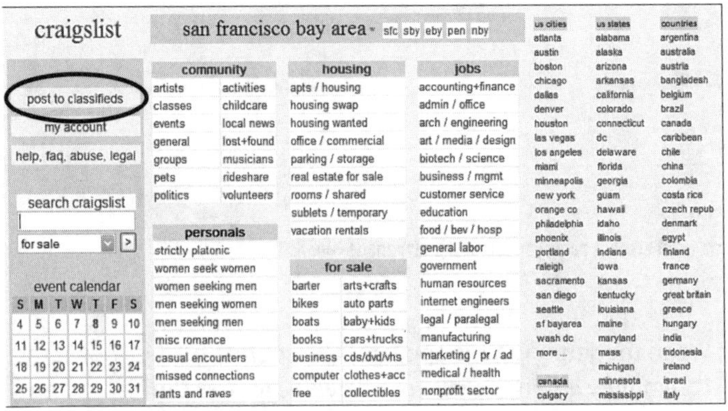

Figure 2.11
Frequently used items on the craigslist home page including the **post to classifieds** link.

Clicking the **post to classifieds** link is one way to create a listing. You'll walk through a series of choices before reaching the Create Posting page. (This is a good strategy for beginners. Chapter 4, "All About the Listings," describes a faster way to post after you've got the hang of it.)

You can perform a basic search by entering keywords, selecting a category from the drop-down list, and clicking the arrow (>) button, as shown in Figure 2.12. (For advanced searching and tips for finding what you want, see Chapter 13, "Responding to Listings.")

Figure 2.12
The basic search function.

Exploring Your Neighborhood

Looking for something to do this Friday? Feel like learning something new? Click any date on the **event calendar**, as shown in Figure 2.13, to display a list of events and classes in your area.

When the date listings page appears, as shown in Figure 2.14, events are listed first, followed by a section for classes. Click any of the individual listings to find out more about it.

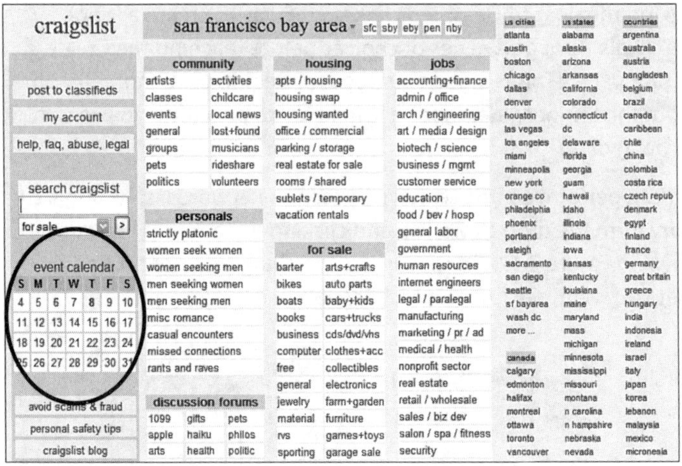

Figure 2.13
Click a date to see what's planned.

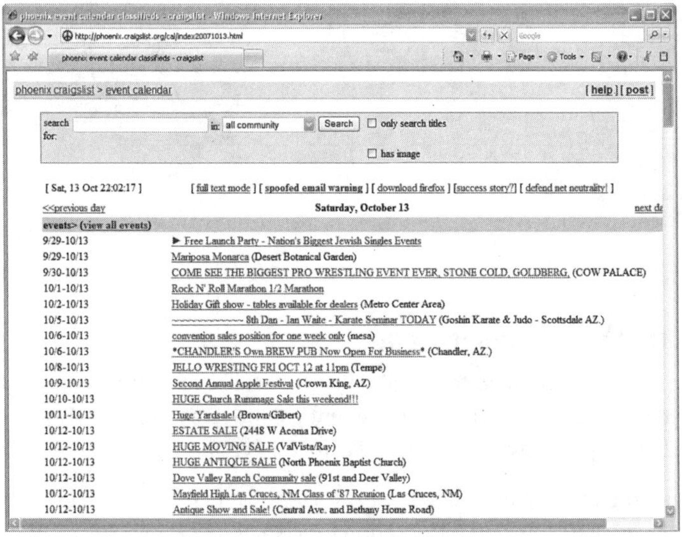

Figure 2.14
Find out about classes and events in your area by using craigslist's event calendar.

For Inquiring Minds

Below the **event calendar** are various links—an assortment of choices for users in need of information and/or entertainment (see Figure 2.15).

Figure 2.15
Links to interesting and helpful information.

You can read about some common Internet scams by clicking the **avoid scams & fraud** link. (See Chapter 3 for more information about staying safe online.) The **craigslist factsheet** link takes you to a page of trivia about craigslist.

One of craigslist's new additions is the craigslist blog (see Figure 2.16). Written by CEO Jim Buckmaster, the blog covers current craigslist happenings, interesting listings, and whatever else happens to be on Jim's mind.

Figure 2.16
Follow the craigslist blog to find out what goes on inside the world of craigslist.

To visit one of the most entertaining areas of craigslist, click the **best-of-craigslist** link to reach the BEST OF page, as shown in Figure 2.17. Postings are nominated by craigslist users and can come from any category and/or community. Most are funny, with a few that may make you stop and think, but almost all offer a unique perspective into the variety of individuals who make up craigslist.

Warning 4U The writings are uncensored and can be explicit in nature, so best to avoid them if you're easily offended.

Click the **craigslist movie & dvd** link to learn about *24 Hours on craigslist*, an award-winning documentary that explores a day in the lives of an interesting assortment of craigslist users (see Figure 2.18).

```
craigslist > best of craigslist

8888888b.   88888888888  .d88888b.  88888888888       .d88888b.   88888888
888  "88b   888          d88P Y88b      888          d88P" "Y88b  888
888   .88P  888          Y88b.          888          888     888  888
8888888K.   8888888       "Y888b.       888          888     888  8888888
888  "Y88b  888              "Y88b.     888          888     888  888
888    888  888               "888      888          888     888  888
888   d88P  888          Y88b  d88P      888          Y88b. .d88P  888
8888888P"   88888888888   "Y8888P"       888           "Y88888P"   888
```

before perusing best-of-craigslist postings below please note:

- postings are nominated by craigslist readers, and are not necessarily endorsed by craigslist staff.
- postings may be explicitly sexual, scatological, offensive, graphic, tasteless, and/or not funny
- if you see copyrighted material not original to craigslist, please let us know and we'll remove it.
- if you are under age 18, please use your "back" button and seek parental guidance
- by continuing you acknowledge being 18 or older and release craigslist from any liability arising from your use of best-of-craigslist

[   ] [search]

03 Sep 2007 - min - RARE Left-hand strung piano

Figure 2.17
Enjoy some creative writing on the best-of-craigslist page.

Figure 2.18
A cultural phenomenon, craigslist has even inspired a movie.

Getting Involved

Click the **craigslist foundation** link to visit the foundation's website (craigslistfoundation.org), where you can find more information on events and resources created to help nonprofit organizations succeed. There's more information on the Craigslist Foundation in Chapter 1, "Putting craigslist on the Map."

Did you know that telephone and cable companies in the United States are trying to gain control over the Internet? Conglomerates such as AT&T, Verizon, Comcast, and Time Warner are lobbying Congress and the Federal Communications Commission to further their agenda. These companies want to tax content providers and control accessibility to websites, giving preference to their own sites and those that can afford to pay. You can find out more about this issue—including what you can do to get involved—by clicking the **defend net neutrality** link. You'll go to Save the Internet (savetheinternet.com), as shown in Figure 2.19, a campaign run by the Free Press Action Fund (freepress.net).

Figure 2.19
Find out how you can help defend Net neutrality by visiting savetheinternet.com.

The Town Square

No town is complete without a local gathering spot—a place for people to make friends, share thoughts, and blow off steam. In a
craigslist community, the **discussion forums** are that place. The
craigslist home page has links to many of the forums, as shown in
Figure 2.20. You can go to a specific forum or click the **discussion
forums** heading to display a list of official forums.

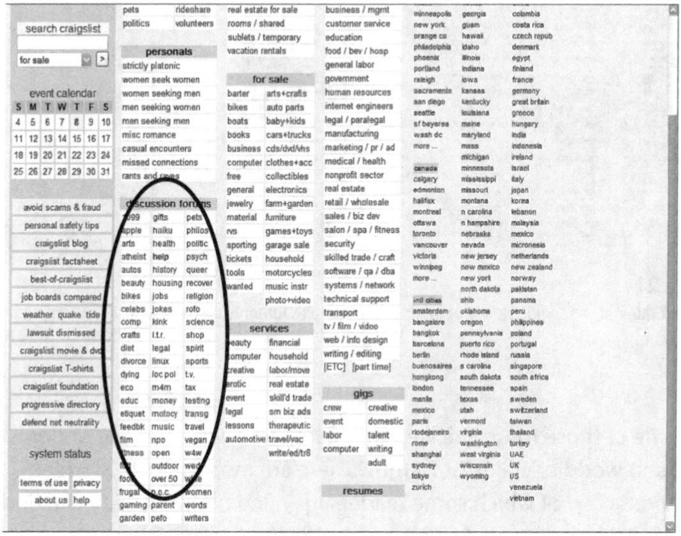

Figure 2.20
You can reach many of the official discussion forums by using links on the home page.

Each link on the discussion forums menu, as shown in Figure 2.21,
displays the number of new postings submitted in the past 24 hours.
Restricted forums display R at the end of the link and require you to
be logged in to post, but you can post anonymously. R+ links denote
that you must be logged in and cannot post anonymously.

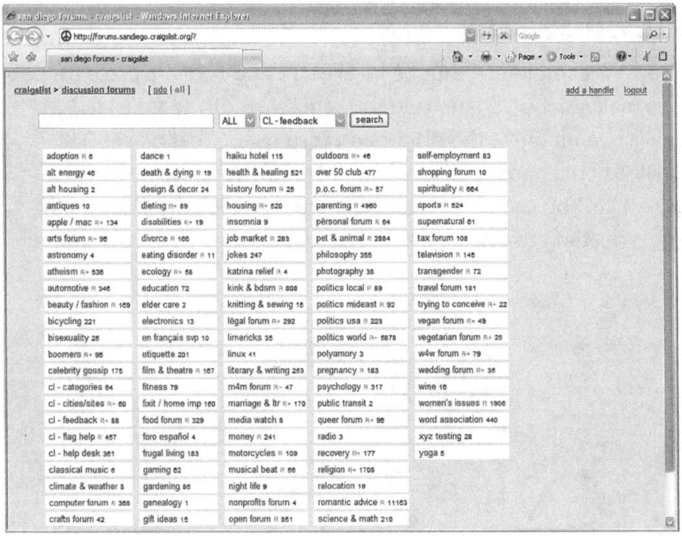

Figure 2.21
Share your thoughts on a wide variety of topics in the 100-plus forums currently on the discussion forums menu.

If none of those forums tickles your fancy, you can enter the underground world of craigslist forums. There are more than 200 hidden forums, a few of which some readers may find offensive. You can find unofficial lists of these forums by visiting the Forums Directory (forums.craigslist.org/?forumID=4111) or the ForumsLister (forumslister.com)—a free, independent website maintained by a veteran poster. Table 2.1 lists a few of the hidden forums you might want to visit.

Table 2.1 Some Hidden Craigslist Forums

Forum Topic	URL
Alternative Health	forums.craigslist.org/?forumID=4300
Alternative Parenting	forums.craigslist.org/?forumID=7676
Arts	forums.craigslist.org/?forumID=3023
Arts Clique	forums.craigslist.org/?forumID=3352

Forum Topic	URL
Confessions	forums.craigslist.org/?forumID=4545
Digital Arts	forums.craigslist.org/?forumID=8478
Forums Directory	forums.craigslist.org/?forumID=4111
I Wish	forums.craigslist.org/?forumID=2109
NASCAR	forums.craigslist.org/?forumID=3058
Newlyweds	forums.craigslist.org/?forumID=1550
Pictures	forums.craigslist.org/?forumID=9090
Poetry	forums.craigslist.org/?forumID=4682
Reading Club	forums.craigslist.org/?forumID=7323
Recipes	forums.craigslist.org/?forumID=7777
Wedding (Unofficial)	forums.craigslist.org/?forumID=1505

Giving Yourself a Handle

Remember the days of CB radios? Forum posters identify themselves with "handles" (nicknames). Some forums allow you to create a handle with each post, but the more active forums require you to use a registered handle.

To add a handle to your craigslist account, follow these instructions:

1. Log in to your craigslist account and navigate to the discussion forum you want.

2. At the upper-right corner of any discussion forum page, click the **add a handle** link, as shown in Figure 2.22.

3. When the new handle forum screen appears, as shown in Figure 2.23, enter your handle choice in the top two boxes. The email privacy setting, URL, and Note entries appear on your forum's profile. The last two settings change the way in which forums display. Click **Submit New Handle** when you're finished. If you enter a handle that's already taken, a message will appear at the top of the box, telling you to enter a different handle.

Figure 2.22
You can access the add a handle link from any discussion forum.

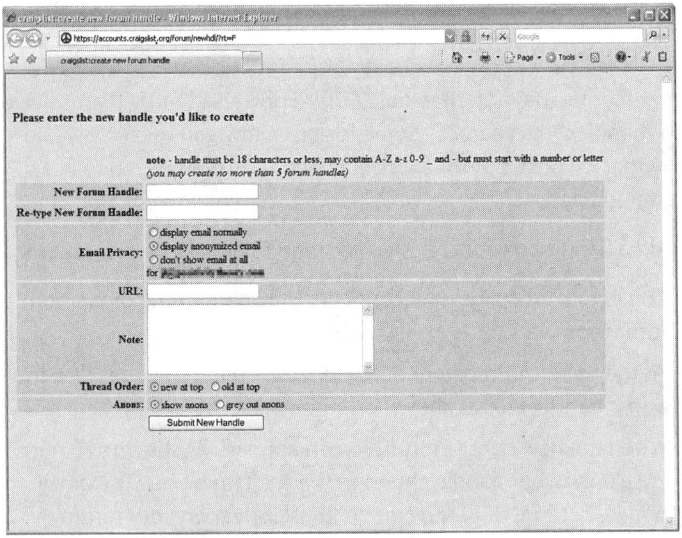

Figure 2.23
Create your forum handle and customize your discussion forums settings.

4. When the confirmation screen appears, you can click **Return to the Forums** and start speaking your mind.

When logged in to your account, your handle displays in red at the end of your posts. Other registered handles appear in green, and craigslist staff handles appear in yellow with a degree sign at the end (see Figure 2.24).

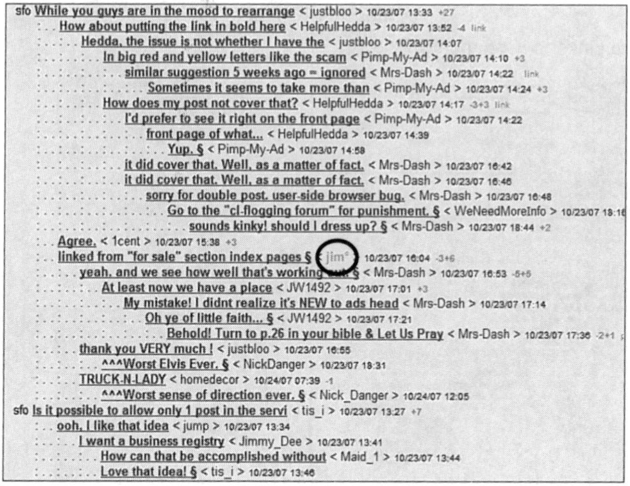

Figure 2.24
Various types of handles appear in different ways.

The craigslist forums have specific rules for handles:

- Each account can have up to five handles.

- Your handle must be registered for seven days before you can use HTML formatting in your posts.

- Ninety days after you create your handle, craigslist allows you to customize your posts by overwriting your handle with each post. Although it's not allowed in all forums, some creative posters use this option to add impact or humor to their posts.

Getting Involved

All forums use the same layout, as shown in Figure 2.25. Find one you like and jump in. Unlike the classifieds sections of craigslist, by default the discussion forums include posts from all craigslist communities. Click the community name link displayed to the right of the breadcrumb navigation at the top of each page to show messages from only your local community.

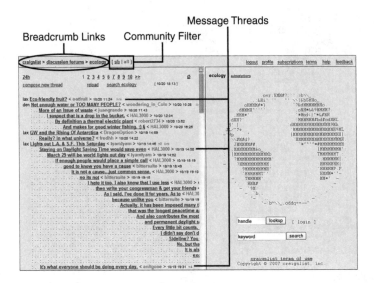

Figure 2.25
All forums use the same layout, as shown here in the ecology forum.

Forums are a place to exchange information—not a place to post ads. Posts are listed in threads to keep related messages together. Message threads display in the left frame, with the most recent posts at the top. When logged in, your handle will display in red and handles of other registered users will show in green. Unregistered or anonymous handles always display in gray.

Warning 4U

In unrestricted forums, anonymous posting is common. *Forum trolls* (malicious posters) sometimes use this opportunity to spam, flame, or annoy others. While it's tempting to post a reply, continuing such a thread only encourages trolling and adds to the problem.

Click any title in a thread to display the full message in the frame on the right, as shown in Figure 2.26.

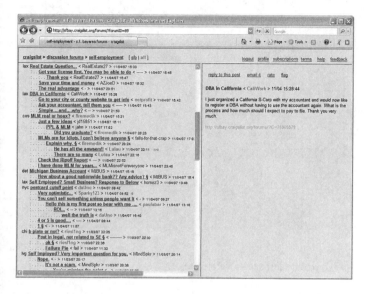

Figure 2.26
The selected post appears in the right-hand frame.

You can post a reply by following these instructions:

1. Click the **reply to this post** link located in the right-hand frame, directly above the message.

2. The compose your reply pane appears, as shown in Figure 2.27, with the original message displayed at the bottom. Fill in the title, enter your message, and click the **preview** button to see how your message will look.

3. When the preview pane is displayed, as shown in Figure 2.28, you can see how your message will look when posted. Check the **email me all new replies to this thread** box if you want to be notified whenever someone posts responses to the thread. If necessary, click **edit again** and make changes. Click the **commit** button when you're ready to post the message.

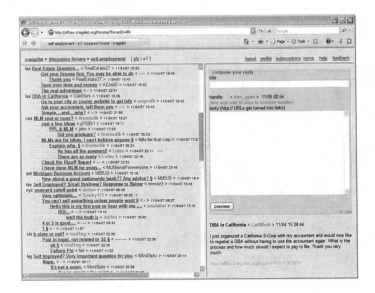

Figure 2.27
Click the **preview** button after entering your message.

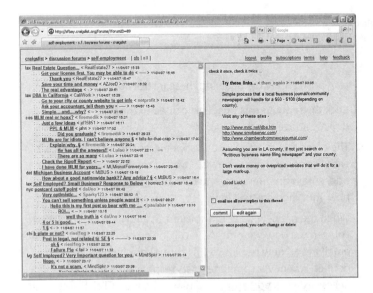

Figure 2.28
Posts cannot be edited or removed after you submit them, so previewing is a good idea.

4. Click the **reload** link at the top of the left frame to see your message added to the thread (see Figure 2.29).

Each thread should be limited to the topic in the initial post. To discuss anything else, start a new thread by clicking the **compose new thread** link in the upper-left corner of the left frame, and follow the preceding directions.

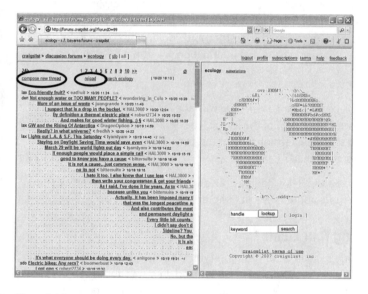

Figure 2.29
The **compose new thread** and **reload** links are key to posting in the forums.

Dressing Up Your Posts

craigslist is simple by design, and many devoted users like it that way, so posting a plain-text message is usually the best way to go. When necessary, you can display active links and images in your posts by using the instructions in this section.

Displaying a Link

Including a link to another website is easy. Simply type the complete URL (for example, http://www.*addresstovisit*.com), starting with http://, and craigslist will turn the address into a link.

Including a Picture

Adding images to your post can be useful, especially in the art forums. If you want to include an image in a forum post, the image must be hosted on the Internet, and you need to know its address or URL. When you have that information, insert the following code:

```
<img src="http://www.test.com/image.jpg">>
```

Replace `test.com/image.jpg` with the location (`test.com`) and file name (`image.jpg`) of the image. The entire address, including http:// and the file extension (.jpg in this example), must be enclosed in quotation marks ("").

Using basic HTML coding is also allowed on craigslist. You can find out more about HTML in Chapter 4.

Staking Your Claim

Ready to share your thoughts with the world, but can't find a forum to discuss your hot topic? Homestead your own forum! Forums are identified by unique four-digit numbers. To create a new forum, enter **forums.craigslist.org/?forumID=*xxxx*** in the address bar. Replace *xxxx* with any four-digit number until you find one that's not being used. Then post an introductory message stating the name and the purpose of the forum. You can also post suggested guidelines for your new forum.

After you've created your forum, post an announcement in the Forums Directory (forums.craigslist.org/?forumID=4111), inviting people to participate. Also, email the information to craigslistforums@forumslister.com to be added to that site. Don't take starting a forum lightly, though. Building a thriving forum can take time and effort. The most successful forums cover popular or controversial topics and have at least a few regular and knowledgeable contributors.

Roadside Assistance

Help is never very far away on craigslist. Although basic information can be found at www.craigslist.org/about/help/ and www.craigslist.org/about/help/faq, questions about specific problems and issues are best posted in the **discussion forums**. To reach the forum, in your browser's address bar, type **forums.craigslist.org/?forumID=** followed directly by the forum ID number from Table 2.2.

Table 2.2   craigslist Help Forums

ID	Name	Topic
9	CL - help desk	Help with technical issues
8	CL - feedback	Post feedback about craigslist
3	CL - flag help	Help if posts have been flagged
1	CL - cities	Suggest new cities
128	CL - categories	Suggest new categories

You can often find the fastest answers by searching in the correct **help** forum. Help desk technical issues include listings that don't show up, login problems, and general questions about the site. Received a notice that your classified listing has been removed (or *flagged*, as craigslist calls it)? Visit the flag help forum to find out why.

The craigslist staffers will respond to some questions, but most help is offered by veteran craigslist users, who volunteer their time. Follow these tips to receive fast, accurate responses to your questions:

- Post in the correct forum. Using the wrong forum slows down the process.

- Briefly state the facts. Include relevant specifics about the actions you took and the results you received. Save lengthy commentary for the feedback forum—or the **rants and raves** section in the **personals** section.

- For questions about specific posts, include the post's URL. You can find message URLs by clicking the message's title from your account home page. You can leave off the http:// if your handle is too new to post links.

▪ If you receive email from craigslist stating that your listing was removed, links to it won't work. Copy the ad from the body of the email you received and paste it into your forum post. To receive the fastest response, include the community, category, and number of times you posted.

▪ Ask for clarification if needed, but don't argue about the answer. The posters are there to help; they don't design the processes or make up the rules.

Follow the Rules

Most of craigslist's terms of use are what you would expect to find on any site, covering items such as site restrictions, usage, and other legal mumbo-jumbo. (Looking for an exciting read? The current version is at www.craigslist.org/about/terms.of.use.html.) There are a few rules that users don't seem to know about until after violating them, so I'll touch on those rules briefly here. If you keep in mind craigslist's goal of being a local classifieds site for individuals, you'll better understand why these rules exist.

▪ Regardless of size, businesses can advertise their products or services only in the **services** section. Even a one-person startup selling handmade items must list under **services**—*not* in the **for sale** section. If you're trying to make a profit and not make some space in your garage, craigslist considers you a business. Multilevel marketing ads are strictly prohibited. This means no selling of products or services and no recruiting.

▪ No third-party posting agents are allowed. All users post their own listings, to prevent the site from becoming commercialized. This also means that users cannot automate the listing process.

▪ Each item should be posted in only one category and on one craigslist community. No cross-posting of listings between multiple cities or in multiple categories. The idea is to keep the site free of spam and over-posting.

From Here...

Now that you know how to "play nice," you can learn more in the next chapter about staying safe while using craigslist.

3

Safety First

The mission of craigslist is to use the Internet to bring people together offline. When using craigslist, you need to protect yourself both online and in the real world. Staying safe on the Internet is a growing concern. There are bound to be more than a few bad apples online, and this chapter shows you how to spot and avoid the rotten ones.

Internet Safety

True Internet security means protecting yourself and your computer. Although the topic may seem daunting, we all need to take the steps necessary to protect ourselves.

Secure Your Computer

Protecting yourself online means keeping your information private and your computer off-limits to cyber-criminals. Here's a brief list of important security measures to take for your PC:

- **Use a firewall.** Firewalls protect your computer from incoming attacks and can also block outgoing transmissions should your computer become infected with a virus or malware. Firewalls can be in either hardware or software form.

- **Update your Internet browser.** Software manufacturers often release updates to address new security issues and fix program bugs. Whether you prefer Internet Explorer (IE) (www.microsoft.com/ie), Mozilla's Firefox (www.mozilla.org), or another browser, be certain to use the most recent version. Both IE and Firefox have settings that allow the programs to update automatically.

- **Run antivirus software.** Viruses can destroy your computer, steal your information, or run malicious programs without your knowledge. Install an antivirus program and keep it up to date. Several free or low-cost programs are available.

- **Run antispyware software.** Spyware can be simply annoying or completely destructive. While some viruses and spyware work together and may be stopped with antivirus software, keep an up-to-date spyware detection program running for increased protection.

- **Secure your wireless network.** Wireless Internet access (WiFi) is wonderful. If you use a wireless device in your home, however, follow the instructions in the user manual to set up security, or you're giving hackers and freeloaders an open door to enter your world.

- **Turn on your spam filters.** Most email programs include a spam filter that you can customize to your liking. Stopping spam before it reaches your inbox is another way to protect your computer from attacks. Antispam programs are available in case you want additional protection. I discuss this topic further in the next section.

- **Back up your computer.** Performing regular computer backups protects your data and your sanity. Depending on your needs and budget, backups can be performed using a mix of external drives, software programs, or online resources.

Although nothing is foolproof, and new threats are always on the horizon, following the preceding recommendations provides a first line of defense. For more information about any of these items, I recommend that novice computer users pick up the latest edition of Michael Miller's *Absolute Beginner's Guide to Computer Basics*, available at most libraries and bookstores. Get Safe Online (www.getsafeon-line.org) offers free expert advice about Internet security, including instructions for Linux and Mac users, and Tech Support Forum (www.techsupportforum.com) offers helpful details on security options, including how to diagnose and resolve security problems.

Now that your computer is protected, we can move on to protecting your information.

Protect Your Information

As in the real world, honest, law-abiding craigslist citizens far out-number the criminals, so this chapter *is not* meant to scare you away. I want to empower you—to give you the knowledge and tools to use craigslist wisely and safely. Most Internet crime starts when unsus-pecting users give out their personal information (directly or indi-rectly). Protecting your privacy is key to staying safe on the Internet. Let's look at ways to keep your information out of the wrong hands.

Choose Your Email Address Wisely

Many people don't realize how much information they reveal in their email address. Personal email addresses should never include your full name, your birth date, or other identifying information.

Guard Your Email Address

Never use your primary email address to register on any community-based or social networking site, sign up for a newsletter, or join a forum or group. Give your primary email address only to people you know and trust. When spammers learn your email address, your inbox will overflow with bogus offers and virus-packing email. Valid email addresses are sold from one spammer to another, so it's nearly impossible to close the floodgates after you start receiving spam.

Spammers use harvesting programs and other devious tricks to steal people's email addresses off websites and from forums. During my research for this book, I was shocked to discover a simple and free technique for gathering email addresses off the Internet. Without sharing the details, I tested it and was able to collect close to 1,000 addresses in less than 20 minutes (which I promptly deleted). But my test was enough to make it clear to me that using my actual email address for replies left me begging to be spammed.

Having multiple email addresses may seem like too much work, but using disposable email addresses (DEAs) can simplify things. A DEA is a temporary email address (alias) that you give out in place of your real email address. DEAs are useful for online shopping, signing up for websites and newsletters, or joining forums and user groups. Email sent to an alias is forwarded to the target address you specify, until the alias is turned off or expires. If you use a separate alias for each contact and begin to receive spam through a particular alias, you will know who compromised your information and can disable that alias without disrupting your other email.

A number of convenient disposable email services are available, but not all offer a way to reply to email by using your alias—and without that feature, you'll still disclose your real address when you respond to email. TrashMail (www.trashmail.net) and spamgourmet (www.spamgourmet.com) are free services with good features and flexibility. Both allow you to reply to forwarded email without disclosing your true email address.

ShieldedMail (www.shieldedmail.com) and Emailias (www.emailias.com) are virtual email services that cost less than $20 per year. These web-based programs act as a protection layer between your inbox and the Internet. In addition to unlimited DEAs, features include virus scanning, multiple target addresses, and email header customization.

The downside of DEAs is that because people use them to send spam or flame mail anonymously, their domains are sometimes banned by group and list owners. Because both ShieldedMail and Emailias allow you to use your own domain name, you can use their services and not worry about this issue, if you want to take the time to set them up. Alternatively, you can use a domain seller, such as One World Domains (www.oneworlddomains.com), to register your own domain name for under $10 per year. This option gives you the freedom to use an address that's more personal (and usually more interesting) than a typical Yahoo! or Hotmail address.

ZoEmail (www.zoemail.com) and Yahoo! Mail Plus (mailplus.mail. yahoo.com) are full-service web-based email programs that you can use as your primary email address. Both allow you to create disposable email addresses for your account to keep your inbox spam-free. ZoEmail pricing starts at $11.88 per year; Yahoo! Mail Plus will cost you $19.99 annually. Both are low-cost solutions when you consider the time saved by avoiding handling spam.

If you're adamant about sticking with a single email address, try Gmail (mail.google.com). Google's free email program offers one of the most powerful and customizable email services available. Part of its appeal is Google's highly effective spam filter, which works with surprising accuracy to identify unwanted email. Spam is sent to a separate folder and deleted automatically after 30 days. Gmail is highly customizable, can act as a command center for multiple email addresses, and works with email clients such as Outlook and Mozilla.

Use Spam Filters and Blockers

If you've followed the recommendations in the previous section, you already have some type of spam filter running. But if you're getting pummeled, this level of protection may not be enough. Consider adding one of the many antispam programs available today. These programs use a variety of technologies to identify, quarantine, and block spam before it hits your inbox.

Compatible filters are available for just about every email program. Here are three of the many available:

- **ChoiceMail One**—www.digiportal.com/homeproducts.html
- **vqME AntiSpam**—www.vanquish.com/products/products_ personal_antispam.shtml
- **MailWasher Pro**—www.firetrust.com/products/mailwasher-pro

Because these filters work in different ways and have different features, take some time to research spam filtering and find the filter that works best for you.

Don't Let Things Slip

You're not obligated to provide your information to anyone, particularly via email. Some Internet scams are designed to steal a person's money outright, but the goal of many cons is to trick users into giving out their personal information, which leads to identity theft and can cause much greater damage.

Even if someone requests your phone number, address, or banking information, you don't have to give it to that person. Share your information only when you feel safe doing so. Also, never provide more information than necessary. If someone responds to an ad and wants to contact you by phone (and only if you're comfortable doing so), send only your first name and phone number; the recipient doesn't need your last name or address until you reach the stage where you're ready to meet. If you're following the craigslist model, there's never a reason to share your financial information.

Spot Scammers Before They Spot You

Internet criminals are trying to steal your money, your information, or both. Because knowledge is power, knowing what to watch out for will greatly reduce your chances of being taken for a ride. This section covers the most common scams.

There are red flags to watch for when dealing online. For example, you should be suspicious of oddly worded email when the buyer isn't local. This doesn't mean that anyone with poor writing skills is a cyber-criminal—only that people unfamiliar with English often give themselves away by using words incorrectly. Like most advertisers, scammers work to create a sense of urgency. They want you to act on emotion, before you have time to think logically. They may also try to build trust by being overly friendly and praising you before you've done anything deserving of praise. Look for inconsistencies. Most criminals are corresponding with many people at a time and will get their lies mixed up.

If you receive messages like the ones described, you might be tempted to respond, either in hopes that the sender is legitimate or even to "play the game." My advice: Don't! Delete the email and go on with your life. At best, you're wasting precious time; at worst, you might get drawn in.

Out-of-Area Buyer

Unfortunately, the out-of-area buyer scam is all too common. The good news is that you can avoid being swindled if you know what to look for. The messages included in these examples are real and unedited. They're the result of test listings I ran on several craigslist communities. In each instance, I ran an ad for electronics or jewelry and overpriced the item. I received few or no legitimate responses, but no shortage of offers to pay me even more than my asking price.

The game starts when someone responds to your listing and is a little too eager to throw money at whatever you're selling, most notably high-ticket items such as computers, electronics, and jewelry (see Figure 3.1). The scammer asks few of the typical buyer questions beyond finding out whether the item is still available (see Figure 3.2).

Dear Seller,

I saw your item listing on craigslist and and i just showed the picture to my client of mine who needs item urgently and he has fallen in love with it immediately.... so we are very much serious and interested in purchasing it. We are willing to offer you $1600.00 USD for it including shipping via Standard Delivery Service and will be making Payment via PayPal which is Fast and Secure . Please do get back to me as soon as possible if this offer agrees with you. We will be responsible for all shipping charges and insurance. Expecting your reply and oblige and i will also appreciate your detailed Name and your PayPal email address so that payment can be made and sent to you asap

Pls do get back asap.
Best Regards

Figure 3.1
If someone is jumping up and down to buy from you, it's likely that he or she is only trying to reach into your wallet.

When you respond, the scammer will begin to press for the sale, as shown in Figure 3.3. There are several tip-offs here:

- Offering to pay more than the asking price before knowing the cost of shipping
- Detailed explanation of why the buyer needs the item shipped to another location—usually as a gift
- Requesting to use little-known or dubious payment methods
- Misrepresenting the security of the payment method

From: jjohnacquah@aol.in
Sent: Sat 12/1/2007 1:17 AM
To:
Cc:
Subject: Sony VAIO Laptop VGN-FZ280E/B Blue Ray · $1500

** CRAIGSLIST ADVISORY --- AVOID SCAMS BY DEALING LOCALLY
** Avoid: wiring money, cross-border deals, work-at-home
** Beware: cashier checks, money
orders, escrow, shipping
** More
Info: http://www.craigslist.org/about/scams.html

Hello,

   I write in response to your advertisement which appeared in the criagslist website, And respectfully request if the item is still available. Let me read from you seller.

John Acquah

Figure 3.2
Poorly worded email that asks little about your listing is typical for scammers.

These are common statements for this type of scam. They play both to people's desire to bring joy (via the gift) and to our desire for the big score (by receiving more than asked).

Hello,

   Thanks for your response.

   I am living in wisconsin, But i want to ship, The Sony VAIO Laptop VGN-FZ280E/B Blue Ray to my son as a christmas gift. I would have done that myself but i have no chance to do that now, Because in my office we work till midnight. My son is a senior staff in the Consulate office in Dubai, He is in a research now somewhere out of his office .

I'll be paying you through payko
online money order or paypal. It's
secure and protects two parties in a transaction. I would like you to provide the below requirements in your reply for me to send it to Payko Office for payment before you ship it.

  Full Name:
  Full contact address:
  Zip Code:

All this information should be provided correctly to avoid wrong payment.

I will forward my son's residential address to you
 for shipping as soon as the payment reaches you. It will be included on the payment comfirmation.

I would be very grateful to hear your response soonest.

Thanks Immensely,
John Acquah.

NB: I will be paying you $1700 for both the cost price and the shipping fee.

Figure 3.3
Overpaying, risky payment methods, and complex shipping terms are red flags for scams.

Most scammers are patient people because they understand the importance of gaining your trust: It's the only way to convince you to ship the merchandise. Almost all the scammer's messages will be friendly and upbeat, happy to address any concern you might have—that is, until the scammer claims to have sent payment. You may receive an obviously fake-looking notice of payment, as shown in Figure 3.4. This one was sent from a webmail account completely unrelated to PayPal (www.paypal.com). It's filled with typos and grammatical errors. As with most criminal schemes, though, over time these email messages may become more difficult to distinguish from the real thing. Two important points to remember are that legitimate services such as PayPal do not hold your money pending proof of shipment and that PayPal never mails out money orders.

Dear Janet,

We hereby inform you that our client (John Acquah) has successfully made the payment using PAYPAL. We are here to inform you that you can now ship out the item he paid for and you should also send us the Tracking Number and the estimated number of days of arrival of the shipment for verification purpose. After this, your account will be processed within 48 - 72 hours of Shipments and the fund will reflect in you Paypal Account. WARNING: PLEASE, DO SEND US A COPY OF THE TRACKING NUMBER AND TO THE BUYER. THIS IS TO PREVENT FRAUDULENT ACTIVITIES AT THE END OF TRANSACTION, AND TO ENABLE US PROCESS YOUR MONEY FAST.

Thanks For Using Paypal,
Paypal Team.
==

PayPal

ATTENTION
The order has been APPROVED, you CAN NOW ship the merchandise to the buyer's shipping address. You are expected to make the shipment with 48 hours of recieving this Payment Approval Notification and get back to our Costumer/Technical Dept. with the tracking number for Shippment Verification.

PLEASE NOTE
The Money OrderSM will NOT be dispatched or get to your resident until the shipment has been verified. This measure is taken in order to protect both seller and buyer interests and to reduce the occurrence of fraudulent activities.

****PLEASE NOTE***
Due to the fact that PAYPAL processes thousands of orders daily, paypal RECOMMENDS contacting the Customer Support Representative that has been assigned to this particular Order directly. This ensures speedy verification of shipment as well as prompt dispatch the Money OrderSM. Send shippment tracking details to **paypaldirectt@mail2expert.com**

Figure 3.4
A bad attempt at tricking a seller into believing that a payment is waiting.

When I received a notification of payment email and didn't promptly supply the "buyer" with shipping information, I began receiving email from the buyer such as the one shown in Figure 3.5. Finished with the friendly words, the buyer now "demands" that I send him the shipping info. When I failed to respond promptly, I continued to receive duplicates of this email for several days.

Dear Janet,

I have done the payment through paypal, Below is my son's shipping information.

NAME : JOHN ACQUAH J

ADDRESS : DEIRA PARK HOTEL

CITY: DEIRA,

STATE: DUBAI,

ZIP CODE: 9714

COUNTRY: UNITED ARAB EMIRATES

I demand for the shipping information immediately.

Thank you,
John Acquah

Figure 3.5
Next, the buyer will begin to pressure you to ship the merchandise.

Of all the scams that I encountered, the most upsetting was from an individual who claimed to be a United States resident currently hospitalized in the United Kingdom. She wanted to purchase a wedding ring set for her son that I had listed. After we exchanged a number of messages over several days, wherein she repeatedly asked me to send her my credit card information so she could pay me, I finally told her I was afraid of being scammed. She responded by emailing me a scanned copy of her driver's license. It appeared to be an authentic California driver's license. I forwarded the information to the local authorities, but I know that tracking down these types of criminals is nearly impossible.

The most outrageous attempt I encountered was from a woman who claimed that her health would not let her leave the house to come pick up her purchase. She wanted to pay me by "echeck," but before she could pay me, she first instructed me to go buy business check paper for only $25 at my local office supply store.

This scam can be played out in other ways too. A housing wanted ad I had placed led to my being contacted by a man who wanted me to lease his nearby home while he did missionary work in Africa. He sent pictures, provided a bogus address, and added that his brother in another state would gladly ship the keys to me overnight as soon as I sent him the first month's rent and deposit.

Overpayment Scam

In the overpayment scam, the buyer wants to pay you with a cashier's check or money order written for an amount well above your selling price, usually offering a less-than-plausible explanation. The scammer asks that you wire the overpayment amount back to him or her or forward it to a third party who is frantically waiting for the funds. The scammer generously offers to let you keep a bonus amount for the inconvenience.

The problem is that the check or money order is fake, and eventually will be returned to your bank. This process can take days or even weeks. You're out the full amount that you wired—plus any fees charged by your bank—and the scammer is long gone.

Nigerian 4-1-9 Scam

The Nigerian 4-1-9 scam, also called the Nigerian Advance Fee Scam, has been around for many years but still claims victims. It's named after the section in the Nigerian penal code that covers it. It isn't directly related to craigslist, but can be attempted on businesses and individuals whose email addresses are harvested off craigslist. This scam is no longer limited to Nigeria, but originates from many other countries.

The scam starts when you receive a somewhat official-looking email message from a person who claims to be in a foreign government or bank (there are various versions). The email explains that because of certain events, such as the death of a high-ranking government official, the sender is in search of someone trustworthy to help transfer tens of millions of dollars out of the sender's country. In return, the sender offers to share a large percentage of the money.

Often, this scam is played out over many months, at first building the victim's confidence and then requesting advance fees when problems arise along the way. The scammer continues to request money from the victim, sometimes attempting to convince him or her to travel to Nigeria to meet with (fake) government officials to complete the transaction.

Although it may seem hard to believe that anyone would fall prey to this scam, it still succeeds on a regular basis. This scam can cost the victim much more than money: One man was killed after traveling to Nigeria, and other victims have gone missing.

If you receive one of these email messages, *do not respond*. Forward the email to the Federal Trade Commission at spam@uce.gov. If you have fallen victim to a scam like this, contact your local branch of the Secret Service. A list of branches is available at www.secretservice.gov/field_offices.shtml.

Safe and Pleasant Transactions

Because craigslist is a local online classifieds site intended to result in face-to-face transactions between buyers and sellers, there are no safeguards in place, such as user feedback ratings, required registration, or transaction guarantees. Whereas many people will tell you "Buyer beware," my best advice is "Buyer be smart." You can avoid most problems by following a few simple rules:

- Deal locally only. It's much more difficult to be scammed in person.
- Never give out financial information.
- Supply only as much personal information as necessary, and only after you're confident that the person is legitimate.
- Meet in a public place whenever possible.
- Never have someone come to your house when you're alone. Have a friend or two with you.
- Expect no-shows. You'll be less frustrated if you realize that it's a small part of doing business.
- Inspect the merchandise.
- Test the item. It may have worked last time the seller tried it, but make certain that it's still working now.

- Review maintenance records when possible.

- Complete a third-party inspection. For vehicles and so on, pay for an expert to look over the item.

- Never assume. If you and the other party have not discussed a specific term of the sale, don't assume that you'll agree on it. Discuss terms early on and keep open lines of communication with the other party.

- Ask for cash.

- For a higher-priced item, consider accepting a cashier's check drawn on a local bank, or a U.S. Post Office money order.

- Get your transaction in writing. Ask for a receipt for high-ticket items. If guarantees are made, get them in writing, too.

- For service providers, ask for proof of any required licensing and for references.

Safe and Sound Online Dating

Many of the previous transaction rules I've mentioned apply to dating, too, but because there's so much more at stake, I felt it was important to cover this topic separately. This section discusses what has become traditional online dating. The **personals** section on craigslist also has categories other than dating, some of which are high-risk.

Warning 4U For those who are not interested in taking it slow in regard to online dating, the best advice I can offer is to trust your instincts. Listen to that voice inside you and get away if you feel even the least bit vulnerable. Also, NEVER meet at anyone's home or a secluded place. Always have your first few meetings in a very public place. Even then, let someone know where you're going and when to expect you back. If you aren't comfortable sharing the information directly, write it on a piece of paper and leave the paper somewhere in your home where people would easily spot it.

Here are some ways to protect yourself—and your heart—when looking for love online.

Take it slow and enjoy the process. This is the best way to protect yourself. It's easier to connect with people online than in person. Anonymous communication frees many of us of our inhibitions. However, that instant attraction can wear off as we get to know each other better. Exchange email and instant messages, and before long you'll know whether the attraction is real or simply the thrill of possibilities.

If the interest is still there after you know more about the person, move on to phone calls. This is an important stage because it's your first chance to communicate directly. Use this time to learn more about each other and see whether you share goals and values. Then move on to meeting in person. By pacing the process, you'll have a stronger foundation and a greater chance of success.

Keep it private. Don't give out your personal information too soon. Knowing a person's first name and general location is fine to start. You can give out your cell phone number when you agree to move forward in the relationship. Because home phones can be traced to addresses, give your cell phone at first. No one needs to know where you live to reach you by email or phone. You don't have to volunteer your contact info to prove that you trust someone or because you don't want to appear paranoid. If the other person doesn't respect your boundaries, it's doubtful that he or she is right for you.

Make it public. If you decide to meet, do it in a public place. Meet for lunch at a restaurant or in the early evening for coffee. Never go to the other person's home, invite him or her to yours, or meet at a secluded place. Remember to use this time to talk and get to know one another better. Avoid going to the movies or anywhere your time will be spent focused away from each other.

Do your homework. When you have information about the other person, do some searching online. You can find out a lot about some people by Googling email address, phone number, name and city, or job info. Although you may feel as if you're spying, keep in mind that knowledge is power, and anything on the Internet is public record. Many employers routinely check out applicants this way, and a potential date or mate is definitely more important than a job candidate.

Enlist a wingman (or woman). In the beginning, tell someone you trust about your date before you go. Provide the time and place information, as well as details about the other person. Keep your cell phone with you at all times, and call from the washroom to update your backup on any change of plans.

Make it equal. For the first few dates, drive separately and pay your own way. If you arrive on your own, you're free to leave whenever you want. By taking care of your share of the check, you ensure that you're both investing the same amount in the date. You won't owe each other anything, and you start on a level playing field.

Don't drink. Alcohol can cloud your judgment and lessen your inhibitions; being nervous can magnify the effects. Stay clear-headed and in control. Not only is it safer, but it's a better choice if you're hoping to have a lasting relationship.

Read the signs. Don't overlook or explain away red flags that tell you the two of you aren't a match. If the other person misrepresents himself or herself, tells lies, is vague, criticizes or is disrespectful to you or others, is closed-minded, doesn't share your values or goals, or abuses alcohol or drugs, those are big flashing billboards that read "Run away!" You'll almost certainly be disappointed if you expect the other person to change. Dragging out the relationship isn't going to improve your chances for happily ever after.

Walk away. If you realize that a date isn't going well for you, end it. Don't be rude or disrespectful, but suffering through it serves no purpose. If the connection isn't there for you, it most likely isn't there for the other person either. Walking away is essential if you feel frightened or threatened in any way.

Value yourself. Respect your heart and your body, and expect the other person to do the same. The value of anything is based on perception. If you don't see your worth, the other person probably won't, either.

Online dating is a wonderful thing. With busy lives, going out to meet quality people has become harder and harder. Use the preceding information to keep out of harm's way and enrich your dating experience.

From Here...

Protecting yourself in our increasingly connected yet segmented world is a real challenge. I hope that the information in this chapter enriches your craigslist experience and helps you to feel safer and more in control. Ready to get started? Chapter 4 gives you some of the vital details on how and where to post your listing.

Posting on craigslist

4 All About the Listings 61

5 Successful Listing Strategies 77

6 Listing in the Community 91

7 Listing in the Housing Section 113

8 Listing in For Sale 139

9 Listing in Services 159

10 Listing in Jobs and Gigs 187

11 Listing in Resumes 207

12 Listing in Personals 225

All About the Listings

This chapter covers posting guidelines and gets you and up running with step-by-step instructions for the posting process. It also explains craigslist's flagging process and what to do if your listing gets flagged.

Each craigslist category displays a list of ads by title with the most recent posts at the top (see Figure 4.1). The price and location are also displayed. Titles with the letters "pic" or "img" at the end include at least one picture or graphic in the listing. craigslist has been experimenting with displaying thumbnails of images alongside the title and will probably roll out this feature soon (see Figure 4.2).

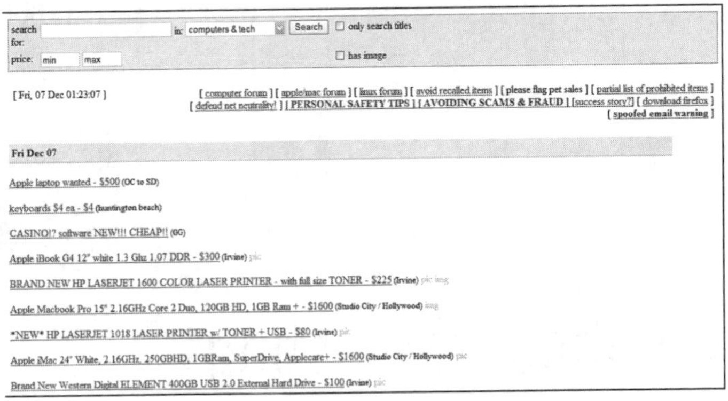

Figure 4.1
craigslist's category listings.

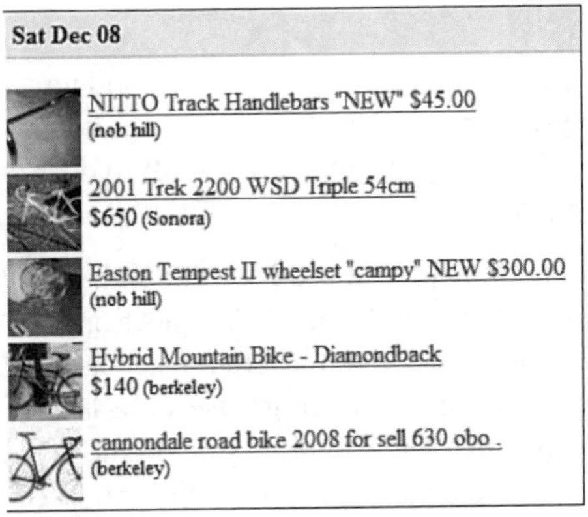

Figure 4.2
Thumbnail images used in some craigslist categories.

Anatomy of a Listing

As shown in Figure 4.3, an individual ad resembles a simple text email and contains standard information, such as a title, price, description, image (where permitted), and location. Flagging links are displayed in the upper-right corner.

Title   Price   Flagging Links

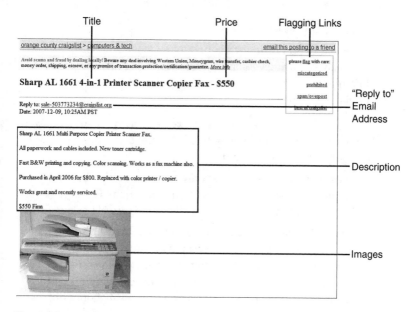

"Reply to"
Email
Address

Description

Images

Figure 4.3
craigslist's ad layout.

The "reply to" information is located below the title. By default, craigslist assigns each post a *disposable email address* (DEA) to display. Responses to the DEA forward to the email address on your account. You can choose to display your true email address, but doing so publicizes your email address on the Internet for spammers to harvest for free. If you prefer not to be contacted by email, you can choose not to display either email address and instead include contact information in the description field. Although this approach may be reasonable for businesses, individuals should never list their personal information this way.

You can upload up to four pictures with each listing in the **community**, **housing**, **for sale**, and **personals** categories. The total size for all image files should be less than 150 kilobytes. craigslist supports several file types, including JPG, GIF, TIF, and PNG. Of these, JPG is recommended for reliability and file size.

Playing By the Rules

Before you start posting, it's important to understand craigslist's policies to avoid having your listings blocked or flagged. There's more information on flagging later in this chapter. Here are some posting guidelines to follow:

- **Post one listing per item, in the correct category.** Although your listing might work in more than one category, choose the category that's most relevant.

- **Post to your local craigslist only.** No cross-posting between communities. craigslist is for local, cash transactions. Postings from outside the community or that offer shipping will be flagged.

- **Post a maximum of once every 48 hours.** craigslist's policies allow multiple posts for different items within the same category. However, many users flag multiple posts from the same person. If you have several items to sell in the same category, it's best to include them in one ad. You can repost every 48 hours, but you should delete the original post first; otherwise, your new ad may be blocked.

- **Spread out your posts.** craigslist will block users who rapid-fire listings over a short period of time. craigslist won't give out specific numbers, which can vary by community and category, but if you have lots of legitimate posts, space them out over a day or so to avoid a problem.

- **Businesses can advertise, but only in the <u>services</u> section.** The <u>services</u> section may not seem like the right place if you're selling merchandise, but it contains a small business category for that exact purpose. The <u>for sale</u> section is for individuals selling their personal belongings only.

- **Post want ads in the <u>for sale/wanted</u> category only.** Although it's logical to post in the category of the item you want, buyers don't like sifting through want ads, and your listing will be removed.

- **No posting agents or automated posting.** List your own items and do it manually.

- **No posting replies to ads.** The classifieds are for advertising only. Send replies directly to the poster. All discussions and commentary are limited to the forums.

- **No pet sales.** You cannot offer pets for sale or breeding. You can post pets in the **community pets** category with a small rehoming fee. Livestock can be offered in the **for sale farm+garden** category.

- **No illegal activities.** Although people try to work around this guideline by using code words, posts will be blocked and the posters banned.

- **No controlled substances.** Besides illegal drugs and paraphernalia, this includes prescription medication and medical equipment.

- **No counterfeit, bootleg, or knock-off items.** This includes anything that would constitute copyright infringement.

- **No weapons and related items.** No selling or bartering of any weapons, including firearms, knives, tear gas, stun guns, ammunition, and accessories.

- **No MLM in any category.** craigslist's terms of use prohibit multi-level marketing or affiliate listings. Even if not caught by the filters, these ads are quickly flagged off.

- **The jobs section is for paying work only.** If there is no compensation, the listing should go in the appropriate **gigs** category.

Following these guidelines will help you ensure successful listings and avoid the frustration of spending your time and energy on ads that no one will ever see.

The Posting Process

craigslist has always kept the posting process simple. Although you're not required to be logged in to your craigslist account, posting through your account will make managing your listings faster and easier.

While logged in to your account, follow these steps to post a new listing:

1. Click the **post to classifieds** link on the home page, as shown in Figure 4.4.

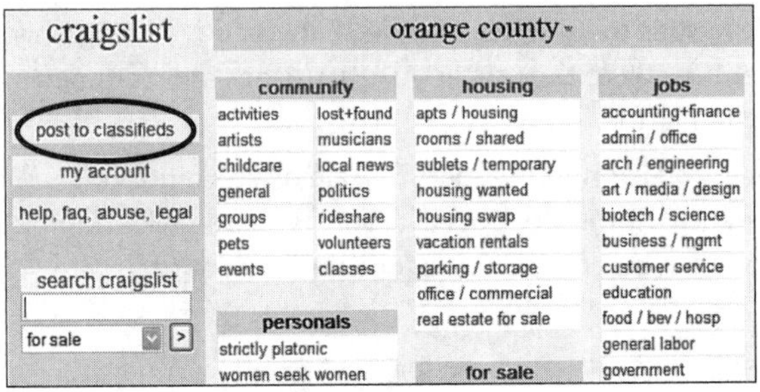

Figure 4.4
Use the **post to classifieds** link on craigslist's home page to start a listing.

2. On the next screen, as shown in Figure 4.5, select the type of posting to continue.

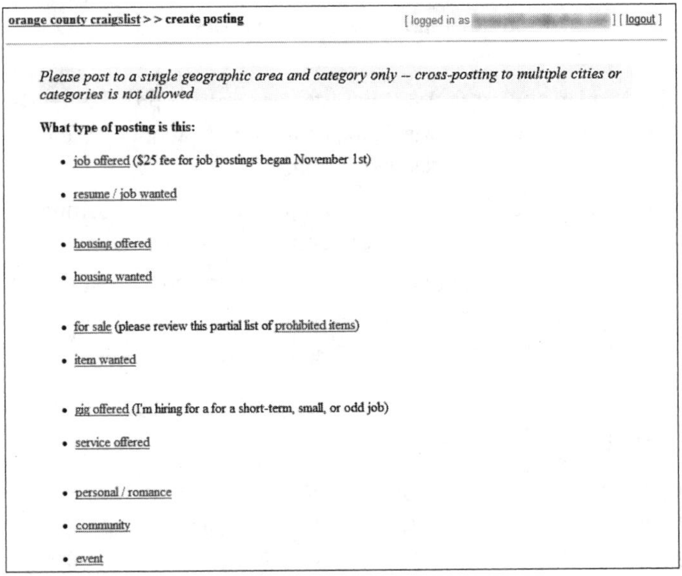

Figure 4.5
Choose the type of listing to proceed.

3. When the list of categories appears, as shown in Figure 4.6, select the appropriate category to reach the listing page.

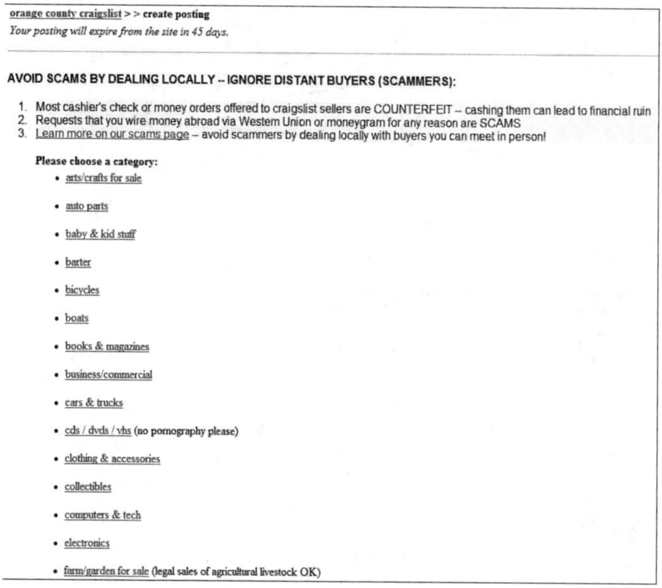

<u>orange county craigslist</u> > > **create posting**
Your posting will expire from the site in 45 days.

AVOID SCAMS BY DEALING LOCALLY -- IGNORE DISTANT BUYERS (SCAMMERS):

1. Most cashier's check or money orders offered to craigslist sellers are COUNTERFEIT -- cashing them can lead to financial ruin
2. Requests that you wire money abroad via Western Union or moneygram for any reason are SCAMS
3. <u>Learn more on our scams page</u> -- avoid scammers by dealing locally with buyers you can meet in person!

Please choose a category:
- <u>arts/crafts for sale</u>
- <u>auto parts</u>
- <u>baby & kid stuff</u>
- <u>barter</u>
- <u>bicycles</u>
- <u>boats</u>
- <u>books & magazines</u>
- <u>business/commercial</u>
- <u>cars & trucks</u>
- <u>cds / dvds / vhs</u> (no pornography please)
- <u>clothing & accessories</u>
- <u>collectibles</u>
- <u>computers & tech</u>
- <u>electronics</u>
- <u>farm/garden for sale</u> (legal sales of agricultural livestock OK)

Figure 4.6
Select a category to continue.

4. On the next page, as shown in Figure 4.7, fill in the title, price, location, and description. As mentioned previously, it's best to leave the email address section defaulted and use the disposable craigslist address. Click the **Add/Edit Images** button, or skip to step 7 if you don't want to add pictures.

5. When the **Add/Edit Images** box expands, as shown in Figure 4.8, click the **Browse** button to add images stored on your computer.

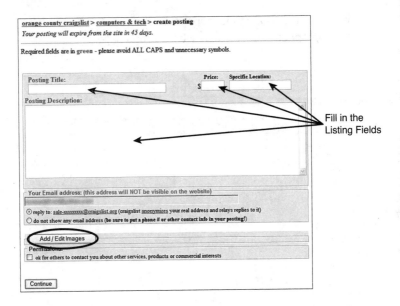

Figure 4.7
Fill in your listing information and add images.

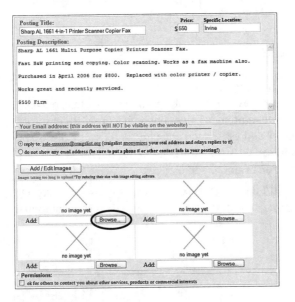

Figure 4.8
Select Browse to locate stored images.

6. When the Choose File dialog box appears, as shown in Figure 4.9, locate the image file you want to add and double-click it. When the file is added correctly, a green circle and the image filename will display in the image box (see Figure 4.10). Repeat this step to add up to four images.

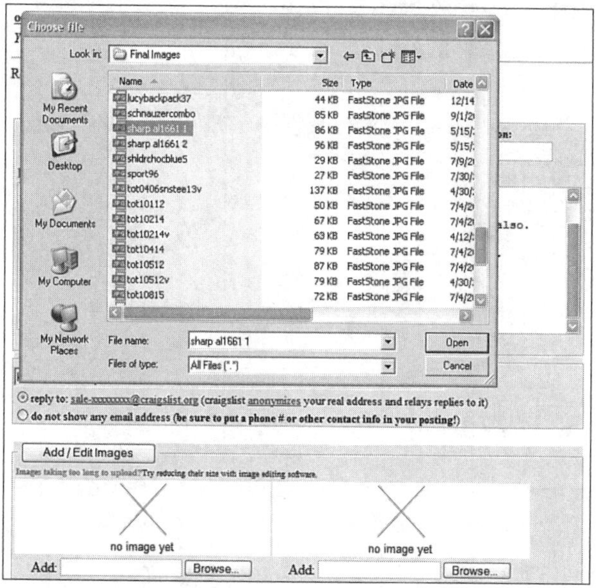

Figure 4.9
Upload a picture using the Choose File box.

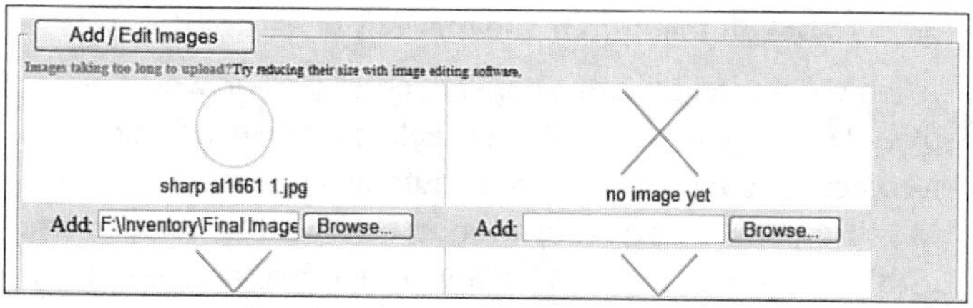

Figure 4.10
The image filename displays below a green circle.

7. After you've added your images, as shown in Figure 4.11, click **Continue** to proceed.

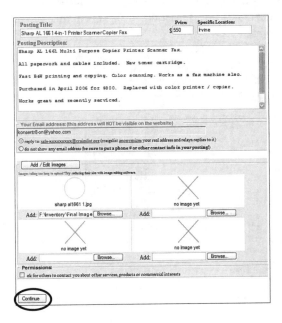

Figure 4.11
Click **Continue** when finished.

8. When the preview appears, as shown in Figure 4.12, you can proofread your listing and check the layout. Click **Continue** to proceed or **Edit** to return to the previous screen.

9. When the "captcha" screen appears, enter the two words displayed on the screen into the text field, as shown in Figure 4.13. A captcha program works to stop automated posting by software programs by requiring a verification word or words to be read and entered correctly. ReCaptcha (www.recaptcha.net) is a free program from Carnegie Mellon University that uses the verification process to help digitize books and preserve literature. There is also an option to play a series of digits to allow sight-impaired visitors to use the process too.

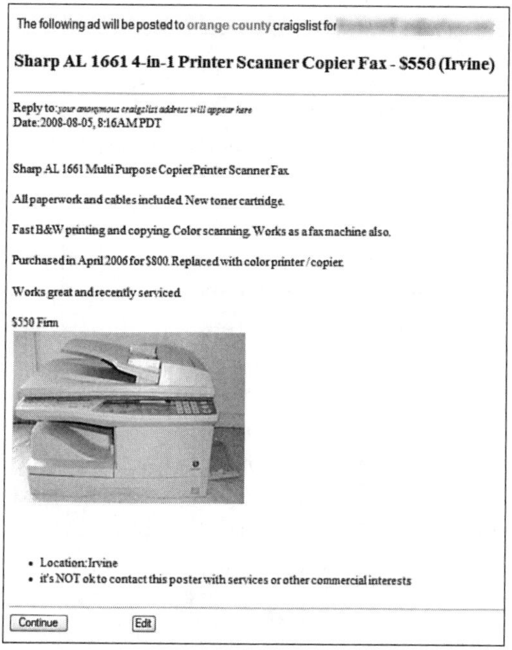

Figure 4.12
Preview your listing for content and formatting before posting.

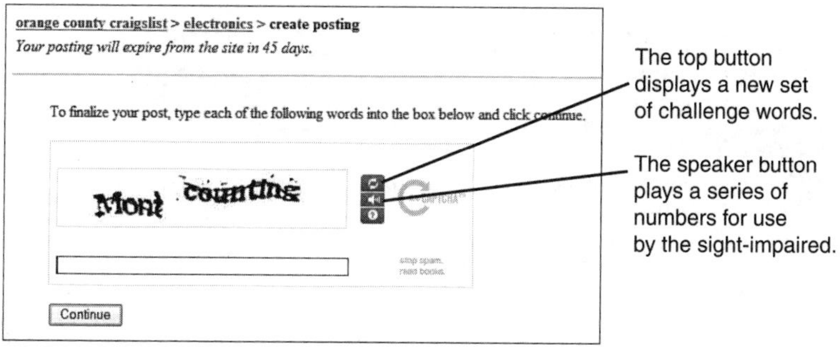

The top button displays a new set of challenge words.

The speaker button plays a series of numbers for use by the sight-impaired.

Figure 4.13
Enter the verification words on the captcha screen and click **Continue**.

10. A confirmation notice should appear, as shown in Figure 4.14, indicating that your listing has been submitted.

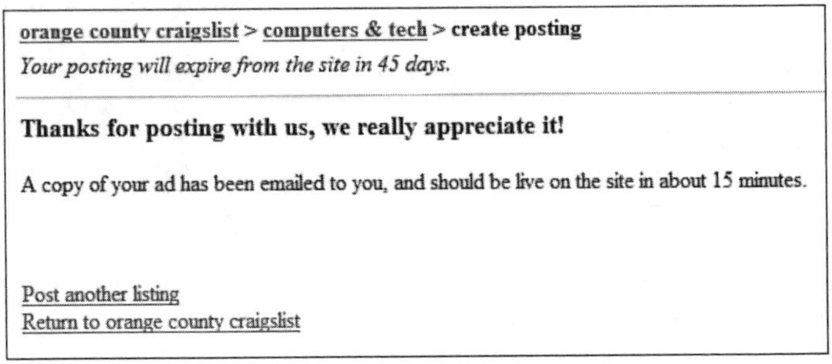

orange county craigslist > computers & tech > create posting
Your posting will expire from the site in 45 days.

Thanks for posting with us, we really appreciate it!

A copy of your ad has been emailed to you, and should be live on the site in about 15 minutes.

Post another listing
Return to orange county craigslist

Figure 4.14
The confirmation page stating your listing has been submitted.

It can take up to 15 minutes for your ad to appear in the category listing and search results. You'll also receive a confirmation email message, as shown in Figure 4.15, that includes a link to your ad.

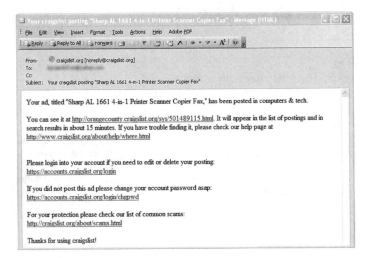

Figure 4.15
Confirmation email with link to your ad.

craigslist recently implemented a phone verification process for posting to the **services** category. It is an undocumented process designed to stop abusers from flooding the category with spam and scams. Management has indicated that this is only one of the steps they intend to put in place to increase security, so there probably will be others shortly. You can read more about it in Chapter 9, "Listing In Services."

Unfortunately, if you encounter posting problems, craigslist usually doesn't display an error message or indicate what's causing the problem. Very often, though, the problem is that the total file size of your images is too large. If you're having difficulty completing the posting process, try reducing the size of the images and posting again. Remember, the total file size should be less than 150KB.

Getting Creative

Although craigslist likes to keep things simple, sometimes it's fun to jazz up your ads a little using Hypertext Markup Language (HTML). Remember that craigslist filters may block listings with excessive HTML, so use it sparingly.

You can display a link to another website in your ad by typing the full URL (for example, http://www.*addresstovisit*.com). Include http:// in front of the address to have craigslist turn the URL into a link. Not all categories allow links to outside websites, so check the terms of use.

If you prefer to host your own images or want to add more than four to any listings, the images must be hosted on the Internet and you need to know the address or URL for each one. When you have that information, insert the following code:

```
<img src="http://www.test.com/image.jpg">
```

Replace *www.test.com/image*.jpg with the real address and the image's correct filename. The entire address, including http:// and file extension (.jpg in this example), must be enclosed in quotation marks ("").

You can also use basic HTML to format your description. If you're not familiar with HTML, www.w3schools.com offers short, easy-to-follow, free tutorials. Tables 4.1 and 4.2 show some basic HTML tags that currently work on craigslist.

Table 4.1 HTML Text Formatting Tags

Effect	Start Tag	End Tag
Paragraph	`<p>`	`</p>`
Line break	` `	`</br>`
List	`<li>`	`</li>`
Horizontal rule	`<hr>`	`</hr>`

Table 4.2 HTML Character Formatting Tags

Effect	Start Tag	End Tag
Bold	`<b>`	`</b>`
Italic	`<i>`	`</i>`
Emphasis (red)	`<em>`	`</em>`
Underline	`<u>`	`</u>`

Put these formatting tags to work by placing them at the beginning and end of any text you want to format. For example, entering `<b>This is bold.</b>` will display as **This is bold.** You can have fun with these tags by visiting the craigslist xyz test forum (forums.craigslist.org/?forumID=21) and trying the tags for yourself.

The craigslist Police

craigslist devotes tremendous resources to eliminating prohibited listings. In addition to staff moderation, craigslist uses filters designed to identify prohibited posts and block them from displaying on the site. Although they won't disclose the filtering criteria, blocked listings often include one or more of the following:

- Excessive HTML (a few tags are fine)
- Selling terms, such as "new in box," "great deal," or "hot buy" (outside the **services** category)
- Shipping or payment terms (such as PayPal)
- Terms associated with illegal activities
- Duplicate or similar postings
- Symbols, especially in the title

craigslist doesn't notify posters if their listings have been blocked. In fact, the poster will receive a confirmation email with a working link to the ad, and the ad will show as active in the poster's account, but it won't display in the category or search results.

If your ad doesn't display on the website, delete the listing through your account page, wait 20–30 minutes, and then repost the ad, omitting any questionable content. It can still take another 15 minutes to have your ad display.

If your ad still doesn't show up, visit the craigslist help desk forum (forums.craigslist.org/?forumID=9) to get help. For the fastest response, include a link to your listing and as much additional information as possible.

craigslist promotes user-moderation, so if prohibited ads do get past the filters, users identify these posts by a process called *flagging*. Flagging links are displayed in the upper-right corner of each listing, as shown in Figure 4.16.

Flagging Links

Figure 4.16
Flagging links are displayed in each listing.

Ads can be flagged as miscategorized, prohibited, or spam/overpost. Each user can flag an ad only one time. Although each category in each community has its own flagging threshold, it takes more than one or two flags to get an ad removed. But when that undisclosed number is reached, the post is removed automatically. While any prohibited listings will likely be flagged, overposting, attempting to sell pets, miscategorizing your item, and asking not to be flagged in your ads are hot buttons for many users.

If you receive an email stating that your ad has been flagged for removal, more often than not there's something wrong with your listing. If you can't figure out why it was removed, visit the craigslist flag help forum (forums.craigslist.org/?forumID=3) for assistance. Include a copy of the listing and as much relevant information as possible.

If your listing gets blocked or flagged for something other posters appear to get away with, don't take it personally. Both the filters and the flaggers are subjective, and both catch as many bad ads as possible.

Another flagging link on each listing nominates a post for the **best-of-craigslist** section. This is an oddly positive category, usually reserved for very unusual or extremely humorous postings. Flagging for the **best-of-craigslist** section will not get a listing removed. Once a listing has received a few "best of" flags, the staff will review it and add it to the **best-of-craigslist** section.

Editing and Deleting Posts

You can manage your existing ads from your craigslist account, as shown in Figure 4.17. Click any title in your account to display the listing with options for editing and deleting (see Figure 4.18). Be sure to delete the post if the item or service is no longer available.

ID	Date	Site	Category	Title	Fee
501489115	Dec 07 07	orc	computers & tech	Sharp AL 1661 4-in-1 Printer Scanner Copier Fax	
493341853	Nov 29 07	lax	computers & tech	Sony VAIO Dual Core Laptop VGN-FZ280 c/b	
493255736	Nov 29 07	isl	computers & tech	Sony VAIO Laptop VGN-FZ280E/B Blue Ray	
493046781	Nov 29 07	orc	photo/video	Nikon D200 Digital 10.2 MegaPixel SLR w/ extras	
492686800	Nov 28 07	sdo	jewelry	18K Gold Diamond Engagement Ring	

5 most recent postings
of 150 maximum returned [change]

[active pending removed by me expired flagged deleted]

Figure 4.17
Manage your postings from your craigslist account.

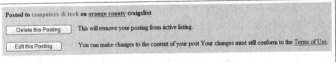

Figure 4.18
Edit or delete your listing.

From Here...

Now that you understand more about listings and the listing process, let's go on to the next chapter and see how you can make the most of buying and selling on craigslist.

5

Successful Listing Strategies

As an e-commerce consultant, I'm often approached for help by people who want to use craigslist but don't know where to start. Some understand the technical posting process but may have heard stories of (or experienced) unsuccessful listings, frustrating transactions, or spam/scams. The information in this chapter has come out of working with many clients, helping them to experience greater success using craigslist.

Over the years, I've found that most successful transactions—whether business or personal—have two factors in common:

- Well-defined goal
- Understanding of the market

The first advice I offer everyone is to approach each listing with a business mentality. Although it might seem as though a business posting would be significantly different from a private party ad, in reality the goals are the same. Whether you're advertising your business, searching for true love, selling personal items, or hoping to find someone to haul away an old refrigerator, the overall goal is the same: a safe, smooth, and successful outcome. You can use the steps in this chapter to achieve this goal. This strategy can make an enormous difference even when using craigslist to give away something free, as illustrated by the following example.

Example of an Unsuccessful Listing

In a meeting with Brandon, a client of mine, my suggestion to include craigslist in his Internet marketing plan was met with a firm "No." With great animation, Brandon went on to recount his experience using craigslist to give away an old couch. He spoke of unwanted early-morning phone calls and how many people chose to email him with lots of questions.

Brandon went on to complain about people who never showed up and how, when a couple did show up, the couch couldn't fit in their SUV. He added that he became so frustrated, he finally paid to have the couch hauled away.

I asked Brandon about the wording of his listing. He said it read, "FREE - Couch, tan. Good condition. Moving, must go." He included his phone number. When I asked him if he had researched the market, he laughed at me and asked why he would waste his time and energy researching something he is giving away.

Then I asked him how much time and energy he had wasted dealing with email, phone calls, no-shows, and finally arranging for someone to pick up the couch.

Brandon could have taken a few minutes and followed some easy steps to simplify the process and increase his chances of having a successful transaction. The rest of this chapter describes these steps, and then shows how Brandon could have applied them in his situation. In the following chapters, you'll learn how best to apply these steps to each craigslist category. Although none of these stratagems are *required* to create a listing, the time invested can result in more responses, faster results, smoother transactions, and increased return on investment.

Steps for Creating a Successful Listing

Creating a successful listing is a matter of four steps. None are complicated, but they do require some effort, so be prepared to invest an appropriate amount of time. (Spend more time preparing an ad selling a high-ticket item or promoting your business, and less on a posting to give something away.)

1. Educate yourself about your item, your customers, and your competition.

2. Set a specific and detailed goal to achieve with your listing.

3. Whether you're selling a tangible item or promoting a service, take pictures to use in your ad.

4. Using the information from the first three steps, write a listing that grabs readers' attention and shows them how'll they will benefit from buying your item.

 For simplicity's sake, in this chapter I'll use the term *item*, but the item could be a service you're offering, an event, or a need that you have.

The following sections provide more details and examples of each step in this process. As you complete each step and as you start working on your listing, I recommend that you keep written or typed notes about what you learn.

Step 1: Educate Yourself

Exploring what's already out there is usually the best place to start. Search craigslist using relevant keywords to find ads for items that are similar to yours. To truly understand the market, you need to do the following:

- Understand the item, service, or event.
- Determine your target audience.
- Find your competition.

As you read through the listings, the item information you want to note includes the correct listing category, terminology, pricing, demand, and so on.

Reading these listings will also give you information about your competition—the posts with which your listing will compete. It will probably become apparent rather quickly that there are various listing styles. As you read through the listings, note anything that catches your eye or turns you off. You can refer to these notes later when writing your listing.

Finally, figure out your target market. Think about the audience you're trying to reach and who will be most interested in your listing. For some listings, the description of your target market can be as comprehensive as gender, age, level of education, location, possible hobbies, and so on. You can increase your chance of meeting your goal by thinking like someone who's looking for what you have to offer.

Although craigslist is the best place to gather this information, you don't have to stop there. Other online sites such as eBay (www.ebay.com), Kijiji (eBay's free classifieds, www.kijiji.com), and Backpage.com (www.backpage.com) can provide you with a larger sampling. Your local newspaper classifieds may be useful too.

Step 2: Set Your Goal(s)

Now that you better understand your product, competition, and target market, visualize your ideal outcome. Write down what you want for your objective. It's easier for you to achieve a positive result if you have a clear goal in mind.

Your objective can be as simple or as complex as you want, but the more details you include, the better chance you'll achieve it. "Sell my car" is a valid goal, but "Sell my 2003 Honda Pilot for $11,000 cash within the next two weeks" is a more well-defined goal. As with any goal, putting it in writing is the first step to making it happen.

Besides writing down your objective, create four lists:

- Specifics
- Preferences
- Requirements
- Deal-breakers

Information you add to each of these lists can help you to define your goal and is also useful when writing your listing.

Preferences, requirements, and deal-breakers are self-explanatory. *Specifics* can include a detailed item description if you're selling an item; or who, what, where, when, why, and so on, if your listing is about a service, event, or need.

Your goal is the starting point for your listing, so the more information you include, the better the text you'll create. Include as much detail as possible at this point because you can always omit what doesn't work.

Step 3: Take Pictures

Including pictures with your listing is far more important than many people realize. Sharp, colorful images are the most effective way to grab someone's attention. craigslist even gives searchers an option to ignore listings that don't include an image. For safety's sake, I would never advise anyone to post a picture in a section like **personals**, but when listing in sections such as **housing**, **for sale**, and **services**, you should always add at least one picture.

Info 4U Why shouldn't you post a picture with your **personals** listing, since you're sort of "selling" yourself with that kind of ad? The answer is that there are no gatekeepers in the craigslist **personals** section. People don't always realize how easy it is to find out personal information about someone from their online trail. For example, a client of mine tried listing in the **personals** section. Someone responded to the ad who sounded normal and decent enough, so they exchanged a few email messages. My client used a disposable email address, and the respondent used what he probably thought was an anonymous address. But people have a habit of using the same login ID for lots of sites and for their email address. My client Googled the guy's login ID and found out that he was into voyeurism—including taking stealth pictures of young girls (the site bio made it clear that it was the same person). Not the sort of creep you'd want to see your picture or have your email address.

The most successful listings are those that include the most information. Pictures give users a wealth of instant information—before they even begin to read your text! They're an outstanding online sales tool. A crisp, well-lit closeup, as shown in Figure 5.1, can increase the number of interested people.

Figure 5.1
A great picture conveys lots of information and captures people's interest.

Use these tips to create pictures that will grab the reader's attention:

- **Shoot the item by itself.** Keep the picture free of clutter and other objects that draw attention from your item. In Figure 5.2, the photo includes too many other items in the image. You want the reader to see just the item you're posting.

- **Use a complementary background.** Whenever possible, photograph an item against a solid background color. Depending on the item's color, white, black, or midnight blue backgrounds usually work well. A pillowcase, sheet, or tablecloth with a solid color makes an inexpensive background. For larger items, such as a car, park the item alongside a wall or fence that's a solid color. (Choose one without an interesting texture that might be distracting.)

- **Zoom in.** Get as close to the item as possible to fill the shot. For smaller items, you may need to use a macro setting on your camera.

- **Focus.** Keep taking shots until you're certain you have images that are crisp and clear, unlike the one in Figure 5.3.

Figure 5.2
A picture filled with other items distracts the viewer's attention.

Figure 5.3
A blurry picture is almost as bad as no picture at all.

■ **Use good lighting.** Natural light works best, so photograph outside when possible. Try shooting slightly off-center if you use a flash or the item is highly reflective. If the flash is too harsh, try covering it with a layer or two of tissue paper. The photo in Figure 5.4 was shot without sufficient lighting.

Figure 5.4
A picture that's too dark or too light makes it impossible to see detail.

■ **Take lots of pictures.** With digital photography, your only real expense is time. The more valuable an item is, the more pictures you should include. Post shots from different sides and angles, and take a closeup of any known damage if you're selling an item in less than mint condition.

When you have all your pictures, preferably in JPG format, you're ready to move on to the next step.

Step 4: Write a Listing That Addresses Your Goal(s)

Now you're ready to write your listing. Although you *can* type your listing directly into the posting tool on craigslist, I recommend using a word processing program such as Microsoft Word or the free open source product OpenOffice.org (www.openoffice.org) to take advantage of spelling and grammar checkers. Don't have access to a word processing program? Most email programs offer spell checking; you can write your listing in a message addressed to yourself.

Before you begin to write your ad, gather as much information as possible, using the following list. To start, you can type the information on separate lines. Use the following headings to help you organize the data:

- Listing title
- Objective
- Specifics/details
- Location
- Price
- Terms
- Preferences
- Requirements
- Deal-breakers

When you have all your information together, you can start editing and formatting. Use punctuation and follow the rules of grammar. Keep sentences and paragraphs short, to the point, and easy to read. *Never* use all caps in your title or listing. In most cases, you should avoid slang unless your target market uses it extensively.

A formula used in advertising works very well. It is called AIDA and stands for the following:

- **Attention.** Grab the reader's attention by making your ad stand out. It's estimated that consumers are bombarded with more than 10,000 messages every day, so it's critical that you catch the reader's eye to avoid getting lost in all the advertising noise.

Because craigslist displays only listing titles in the search results, you need to write a headline that stops readers in their tracks, giving them the feeling they *have* to know more. Appealing to emotion and/or curiosity is one of the common ways to do this. Write a title that strikes an emotional chord or makes the reader curious.

Remember that the user is trying to fill a need or solve a problem, or they wouldn't be searching in the first place. Think about what that problem might be. Strengthen your headline by including one or two benefits that solve that problem. The caveat is that whatever headline strategy you use, it must be true and the body copy must support it or the reader will feel duped and angry.

Interest. After you've caught the reader's attention, you must keep it. As you write the body of the listing, keep in mind that every sentence should be written to keep the reader engaged. The most effective way to do this is to realize that a person's main reason for reading your post is to find out what's in it for him or her.

Although it might be hard to believe, your prospects don't really care about you, your product, or your problems. They want to know what you can do or what you have to offer that makes their lives easier and better. Keep writing with that goal in mind, and you'll do a much better job of holding their attention.

Desire. Next, you want to build up a desire in the reader to have whatever you're offering. Again, the best way to do this is to show them how you can make their lives easier/better. Besides showing the benefits, explain how quickly readers can enjoy those benefits. In today's world, people are rabid about "fast" and "easy."

People buy things based on their emotions and then justify their purchases with logic, so if you trigger those emotional hot buttons and then give them reasons to back up the purchase with logic, you'll experience greater success. For example, if someone is buying a couch, she'll choose one based on emotional cues, but you can shorten the selling process if you can also show that it's a high-quality couch at a great price.

- **Action.** This is the one step that most people miss when writing their listings. However obvious it seems to you, include a "call to action"—a directive for the reader to "act now," "call today," or "stop by before 1 pm."

  Part of getting readers to act is creating a sense of urgency. Give them a reason *not* to wait; show them what they'll miss if they do. The vague pitch is "Hurry, this offer won't last long," but you'll get better results if you can be more specific, offering a limited-time discount or bonus.

Apply the AIDA formula to your ads, to write appealing listings that get great response rates.

To make it easy for the reader to scan your listing, use a short paragraph at the top to cover the description, and then a bulleted list for specifics. See Chapter 4, "All About the Listings," to learn more about formatting with HTML.

Include relevant terminology within your listing when it makes sense to do so, but don't pepper your listing shamelessly with keywords—or your ad will probably be flagged.

Your deal-breakers can help you to visualize your goal, but tread lightly when including them within your listing. People tend to be turned off by ads that sound demanding or come across as negative. If you want to include a deal-breaker, write it as a positive. For example, the deal-breaker "No checks or money orders" can be rephrased as "Cash only."

In most craigslist sections, a lighthearted, casual tone works best for listing. A little humor can help you bond with the reader, but avoid anything controversial. Don't turn the listing into a witty dissertation, or you risk your audience losing sight of your true goal.

If you're intent on including your contact info, rather than using craigslist's safer anonymous email response system, be certain that your info is correct and easy to spot when scanning the ad.

When writing your listing title, include the main point of the listing and positive descriptors that quickly tell the reader why your listing is better than all the rest. By default, craigslist searches titles and listings, so you don't have to pack your title with every known keyword.

When your listing is complete, you can repost it as often as every two days if you delete your previous post first. This is a good way to stay higher in the page results, especially for high-volume categories. Using your account makes managing your listing easy.

Strategies in Action

I hope you've begun to see how Brandon could have used these steps for his giveaway and saved himself time, energy, and money. A quick search for other couches would have showed him specific information to include, such as fabric type, style, measurements, and a detailed description of the couch's condition.

Giving readers more information would have spared Brandon from spending time answering questions through individual email messages. Some readers will email questions, but others just move on to the next listing. Brandon's barebones listing put up an invisible roadblock to a successful listing.

For Brandon's listing, I would have recommended including a general location. Many craigslist's communities span large geographical areas. Some users may end up being no-shows when they find out how far they have to travel. Also, in this case, picking up a large item may require some planning, so giving the reader this information upfront can help to avoid logistical snafus later. By providing measurements, Brandon would have reduced the chance of someone showing up with a vehicle that wouldn't hold the couch.

When looking through the listings, Brandon also may have perceived the difference between listings with images and listings without. People are naturally drawn to listings that include a picture because a picture offers solid information. The words "tan couch" can conjure up a variety of different images, but when the listing contains a picture of the tan couch, a lot less is left to the imagination.

As for contact information, Brandon would have avoided unwanted phone calls by using craigslist's anonymous email system. He also wouldn't have compromised the privacy of his phone number by publishing it on the Internet for the duration of the listing.

These are only some of the benefits Brandon could have experienced had he been aware of these strategies. For the research involved and for taking a picture, Brandon probably would have spent less than 30 minutes—a small investment to increase the chances of a successful listing and save him time, energy, and money.

I think you'll find this approach a valuable tool in getting the most out of your craigslist experience.

From Here...

In Chapter 4, you learned how to post a listing. Here you've learned how to compose a successful listing. The next few chapters discuss the various craigslist sections and how to make the most of your postings in each section.

Listing in the Community

The **community** section of craigslist (see Figure 6.1) is a great place to find people with common interests, publicize local events and news, or get involved with the community. There's a connection for every craigslist member. Although blatant business advertising will likely get your listings flagged, strategic marketing can help you to make a contribution to your community while promoting your business or cause.

craigslist		orange county ▾			
	community		**housing**		**jobs**
post to classifieds	activities	lost+found	apts / housing		accounting+finance
	artists	musicians	rooms / shared		admin / office
my account	childcare	local news	sublets / temporary		arch / engineering
	general	politics	housing wanted		art / media / design
help, faq, abuse, legal	groups	rideshare	housing swap		biotech / science
	pets	volunteers	vacation rentals		business / mgmt
search craigslist	events	classes	parking / storage		customer service
			office / commercial		education
	personals		real estate for sale		food / bev / hosp
for sale ▾ >	strictly platonic				general labor
	women seek women		**for sale**		government
event calendar	women seeking men		barter	arts+crafts	human resources
S M T W T F S	men seeking women		bikes	auto parts	internet engineers
10 11 12 13 14 15 16	men seeking men		boats	baby+kids	legal / paralegal
17 18 19 20 21 22 23	misc romance		books	cars+trucks	manufacturing
24 25 26 27 28 29 30	casual encounters		business	cds/dvd/vhs	marketing / pr / ad
31 1 2 3 4 5 6	missed connections		computer	clothes+acc	medical / health
	rants and raves		free	collectibles	nonprofit sector

Figure 6.1
Find like-minded people and new adventurers in the craigslist **community** section.

Get Out There: Activities

When you have an adventure in mind and don't want to go it alone, come to the **activity partner** section, where a new friend is merely a post away. (Although the link on the home page reads *activities*, the actual category is called "activity partners.") Whether you're looking for a museum companion, a chess opponent, or some workout buddies, you can find them here.

Start by doing your research. Search the **activities** section for postings with activities that interest you. See what other people are writing, what keywords or terms are used. Note what appeals to you and what doesn't.

From there, write down the basics and what you've learned. Use the following 10 questions to get started:

1. What's your initial goal?
2. How would you describe your ideal outcome?
3. How often do you want to gather?
4. What specific times or time of day does the activity or your schedule require?
5. Do you want to meet in any specific location(s) or area(s)?
6. What do you hope to get out of the activity?
7. What's your target audience?
8. Any preferences regarding the event or your partner(s)?
9. What are your requirements?
10. What are your deal breakers?

Use the information you've compiled to write a detailed goal. Describe your ideal outcome and use it to write your listing. Include the relevant information using bullet points or short sentences. Include as much information as possible. Use positive words and invite the reader to contact you.

A reader's first impression will come from your title, so take the time to do it right. Remember to sell the benefits, as suggested by the following examples:

- Let's get in shape together for bikini season!
- Would you like to tee-off at Marbella on Friday mornings?
- Want to share some popcorn and a few good laughs?

Notice how the titles describe an action and get the reader to say yes before even reading your listing. Grab the reader's attention and create a mental image that makes him or her want to find out more.

Get Together: Events, Classes, and Groups

The **groups**, **events**, and **classes** categories offer valuable networking opportunities within your community. For easier browsing, postings in the **events** and **classes** categories are also displayed by date, using the event calendar on the left side of the home page (see Figures 6.2 and 6.3). The following paragraphs cover ways to use these categories to contribute to the community while marketing your business, but you can use the same steps to create a group, event, or class posting for your personal life!

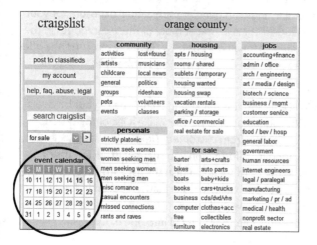

Figure 6.2
The event calendar on the craigslist home page gives users another way to browse events and classes.

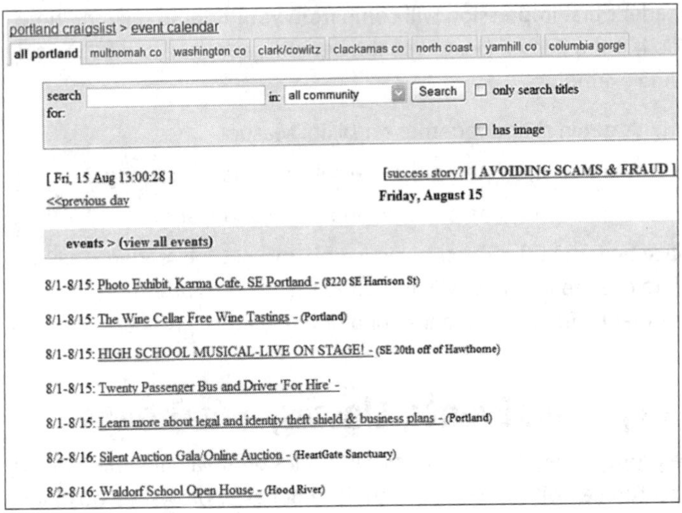

Figure 6.3
Select a date to display a list of happenings.

These community categories provide free advertising for any type of activity. In most craigslist communities, the **community** section is very active, and listings can generate substantial exposure for your business. I include listings in one or more of these categories in the marketing strategies for all my business clients. If you currently offer a class, hold an event, or lead a group, you're ready to start your research.

If you would like to add this marketing technique to your business plan, start with your areas of expertise. Make a list of the questions you most often receive from customers. Next, add a second section that lists any standard information you share with customers on a regular basis. In the third section, finish the list with advanced information, such as tips and tricks, or information that an industry professional or subject expert would know. You now have a basic outline for one or more presentations that fall into one of the following categories.

Events

events is a broad category that can refer to almost any type of gathering, including seminars, social functions, and open houses. Whereas classes are normally presented in a formal setting and groups have scheduled meetings, events can be one-time or recurring, and offer you a free-flowing structure to meet your needs.

Informational seminars are a great way to expand your customer base and increase sales. The most successful introductory seminars are free, run 1–2 hours (including some Q&A time), and cover all or part of the information in the first two sections of your outline. The goal of the seminar is to expand your customer base. By presenting the same information you would provide to any potential customer, you're demonstrating your expertise, building rapport and trust, and opening the door to additional revenue through future sales and/or an advanced fee-based seminar.

Besides being fun, social functions can be highly effective marketing tools, particularly for retail stores. Grand openings (or reopenings), open houses, and holiday parties are social events that can bring joy to your community while bringing customers to you with just a few refreshments, a door prize, and some discounts.

Classes

Although similar to seminars, **classes** are usually offered in a more formal setting, follow a set curriculum, and present information in an instructional step-by-step format that includes printed materials. Introductory or basic care and maintenance classes for a product can be offered free to attract customers, but consider charging a fee for advanced-level classes.

Pricing for classes can be based on the value of the information presented, the cost of materials, and your reason for offering the class. Charge appropriately if the class is advanced or gives insider information and your goal is an additional revenue stream. Offer free or nominal-fee classes if the goal is to gain exposure for your business and increase sales.

Groups

Many **group** posts are started by craigslist users as a way to find other people who share a specific interest. Support groups, user groups, social groups, and athletic groups are four common groups. You can start a group related to your business or industry that gives value to the community and also brings customers to your door. If you can offer meeting space or other benefits on behalf of your business, you can start a group for personal reasons that generates goodwill in your neighborhood and is a low-cost marketing tool.

If you sell a unique or complex product, consider starting a user group. This gives you an opportunity to create a recurring revenue stream by driving customers back to your store on a regular basis. Potential customers also have the opportunity to learn about a product and receive in-person endorsements from existing customers.

If you operate a retail store, organize a walking or running club, using your store as the meeting place. Lay out a simple route, post your listing, put flyers in your store, and have a case of bottled water ready to go. Many people like the idea of having scheduled group exercise but wouldn't organize it themselves. This strategy requires little effort or expense yet can generate a recurring stream of traffic to your store. Your listing should state that the event is sponsored by your business; craigslist users don't like to be mislead.

Financial advisors, accountants, and insurance agents can run a local personal finance group. You can target specific areas, such as stock market investing, credit repair, or preparing for retirement. Bring together a group of individuals with a similar desire to share their advice and experience in an informal setting. As the leader, you can facilitate the group and offer limited insights. This group can provide you with warm leads and a chance to build trust and rapport within your community.

Table 6.1 suggests additional marketing strategies.

Table 6.1 Marketing Strategies

Product or Service	Suggested Activity
Accounting	Investment group, budgeting seminar
Appliance sales or repair	Basic maintenance seminar, advanced usage class
Artist	How-to class, museum or exhibit group
Automotive repair	Seminar on buying a used car
Bakery	Cake decorating or baking class
Beauty consultant	Skincare, makeup, fashion, or hairstyles seminar
Bike shop	Buying or basic maintenance seminar, riding group
Business consulting	Networking group, public speaking seminar or group
Financial advice	Investment group, stock market info seminar
Hobby shop	How-to class, trade group
Insurance	Retirement planning seminar or group
Medical care	Support group, informational seminar
Mortgage brokerage	Home loans seminar, credit repair seminar
Nursery/gardening	Lawn care or landscaping seminar
Pet shop	Seminar on basic pet care or choosing a pet
Real estate	Seminar on buying or selling a home
Restaurant	Tasting, cooking class, fundraiser
Technology consulting	Software or Internet users group, how-to class
Veterinary care	Seminar on basic pet care or choosing a pet

Now that you have an event, class, or group in mind, do some research on your competition and write down the following information:

1. Identify your initial goal (generate revenue, increase customer base, and so on).
2. Describe your ideal outcome.
3. Indicate whether you're planning an event, class, or group.
4. Describe the mission or purpose.
5. Describe the content or what you're offering.
6. Describe your target market.

7. Specify the date, time, and frequency of gathering.

8. List the location.

9. Specify the maximum number of attendees.

10. List any prerequisites for attending.

11. Indicate how attendees will benefit.

12. Describe the supplies required or provided.

13. Indicate any fees and/or the cost of supplies.

14. List preferences you have.

15. Identify your requirements.

16. Specify your deal breakers.

Using this information, you can write a listing that gets results. Tell readers how they will benefit by attending and promote ways in which it will make their lives better or easier. Readers wouldn't be interested if they didn't have a question to answer or a problem to solve, so think of the most common questions or problems that your customers bring to you; that will tell you the hot buttons to mention in your listing.

A little humor in your listing is another great way to connect with the readers. Put a little bit of "you" in your marketing to make it unique and believable. It's called *personality marketing*, and it gives you a way to connect with people and stand out from the competition. People like to see pictures, so if you have a relevant picture, add that to your listing. You can also include a business logo, although some communities may frown on it.

There's an endless number of strategies you can apply to make use of the **groups**, **events**, and **classes** categories. Let your creativity run free and contribute to the community while building your business.

Find What's Missing: Lost+Found

Most craigslist communities have active **lost+found** categories, making them a great place to post if your pet goes astray or a new one shows up at your door. Posts in **lost+found** can be for lost animals or lost belongings. For simplicity's sake, I'll refer only to pets in this section, although much of the following information applies to both pets and objects. The most important thing to do if something is missing is to act fast! Initiate your search as soon as you realize your pet may have wandered off. The longer you wait, the less chance you have of bringing home your beloved friend. craigslist is a good place to start because you can get a listing up in minutes, but it doesn't replace a local search. In addition to your craigslist post, hand out and post flyers within the surrounding area and contact all local shelters.

The listing strategy for this category is a little different. Start by listing the specifics:

1. Identify your goal.
2. Describe the animal in detail.
3. List medical or physical issues.
4. Indicate the date and time lost/found.
5. Specify where the pet was lost/found.
6. Specify details indicating when it was lost/found.
7. Describe the animal's home life.
8. Mention a reward, if applicable.

As usual, use your notes to write your post. Within the listing, include specifics about the date and location where the animal was lost or found. When describing an animal, include enough information about breed, size, and color to give readers a clear picture, but leave out identifying marks or specific details that you can use later to verify ownership.

For missing pets, be certain to describe any medical or physical issues, such as required medicine or injuries, that heighten the sense of urgency. Personalize the listing by including a sentence or two about your home life. A few words about your sorrowful child or lonely companion pet may make your plight stand out in the reader's mind. This kind of information betters your chances of someone seeing your pet at a later point and recalling your listing.

Include information about any reward you are willing to offer. If you have any reason to believe that your pet may have been taken by someone, include a "no questions asked" statement. If a pet was kidnapped, a reward may motivate thieves to return the pet for the money—but only if they feel it's safe to do so.

Start the title with either "LOST:" or "FOUND:". This is the only time I suggest using all caps for a title word. Include a basic description of the pet and state "Reward," if offered. If there's room, you can include a location, but the city will display after the title on all search results.

Some posters include a picture of their lost pet. While odds are slim that someone could use the picture for errant reasons, I would include only a face shot. Stories have surfaced of faked pet kidnappings, with strangers demanding a hefty ransom for the pet's safe return. Putting a full-body shot in your listing gives a criminal detailed information to use against you. When someone responds to your ad and seems like a match, you can email a better picture at that time or take it with you when you go to reclaim your pet. Also, never respond to people who claim to have found your pet and then ask for money up front to return it.

Express Yourself: Artists and Musicians

The **artists** and **musicians** categories are valuable resources for your creative side: promote your work, start a band, find a studio, line up a gig, and so on. Each category serves as a gathering place, promotional tool, and overall resource, where industry vendors also advertise applicable products and services. There are posts in each category offering lessons. If you teach beginner level, the **lessons** category in the **services** section probably will get your listing in front of a wider audience. Take some time to research the other types of posts.

If you're promoting your work, a gig, or a showing, start with the following information:

1. State your initial goal.
2. Describe your ideal outcome.
3. Determine what type of event you have in mind.
4. List scheduled date(s) and time(s).
5. List the scheduled location.
6. Describe the event.
7. Describe your work.

8. Describe your target market.

9. Explain the benefit in attending.

10. List preferences you have.

11. State your requirements.

12. Specify your deal breakers.

Use this information list instead if you're offering a product or service:

1. State your initial goal.

2. Describe your ideal outcome.

3. Describe the product or service.

4. Identify what features are included.

5. Describe your target market.

6. State how the product or service benefits the customer.

7. List the location.

8. Identify the costs.

9. List preferences you have.

10. State your requirements.

11. Specify your deal breakers.

Some artists and musicians have told me that they have difficulty putting the benefits into words. I tell them to think about the experience people have. Depending on the event, attendees can enjoy great music or world-class art, have a great time dancing or relaxing with friends, get out and make new friends, have a girls' night out. There are many other ways to look at it. Think of the big picture, think of the emotions, and think of the fun! Always include a "call to action" sentence that asks the reader to visit, call, or email.

If your work is available online, include a link to that website. Linking to another shopping site is prohibited, but many artists have online galleries, and musicians often upload their tracks to a MySpace (www.myspace.com) page, which gives them additional exposure.

Because of the variety and number of posts in these categories, using a catchy title will help your listing to stand out. Try using a question about one of the selling points or include a call to action:

- "Want a Great Retro Band to Liven Up Your Party?"
- "Want to Enjoy a Peaceful Day Surrounded by Beautiful Works of Art?"
- "Bring Your Girlfriends and Dance the Night Away for Free"

Include your logo and a picture or two, either of your work or of your performance. Use action shots that capture the fun whenever possible. For showings and gigs, include a picture of the front of the location, if possible, to make it easier for first-time visitors to spot.

Take Care of Baby: Childcare

In the craigslist **childcare** category, you can promote your childcare services or find a daycare, nanny, or sitter. This is a very active category in most of the craigslist communities. Because this category promotes a service, rather than a product, the ads need to cover the scope of the services being offered. Service ads usually rely heavily on selling benefits, rather than features. A well-written ad in **childcare** will truly stand out, so start by doing your research.

As you read through other listings, you'll likely see that many ads in this category are vague and poorly written. Note do's and don'ts from these listings. Writing a top-notch service listing requires a little more thought than a listing for a tangible product. After you've seen what's out there, use the following list to organize your information:

1. State your goal.
2. Describe your ideal outcome.
3. State whether you want or your service is a daycare, live-in/out nanny, part-time babysitter.
4. Specify location or travel area.
5. Indicate days and hours available/needed.
6. List the number of openings or children.

7. List the desired/acceptable age range or age(s) of child(ren).

8. Indicate the childcare duties offered/requested.

9. Specify any additional duties offered/requested.

10. Specify the background and experience required/supplied.

11. List any certifications and proof of citizenship.

12. Describe the facility or home.

13. Note the rates or compensation/discounts.

14. Specify who provides meals/snacks.

15. State your preferences.

16. List your requirements.

17. Identify your deal breakers.

Start with a sentence or two about what you're offering or what you require. Use bullet points to list specifics. Provide as much information as possible, including your preferences, requirements, and deal breakers. Unlike with other advertising campaigns, if the provider and family aren't a match, there's no reason to prolong the marketing effort.

Watch your grammar, use a spell checker, and include common punctuation, especially if you're a provider. Parents want to entrust their child to someone who is professional, detailed, and organized, and those qualities should be reflected in your listing.

State clearly in your headline if you're offering or in need of childcare. Use words like *fun*, *loving*, *learning-oriented*, *healthy*—active words that paint a picture of a place where you would be comfortable leaving your child. Other title words cover certifications and experience that would be appealing to a parent.

If you run a childcare facility, include a picture or two that showcases your center. Make certain that the rooms in the pictures are clean, organized, and bright. Show the children playing, but avoid face shots.

What's Happening: Local News, Politics, and General

In almost all craigslist communities, <u>**local news**</u>, <u>**politics**</u>, and <u>**general**</u> are low-traffic categories filled with posts that would likely be flagged off in a busier category. Although I wouldn't advise anyone to spend a great deal of time marketing directly to the readers of any of these categories, listing in one of them still serves a purpose: exposure. Search engines pick up craigslist postings for their own databases and also feed them to other search engines. Google identifies craigslist as an authority site and indexes it regularly.

You can make the best use of these categories by posting a press release. Decide on one newsworthy aspect of your business, event, or cause. A new business or product release, an event, and a new employee are a few notable happenings. Promote your news in a press release. Media relations expert Joan Stewart offers a free tutorial on creating consumer-targeted press releases on her site (www.freeprinfo.com).

Search engines aren't the only reason to list here. Stewart, a former journalist and newspaper editor, sums it up best: "When I worked as a reporter 30 years ago, we had to find news stories the hard way— by developing and using sources, waiting for somebody to call in a good tip. Today, all a journalist has to do is lurk at the local craigslist site, a virtual treasure trove of story ideas. As a publicity expert, I've heard from many people who posted on craigslist and were later called by reporters. I recommend that anyone promoting a product, service, cause, or issue post press releases or other items on their local craigslist. More people probably read craigslist than read the classifieds in their local newspaper."

Use this information list to get started:

1. State your initial goal.
2. Describe your ideal outcome.
3. State the reason for the press release.
4. Describe the product or service.
5. Identify the features.

6. Describe your target market.

7. Indicate how the product or service benefits the customer.

8. List the location.

9. Specify your rates.

10. List preferences you have.

11. State your requirements.

12. Identify your deal breakers.

Some of these items may not apply, but complete the ones you can and then use that information as the basis of the press release. Post the press release to one of the three categories. Remember, duplicate posting is prohibited. This is another instance in which correct grammar, spelling, and punctuation are a must. As with all types of advertising, typos and bad grammar hurt the image of your business. Plant a seed by posting a well-written press release; you never know how big a public relations tree you might grow.

Live Green: Rideshares

You can find rides and riders for local and long distance trips, as well as daily commuting, in the **rideshare** category. Most craigslist **rideshare** communities have a moderate to light stream of posts and visitors. Two key elements to successful **rideshare** postings are timing and details. Post your listing as far in advance of your travel date as possible to give yourself time to find an ideal match. Know what you want and what you're willing to offer to avoid problems later. Use the following list to clarify the details:

1. State your goal.

2. Describe your ideal outcome.

3. Indicate whether you need a ride or are offering a ride.

4. Specify the origination point or general location.

5. Specify the destination or general location.

6. Indicate whether this is a one-time or regular commute.

7. Specify one way or round-trip.

8. List travel date(s) or date range(s) you have in mind.

9. Specify the planned route.

10. Identify whether driving responsibilities will be shared.

11. Indicate any compensation/contribution expected or offered.

12. Specify whether room will be available/provided for luggage, pets, and so on.

13. State your preferences.

14. List your requirements.

15. Identify your deal breakers.

Remember, even the most ideal rideshare will probably include your spending an extended amount of time in a small confined space with someone you recently met and know very little about. There are a lot of variables in that situation. Here are some tips to increase your odds for a successful experience:

- State any flexibility on departure/arrival dates and times.

- For regular commuting, agree to an initial trial period in case things don't work out.

- For longer distances, include in your listing any major cities along your route, as possible drop-off points.

- Check coverage with your insurance company before sharing driving responsibilities.

- Consider requesting a driving record printout and proof of insurance before letting someone else drive your vehicle. Printouts are available from most motor vehicle departments for a small fee.

Because you're asking someone to spend at least a few hours with you, clearly communicating your offer and your expectations is important. In this category, I suggest always including any deal breakers in your listing. Failure to communicate about smoking, pets, luggage space, and so on can cause serious problems when you begin your trip. Although humor is always a good way to connect, use it sparingly in these listings because sometimes it can be misconstrued.

Another important issue can be ride-time activities. If your intent is to blare Megadeth the entire drive, you don't want to end up with someone looking to share his or her unabridged life story along the way. If you have a preference or deal breaker, state it in a positive manner.

A good listing title should make it clear whether you're offering or looking for a ride, the destination, and a general time frame. You don't need to go for a hard sell here; the facts alone should suffice.

Get the Help You Need: Volunteers

Many a good cause can be furthered with the help of willing volunteers, and the **volunteers** category in the **community** section is just the place to find them. This category is active in most of the larger communities but can be slow in smaller ones. Research other postings to see terminology used, things that appeal to you, and things to avoid. Here's an information list for this category:

1. State your initial goal.
2. Describe your ideal outcome.
3. Describe your business or cause.
4. Identify what volunteer work is needed.
5. List specific qualifications required.
6. List days and times needed.
7. List location(s).
8. Specify what training is offered, if any.
9. Identify what the volunteer will experience or gain.
10. List preferences you have.
11. State your requirements.
12. Identify your deal breakers.

As you write your listing, remember to keep your statements brief. Use affirmative wording that appeals to a person's desire to enact positive change in the world or to be a part of the greater good. This is one situation in which you want to make it as easy as possible for someone to contact you, so I strongly recommend including a link to your website. The link will invite the user to learn more about your mission. If possible, indicate a specific contact person who is familiar with the listing and can build on the existing connection.

Keep requirements and deal breakers to a minimum in your listing. You can cover those when someone contacts you. Even if the person isn't suited for this need, he or she may have another skill or a contact that will be a blessing. You'll never know about it if you prequalify the person in the listing and he or she moves on to the next one.

Unless you're asking for a licensed professional, such as a lawyer, focus your listing title on the mission, not necessarily the duties of the volunteer. Which of the following titles would interest you most?

- File Clerk for Nonprofit
- Nonprofit Working to End Hunger in Africa - Office Help Needed

Including your logo and some pictures of the work you do will definitely help.

As you can see, the **community** section offers a wealth of opportunities to bring people together for social, business, and service activities. When you're ready to post, take the time to do the research and complete the information list. It will help you to build a better listing and achieve your ideal outcome faster and with less effort.

Pets: A Controversial Issue

Most **pets** categories on craigslist are very active—and often controversial. Most listings in this category are made by individuals looking to find a new home or a temporary foster home for a house pet—dogs, cats, primates, caged birds, rodents, reptiles, amphibians, and fish. Only listings that offer pets for adoption (called *rehoming*) are permitted. craigslist expressly prohibits posting for the sale or trade of a pet. Pet wanted ads are not a direct violation of craigslist's terms, but some users believe that such ads are golden opportunities for puppy mills to further their business, and the listings are subject to aggressive flagging. Livestock can be offered for sale in the **farm+garden** category of the **for sale** section. According to craigslist's terms of use, listings for pet breeding or stud services are prohibited (whether that includes livestock seems to be open for debate).

Listers in this category are encouraged to request a small adoption fee as a way to ward off "bunchers" who gather animals for illegal purposes. More information on "bunchers" can be found here:

www.craigslist.org/about/PETA.html

The amount of the adoption fee should be no more than the costs incurred to prepare the animal to place it in a new home. You cannot attempt to recover the cost of the animal or any supplies.

Although craigslist CEO Jim Buckmaster has stated that the **pets** category is "a petpourri not to include selling animals or stud/breeder stuff," some communities prefer to permit only rehoming ads in the **pets** category and will flag other types of posts. Craigslist prohibits "discussions" in the **community** section because those posts are best suited for the **discussion forums** (forums.craigslist.org/?forumID=26), as shown in Figure 6.4. However, an ongoing debate has ensued about what constitutes a discussion. Some communities allow posts that announce free or low-cost resources, such as vaccination clinics or dog parks, whereas other communities classify announcements as "discussions" and will flag down posts rather quickly. Research the listings in your **pets** community to see what's allowed.

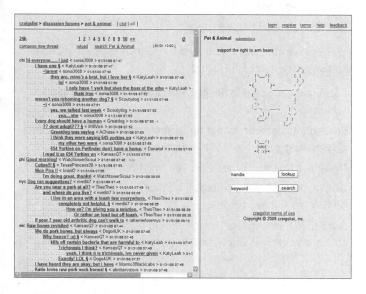

Figure 6.4
The **pets** forum is a great place to share information with other animal lovers.

If you need to find a new home for one of your pets, use the following list:

1. State your goal.
2. Describe your ideal outcome.
3. Describe the animal.
4. Specify any interesting/required personality traits.
5. Identify the pet's activity level.
6. List any training.
7. Specify whether the pet is housebroken.
8. Indicate whether the pet is good with other animals or with children.
9. Specify the reason for rehoming.
10. List recent vet visits, shots, and treatments.
11. Indicate whether you want the pet to be adopted by a specific date.
12. List supplies or accessories included.
13. State your preferences.
14. List your requirements.
15. Identify your deal breakers.

As you begin writing your listing, use the following tips to increase your chance for a successful listing:

- Post animal supplies in the **general** category of the **for sale** section.
- Post announcements under the appropriate category for **events**, **classes**, or **groups**—and in the **discussion forums**, too.
- Never use "for sale," "best offer," or "will trade" in a listing.
- Don't talk about the animal as if it's property or dinner; both will be flagged in a heartbeat.
- State the rehoming fee. This fee should be no greater than the cost of any vet fees, shots, and so on to prepare for rehoming.

- If you need to find a temporary home for your pet, include the reason, time frame, compensation, and support you're offering.

- Don't try to recoup the cost of the animal or supplies.

- Don't try to sell the supplies and offer the animal free. Include all supplies free, to be certain that the animal's needs are met. Alternatively, you can offer the animal for adoption with a disclaimer that supplies are also available.

- Include a sentence or two about why you have to give up the animal.

- List the animal's positive qualities and overall temperament.

- If the animal has issues, include them in the listing. Omitting known problems isn't fair to the new family or the animal.

- Include a picture or two of the animal.

- Never mention flaggers or being flagged in your listing.

- The listing title should state new home or foster, as well as a description of the animal.

- If your post gets flagged off, visit the flagging forum (forums.craigslist.org/?forumID=3) if you don't understand why it happened.

Include the preceding information in short, bullet-point sentences. People in this category often write extensively about personal issues causing them to rehome an animal. Avoid doing that. A general sentence about "personal commitments" or "financial considerations" is enough.

Screen anyone looking to adopt your animal to ensure that he or she is placed in a loving home where he or she will thrive. You can find helpful free information on finding a good home for your pet here:

www.hsus.org/pets/pet_care/guidelines_for_finding_a_
responsible_home_for_a_pet.html

Use these tips for a successful experience in the **pets** category. Your pet deserves it!

From Here...

Now that you know how to get the most out of postings in the **community** listings, we'll spend some time examining the other major sections: **housing**, **for sale**, **services**, **jobs** and **gigs**, **resumes**, and the ever-popular **personals**.

Listing in the Housing Section

The **housing** section on craigslist (see Figure 7.1) is one of the most popular sections in almost all communities. Stories of people finding a place to live or a new roomie abound. With a high number of postings in many communities, using successful listing strategies is extremely important.

$1295000 Amazing Opportunity to Purchase in Laguna Niguel! - (Laguna Niguel)
NOT A SHORT SALE..JUST A GREAT BUY IN RSM 4BED/3BATH FOR UNDER $700K - (RANCHO SANTA MARGARITA, CA)
$617000 Casually Elegant Huntington Home - (Huntington Beach) img
$2200 ORANGE COUNTY HOME OWNERSHIP - (ORANGE COUNTY)
PANORAMIC OCEAN VIEW 3BED/2.5BATH PROPERTY IN SAN CLEMENTE UNDER $650K - (SAN CLEMENTE, CA)
$61900 OC Affordable housing---2BR-2BA Manufactured Home - (Costa Mesa) pic
$509000 Gorgeous Condo on Greenbelt, SELLER MOTIVATED!! - (Laguna Niguel) pic
$639900 *****OPPORTUNITY - DETACHED HOUSE IN DANA POINT 2,465 SQFT ONLY $640k -
$995000 SAN CLEMENTE/CAPO BEACH GEM! 4 BED/3.5 BATH,2 MASTER SUITES, WOW!!!!!! - (San Clemente / Capo Beach) pic
$524900 SINCE A GREAT LOCATION ISN'T EVERYTHING LOOK WHAT ELSE YOU GET! - (DANA POINT, CA)
$399900 ****UNBELIEVABLE 3 Bedroom DETACHED HOUSE in Mission Viejo UNDER $400K -
BEAUTIFUL 5BED/3BATH/2500 SQ. FT IN DANA POINT FOR $980K - (DANA POINT, CA)
$799000 New Construction, SELLER MOTIVATED!!!! - (Costa Mesa (East)) pic
Bank Owned - In Anaheim - (Anaheim) pic
$399700 >>>>>> 3 BEDROOM 1,630 SQFT 2-LEVEL BUILT IN 2003 SOUTH OC $39 -

Figure 7.1
Both real estate pros and private individuals post ads in the **housing** section.

The beauty of classified ads, unlike other types of advertising, is that people who read them already have intent. Most people don't seek out classified ads just to pass time; if they're looking in the **housing** section, they're at least thinking about buying or renting a home.

Selling Solo

Although plenty of real estate agent ads are found on craigslist, there's a growing trend of homeowners who want to eliminate the middleman. And craigslist is a great advertising tool for that purpose. Current estimates put home sellers not affiliated with an agent as high as 20% and climbing.

One reason offered by those sellers for going it on their own has been to maintain greater control over the selling process. In an informal survey, sellers mentioned being able to decide who views their home and when. Other comments included the opportunity to know the buyer better—and, of course, eliminating the agent commission.

Done right, selling your home without an agent can provide you with a substantial savings. But you must be willing to put forth the time, effort, and financial investment of selling it yourself. Before you decide not to use a real estate agent, be certain that you understand what that means.

When you sell your home using a real estate agent, you'll pay (on average) 6% of the selling price to the broker as commission. So, on a $250,000 home, you'll be handing over $15,000 at the close of sale to be split among the agents involved. That can be a serious chunk of change—especially in a down market!

In return for that commission, listing agents work to protect your interests and do everything possible to sell your home for the highest price. They'll also research and report on home sales prices, recommend a listing price for your home, give you advice on preparing to show your home, list your home on the Multiple Listing Service (MLS), and advertise and handle advertising and showing your home.

If you want to save a good portion of the commission, you can take on the job of selling the home yourself. Of course, you'll still need an expert or two in your corner. At the very least, consult with a real estate attorney who can go over any contracts (search "real estate attorney"). I also suggest that you team up with a mortgage lender who can help you qualify buyers, so you don't waste your time (search "mortgage lender").

One way to make things easier for you is to find some expert advice. Some very good information sources are available on the Internet. As for do-it-yourself real estate selling, Owners.com (www.owners.com), FSBO.com (www.fsbo.com), and ForSaleByOwner.com (www.forsale-byowner.com) all offer free information on a wide range of topics.

Real estate forms are available for a price at Socrates.com (www.socrates.com) and FindLegalForms.com (www.findlegalforms.com). Owners.com also offers three levels of home sale packages for you to purchase, depending on your needs.

Whether you're looking to sell your home yourself or find a good roommate, understanding the market and knowing your competition can help you to achieve greater success. Even if you plan to use an agent, learning about the real estate market will help you to make more informed decisions.

Move That Property in Real Estate for Sale

Getting ready to sell your home? Are you a real estate professional with a listing, in search of some buyers? Used wisely, craigslist is a fantastic marketing tool, but unless it's a red hot seller's market, a poorly designed listing will bring you no joy. The goal is to reach prospective buyers and show them what makes your offering unique. If you're serious about selling your home, take the time to make a list of the property's features.

An Agent's Best Friend

Most real estate agents won't find a better advertising venue and value than craigslist. It's hard to beat "free," especially given the millions of hits craigslist gets every month. Many agents recognize this fact and use the site as a primary advertising channel.

And that can be great, *if* the agent understands the typical craigslist user. A community user appreciates the simplicity of the site and the guidelines set up to deter spammers. Many users are turned off by graphic-laden listings and will click away from listings that look too polished or cloned. Several agents I spoke with told me that they had far better response rates when they stuck to simple text-based listings, rather than using a template tool like Postlets (www.postlets.com).

Another point that many agents fail to realize is that they should post listings only for homes they personally represent. Often, agents pull details of a home off the MLS and create a listing for homes they don't represent. This is a common lead-generation tool, but one that turns off many prospects. These listings usually are easily identifiable. Although they contain basic information about a property, they don't offer in-depth descriptions. Often they won't include an address but will have a disclaimer that the information is taken directly from the MLS. While this attempt at finding buyers and renters to represent isn't illegal, it also isn't keeping within the spirit of craigslist. A better way to engage buyers is for the agent to post a benefit-filled listing in the **real estate** category of the **services** section.

The last "don't" for agents is this: Don't flood a community with listings, especially if the listings are not located within that community. The wisest agents realize that listing properties in the community where they are located is the most successful way to advertise. If someone from Boston is moving to Orlando, most know to visit the Orlando craigslist to check out Orlando's real estate market. Agents will gain a positive following by respecting craigslist's listing guidelines.

What Do You Have to Offer?

Do you recognize all your home's selling features? A good marketing strategy includes understanding what's important to potential buyers and highlighting it in your ad. Not everyone has the same hot buttons; although it's easy to name the things that you love, you may be missing other important selling points.

Get an idea of what your home has to offer by using the checklist in Table 7.1. Note the condition of each feature, too. While "painted walls" may be accurate, a "freshly painted interior" can be an important selling point. Write down as much information as you can. You never know where the gem might be hiding.

Although you can complete the checklist at any time, it's best to do this when the property is ready to sell. You're looking for selling points and getting a feel for what a prospective buyer will experience, so the evaluation should take place when the home is ready for showing.

Table 7.1   Home Features Checklist

General

Location/neighborhood/development _____

Type (detached/townhouse/condo/duplex) _____

Style _____

Number of stories _____

Age _____

School district(s) _____

Local house(s) of worship _____

Interior

Square footage _____

Bedrooms _____

Baths _____

Living room _____

Dining room _____

Kitchen (eat-in/galley) _____

Den _____

Office _____

Basement (finished/unfinished) _____

Attic _____

Flooring _____

Interior closets/storage _____

Security system _____

Interior, continued

Central heating _____

A/C (central/wall/window) _____

Ceiling fans _____

Heating (gas/electric/oil) _____

Water heater (gas/electric/instant) _____

Fireplace _____

Dishwasher _____

Stove/oven(s) (gas/electric) _____

Garbage disposal _____

Trash compactor _____

Sewer (municipal/septic) _____

Water (municipal/well) _____

Other appliances _____

Exterior Features

Exterior (brick/siding/stucco/wood/other) _____

Gutters _____

Windows: type (single/double/triple/low-e) _____

Windows: brand _____

Roof (type/condition/age) _____

Private driveway _____

Off-street parking _____

Garage (attached/detached/direct access) _____

Carport/covered parking _____

Attached storage _____

Detached storage _____

Additional structures _____

Additional living quarters _____

Yard size _____

Porch _____

Exterior Features, continued

Fencing _____

Patio/decking _____

Pool _____

Spa _____

Playground _____

Street (cul-de-sac/quiet/high-traffic) _____

Community amenities (pool/spa/tennis/park/playground) _____

Other: _____

Other: _____

Other: _____

Other: _____

Questions

What is the first thought that came to mind when you looked at the front of the house? _____

_____

What is the first thought that came to mind when you looked at the backyard? _____

_____

What room do you like best and why? _____

_____

What room do you like least and why? _____

_____

What three things would you change about the house and why? _____

_____

Additional comments: _____

_____

_____

_____

_____

Consider having other people complete the checklist, too. Ask everyone living in the home to complete a checklist, including your kids. Get everyone's take on the house to get a greater perspective on what might get a buyer's attention.

Also ask someone less familiar with your home. There's no substitute for a fresh set of eyes. Having these views will give you a better idea of what a buyer might experience when touring the home.

If you find it awkward asking friends to complete this checklist for you, start by telling them that you appreciate their insights and value their honesty. Approach them with the attitude that you trust and appreciate their feedback because of their intelligence and/or experience. Most people will be more than happy to help you when they hear that.

When you have the information, study any valid negative comments. You can't please everyone and don't need to try, but if the complaint is accurate and there's a reasonable solution, by all means, do it.

I toured a home where the teenage son had his room plastered with posters of his favorite heavy metal bands, some of which were borderline offensive. As much as I may have liked that house, that room stuck out in my mind—and not in a good way. I wasn't the first to give that feedback to the listing agent, but the homeowner wouldn't hear of taking down the posters to make the sale. Those posters definitely slowed the selling process of that home. That's fine if you're not in hurry, but if you want to move your home as quickly as possible, use the checklist to identify any problem areas and listen to the feedback from anyone who views the property.

What's Going on Next Door?

Now that you know what you have to offer, see what else is out there and what's happening in the market. Don't assume that national trends headlining the news apply to your general area or even to your neighborhood. Regardless of the overall market, every locale has some neighborhoods that are always in demand and others that are harder to move.

Exploring craigslist is a great place to see other listings, but don't overlook the real estate section of your local newspaper, still a popular resource for both buyers and sellers. For online resources, visit Zillow.com (www.zillow.com) and Domania (www.domania.com) to access local home sales data. Altos Research (www.altosresearch.com) provides free and paid market information for more than 20 U.S. metro areas. Gathering information from these sources will help you to create a more successful listing.

Map Out Your Information

In addition to the home and market specifics you've already gathered, use the following information list to better define your goal:

1. What is your initial goal?
2. What is your ideal outcome?
3. What are the property's features?
4. What is the home's single best feature?
5. What are the weaknesses?
6. Will you offer help with financing or closing costs?
7. Will you offer credits for repairs/replacements?
8. What preferences do you have regarding the sale?
9. What are your requirements?
10. What are your deal breakers?

Use these questions to visualize the various steps of the process. The easiest way to hit a bull's-eye is with a clear view of the target, so create a detailed vision of what you want to happen from start to finish.

Now that you have your goal, an understanding of your local housing market, and a good understanding of your product and its features, you're ready to look at the last piece of the puzzle—your prospect.

Talk the Talk

Are you doing a "for sale by owner" (FSBO)? Should you offer a lease option? Will your lender do a short sale? If these questions strike fear into your heart, you're not alone. With all the acronyms and industry slang, many people find the real estate market intimidating. You can use the definitions in Table 7.2 to understand some of the more frequently used terms on craigslist.

Table 7.2 Common Real Estate Industry Terms

Term	Definition
55+ or over 55 community	Any housing development that's limited to those aged 55 and over. Sometimes called Senior Housing.
Adjustable rate mortgage (ARM)	A loan whose interest rate changes based on the movements of a stated market indicator or index, either over the life of the loan or for a set number of years. Most ARMs include stipulations as to when, how often, and how much the interest rate can change.
Amenities	Any number of benefits available for use by an owner or renter of a property, such as a community swimming pool, fitness center, children's playgrounds, or a clubhouse.
Appraised value	The statement of a property's value at a specific time, given by a certified appraiser.
Appraiser	A person qualified by education, training, and experience to estimate the value of real property based on industry-accepted criteria.
ARM	See adjustable rate mortgage.
Assumable loan	An existing mortgage on a property that can be taken over by the buyer. Often the lender will charge a fee for doing this.
Balloon mortgage	An installment loan with a larger lump-sum payment due at the end.
Balloon payment	The final lump-sum payment due at the end of a balloon mortgage.
Bank owned	Property that has gone through the foreclosure process and the lender has taken possession.
Climate control	In referring to storage facilities that offer reasonable protection against temperature extremes for some or all of their units.
Closing costs (CC)	Expenses buyers and sellers incur to complete a real estate transaction.

Term	Definition
Commercial property	Property used for business purposes, such as office buildings, malls, standalone buildings, and so on.
Common areas	Areas within a subdivision or condo complex that are for use by all residents, such as a community pool, clubhouse, tennis court, or greenbelt.
Comparable sales (comps)	Recent sales of similar properties in the surrounding area, used to determine the market value of a specific property.
Condominium (condo)	A type of multi-unit ownership where all owners hold sole rights to the interior of their individual unit and ownership of all common areas and buildings is held jointly with all other owners.
Contingency sale	A sale that includes a condition that must be met before the sale is finalized. Often used when a buyer is making an offer on a home with the stipulation that the transaction will not be completed until the buyer sells his current residence.
Contract for deed	An installment contract in which the buyer may occupy the property, but the seller retains title until all or a specified part of the selling price has been paid. Maybe structured as a balloon contract. Also called a *land contract*.
Cooperative (co-op)	A type of multi-unit ownership where all owners hold shares in a cooperative corporation that owns the property, with each owner having the right to occupy a specific unit.
Cul-de-sac (CDS)	The end of a residential street where there is no outlet. Generally a desirable location for a residence because of limited traffic.
Default	When a buyer fails to make his agreed-upon mortgage payment. Generally, if a buyer fails to make his payment within the first 30 days of the due date, the buyer is considered to be in default.
Drive-up unit	An outside self-storage unit located on the first floor of a storage facility, which allows you to drive up to the door for loading and unloading.
Duplex	A residential building consisting of two separate residences that share a common wall.

Term	Definition
Escrow	In real estate, when monies or other items of value are held by a third party until the close of the transaction.
Escrow account	Pending close of a transaction, an account set up to hold monies, such as earnest money. After close of a transaction, an escrow or impound account may be established by the mortgage company to hold monies the property owner pays toward taxes and insurance.
Equity	An owner's financial interest in a property. The difference between the fair market value of a property and the amount owed on that property.
Eviction	The lawful removal of an occupant from a property.
Exclusive listing	A contract between a homeowner and a real estate agent, giving the agent the sole right to sell a property for a specific period of time.
Fair market value	The price of a home at any given time at which a buyer is willing to buy and a seller is willing to sell.
Fannie Mae (FNMA)	The Federal National Mortgage Association, a federally created, shareholder-owned company that is the largest supplier of home mortgage funds.
Federal Housing Authority (FHA)	An agency of the U.S. Department of Housing and Urban Development (HUD). The FHA's main purpose is to insure mortgage loans made by private lenders.
FICO score	FICO stands for Fair Isaac Corporation, a California-based company that assigns a nationally accepted credit score to individuals based on a formula it created.
Foreclosure	The legal process used by lenders when buyers default on a mortgage or fail to make their loan payments. Usually, this is to force a sale of the property with the proceeds being applied to the outstanding mortgage.
For sale by owner (FSBO)	Any property for sale where the owner is selling the home without the use of a real estate agent. Either the property or the owner can be referred to as a FSBO (pronounced "fiz bo").

Term	Definition
Homeowners association (HOA)	An organization composed of homeowners within a subdivision or condo complex. These associations take on issues such as maintaining common land and recreation areas and collecting dues from residents. The homeowners association also enforces any covenants, conditions, and restrictions that apply to the property.
HOA dues	Fees paid to a homeowners association for maintenance, repair, and improvements of common areas of a development.
Lease option	A lease agreement that gives the buyer an option to purchase the home at or by the end of the lease. A portion of the monthly lease payment may be credited toward the down payment.
Lease purchase	See *lease option*.
Lien	Granted (either voluntarily or involuntarily) interest in a property as security for a debt owed.
Manufactured home	Sometimes still referred to as a *mobile home* or *trailer*. A manufactured home is built on a permanent chassis at a factory and transported to a building site in one or more sections.
Multiple Listing Service (MLS)	A company for real estate professionals that maintains a detailed database of all current property listings.
Mobile home	See *manufactured home*.
Model home	One of the first homes built by a developer when opening a new subdivision. Often filled with upgraded features, a model home acts as a permanent open house, allowing prospective buyers to tour a finished home before construction in the subdivision has even begun.
Modular home	A home that is built and transported to a building site in individual components. The quality of a modular home might be comparable to a home constructed from scratch at a home site.
Prefabricated home	See *modular home*.
Pre-foreclosure sale	When a buyer has defaulted on a loan and the lender allows the buyer to sell the property below the amount owed, to avoid going into foreclosure.

Term	Definition
Real estate agent	In most states, an individual licensed to handle the steps of negotiating and selling property. Must be supervised by a licensed real estate broker.
Real estate broker	In most states, an individual licensed one step above a real estate agent. Licensed to handle the tasks of negotiating and selling property. Can own and operate his or her own business.
Realtor	A real estate agent or broker who is a member of the National Association of Realtors. (The term "Realtor" is a registered trademark of the NAR.)
Redevelopment	A partnership between local government and private builders to revitalize a declining neighborhood by replacing older, rundown, and dilapidated buildings with new construction.
Rent control	Laws governing the amount of rent a landlord may charge and how and when rents may be raised.
Real estate owned (REO)	Property acquired by a lender through the foreclosure process and held in the lender's inventory.
Self storage	Short for *self-service storage*. A storage facility with multiple rental spaces or "units" that are rented individually with access available only to the renter.
Seller carry	The homeowner will finance all or part of the home for the buyer.
Short sale	A home sale where the selling price is less than the amount owed to the lender.
SFR	Single family residence.
Spec home	A house either currently being built or finished, but not yet purchased.
Sublet	When a lessee (renter) enters into a rental agreement with a third party.
Townhome/townhouse	A residence that usually has at least two stories and shares a common wall with one or more units.
Turnkey	Ready to occupy with little or no changes or additions.

If you want to immerse yourself in the real estate industry, the Federal Trade Commission offers a wealth of free information at www.ftc.gov/bcp/menus/consumer/credit/mortgage.shtm, as do RealtyTimes.com (www.realtytimes.com) and Realtor.com (www.realtor.com). The website City-Data.com (www.city-data.com) has lots of valuable information about cities across the United States. In addition, it has forums (www.city-data.com/forum/) on real estate, mortgages, and renting where you can post questions.

Focus on Your Target

When it comes to effective advertising, one of the biggest secrets of success is to focus on your target market. Many products and services have mass appeal, but your advertising time and money are best spent reaching one market at a time. Although advertisers often have a tendency to want to avoid excluding anyone, if you try to entice everyone, you'll likely interest no one.

Begin to focus in on your target market by looking at the people you believe would most enjoy the benefits your home has to offer. Several obvious things to consider are number of bedrooms, lot size, floor plan, and local community. If you're trying to sell a two-bedroom condo, it isn't a wise choice spending time and money focusing on a family with kids.

Some of these questions can easily be answered in more than one way. You can also narrow your audience by considering your method of advertising. Although craigslist's anonymity prohibits us from having any hard data, you can assume that most of the craigslist users are intermediate to advanced computer users. They probably identify with craigslist's mission of using the Internet to bring people together offline, and they appreciate the clean and simple approach of craigslist. They tend to lean toward being community-oriented and eco-friendly.

Imagine a day in their life. Are they married or single? How old are they? Do they have children? Pets? What type of job might they hold? Where do they shop? What do they do for fun? Are they homebodies or the "outdoor type"? What are their hobbies?

When you have a clear picture of your target market and the benefits your home gives them, you can create an ad that will have them running to your door.

Leave Them Wanting More

Applying the AIDA formula (as covered in Chapter 5, "Successful Listing Strategies") to real estate ads is extremely important. Unlike most small-dollar sales, purchasing a home is an extended buying process. Unless the number of homes for sale is low and buyer demand is sky high, it isn't likely someone will respond to a real estate ad and make an offer on the spot. The goal of your listing is to grab the attention of potential buyers and create the desire for them to find out more and then finish with a call to action.

The four elements that all ads need to include are location, number of bedrooms, number of bathrooms, and price. Don't try to entice people to call by leaving out these details; you will only annoy them. With location, it's best to stick with something broad, such as the city or a general part of town, unless your specific location is one of the hot selling points.

Keep in mind that people are not buying a house, they are buying a lifestyle, and they want the best one they can afford. Home buyers often rethink their priorities after they actually start viewing homes that are for sale. Given the uniqueness of each home, there is value in painting a panoramic visual that doesn't have readers getting caught up in facts and figures. Create an enticing mental image with the basics and focus on the benefits; then encourage the readers to take action.

Your best ad will come about if you think like a buyer and not like a seller or an agent. For most human beings, our prevailing thought is most often, "What's in it for me?" That is especially true when money's involved. The most effective advertisements are created when the person creating it gets inside the mind of his customers.

When writing advertising copy, keep that image of your target market in your mind at all times. To start, I usually envision one person standing in front of me with hands on hips and a look of impatient expectation. I'd better have a good reason for interrupting his day and that reason had better include a bonus for him.

No matter how important the reason is to me as a seller, my prospects couldn't care less that I need to make a sale so I can keep the money flowing in and afford to take care of my family. They have their own issues to deal with, and if I'm going to get their attention, I absolutely must show them how I can make their lives better, not how they can help me.

You have only seconds to engage those prospects, so you need to grab their attention and do it quickly. Two strong attention-getters are curiosity and emotion. Many ads go straight for a list of features, covering the number of bedrooms, bathrooms, garages, and the like. While that approach isn't horrible, just describing the home won't have them picturing their new life there.

A "16' x 20' master bedroom" isn't a bad thing, but "Enjoy relaxing days and nights in your spacious master suite" certainly sounds more inviting. And it doesn't lead people into visually calculating a 16' by 20' room. By nature, most people will visualize a spacious room as being at least somewhat larger than what they currently have. And that's the first step to getting their attention.

Focusing on benefits is a great way to make your listing stand out in the crowd. You'll have buyers picturing their new life. You note a feature when you tell them the home has a "sparkling pool and spa," but you give them a lifestyle if you write "Enjoy early morning laps and poolside entertaining in your private oasis."

A common kitchen feature is "lots of storage" or "ample cabinets," but you bring buyers into the picture when they read, "You'll love having all your kitchen items organized at arms' reach with wall-to-wall kitchen cabinets."

Use positive descriptors when writing any ad. A "15-foot by 20-foot living room" doesn't strike a chord nearly as well as "Entertain friends and family in your elegantly styled living room." The following terms will help you create enticing visual imagery in your listings:

Descriptive Terms

airy	expansive	luxurious	soothing
attractive	extensive	magnificent	sophisticated
beautiful	fashionable	masterpiece	spacious
bold	fresh	modern	stately
captivating	gorgeous	open	striking
casual	gourmet	opulent	stylish
charming	graceful	park-like	subtle
cheerful	gracious	peaceful	subdued
chic	grand	pleasant	tasteful
classic	homey	prestigious	timeless
comfortable	huge	private	traditional
cozy	immaculate	refined	tranquil
delightful	impressive	relaxing	tropical
distinctive	informal	restful	turnkey
distinguished	intimate	ritzy	understated
dramatic	inviting	roomy	welcoming
elegant	laid-back	secluded	well-appointed
enchanting	large	serene	
engaging	lavish	sheltered	

Another thing that really catches a buyer's eye is including any financial terms you'll accept, such as "seller carry," "seller pays closing," or a "lease option," so consider including the appropriate terms in your title. You also need to identify the one feature that truly makes the house stand out. This could be a unique feature, such as a master bedroom suite or a newly upgraded kitchen; or it might be something in high demand, like being in a prized development or within a high-ranking school district.

An even more effective tactic can be to draw in prospects with a good (and true) story. A recently wed Atlanta resident drummed up publicity for her condo by highlighting the fact that she, as well as the two prior owners, had bought the condo while single and, shortly after, found a future husband there. Even in a down market, she had scores of women (and their agents) lining up at her door.

People are drawn to an interesting story. Not only that, many will jump at the chance to get involved. As human beings, we love to be connected with each other and with notable people, places, and things.

What story does your home hold? Think creatively! Start with the home itself. Is something unique about its history? Did any of the previous owners have an interesting story? Do you know anything about how or why the home was originally built or remodeled? Is there history in the land it was built on?

Another topic can be why you're selling the home. Are you headed on an adventure? Have you been called to complete a mission? Will selling your home give you the freedom to pursue your dream? Maybe you found your true love—or lost it?

People like to be helpful and make a difference in the world. By nature, we want to be a part of something that's bigger than us. By sharing your story with prospective buyers, you give them a chance to take part in it. If they understand that buying your home helps you further your goals, they also can get caught up by knowing they play a role in helping others achieve their dream.

Put It on Paper

Start with your ad copy and save writing the listing title for last. Unlike with a newspaper classified, in a craigslist listing you have unlimited space and can use it to make your ad easier to read.

Other than your headline, the first sentence is the most important. Work to engage readers by using a conversational or informal tone. Avoid abbreviations, clichés, and slang.

Many people like to scan ads before they start reading, so stick to a few short sentences that paint a picture of the home, followed by a bulleted list of benefit-laden features. You can use boldface and italics to emphasize the most important information.

If you're going with a story, work to draw in readers by writing as if you're telling your story to a stranger. Choose words that paint a positive and clear mental image. Break up any long sections of paragraphs with subheadings to draw in skimmers. After you've told your story, go on to include a description of the home, using benefits.

At the end of your listing, include a "call to action." You can do this by simply saying, "Call today," guiding readers to stop by during a specified open house time, or requesting they email for additional information. Overall, asking them to email is the least effective response.

Although I normally don't recommend including phone numbers in listings (except for businesses), in real estate, people are used to having instant contact. You can decide what works best for you, but I suggest including a phone number and direct email address in each listing. You can read in Chapter 3, "Safety First," about disposable email addresses, and you can always set up a low-cost temporary phone number through Skype (www.skype.com) or using a prepaid cellular service. This is a small price to pay for keeping your personal contact info from falling into the hands of the wrong people.

A Flashing Neon Sign

Your headline is your one shot to stand out and grab readers' attention. Read what others are doing and avoid doing the same, if at all possible. Leading with a benefit can be very good, so look for ways to incorporate a main one in your title.

If you have agreed to any financing help such as covering closing costs or carrying a note, including that information in the title will likely increase the number of people who visit your listing. But don't waste your title with generic terms like "great deal."

If you have a recent appraisal and are considering selling your home for a lesser amount, that can be a great attention-grabber. Say your home was appraised two months ago at $160,000, but you will accept $155,000. Include "$5,197 under recent appraisal" in your title. Why not a straight $5,000, you ask? First, because of the law of specificity. People find specific numbers more credible and they have greater impact. And, studies have also shown that buyers are less likely to negotiate an amount down as far when you start with a precise asking price.

Headlines can play on emotion, offer a benefit, or pique someone's curiosity. The appraisal headline I discussed offers implied benefits: both financial savings and the possibility of built-in equity. If you're going with a story of why you need to sell, you could use a headline like, "I've got to get out of here," or "I'm on a mission." Headlines give readers a taste of something good. And, they promise the readers there's more where that came from.

Whatever tactic you use, make certain that it's honest. Whatever promise your headline makes, if your listing doesn't deliver, people will feel tricked, and you'll be left wondering why no one called.

A Picture Is Worth...

Nothing takes the place of distinct and colorful pictures. Include as many images as possible. Have a front shot of the house and any other relevant picture near the top of the listing, especially those that highlight the main selling points. You can pepper the rest of your listing with other images as you go.

At a minimum, pictures should include a front shot, the family or living room, kitchen, and the master bedroom or other selling point. Most people do enjoy having a large selection of pictures to study, so include as many as possible.

Try different angles when taking photos, so you can have the best selection to choose from. Remember to remove all clutter from view. You want the house looking as close to model-perfect as possible.

Filling a Vacancy

Just as in the __real estate for sale__ category, craigslist makes finding a tenant a snap. Most of the information provided in the preceding sections of this chapter applies to any type of rental property, too. In the rental listings (__apts/housing__, __rooms/shared__, __sublets/temporary__, and __vacation rentals__), you include the same information you would in a sale listing, with the obvious exception of price. Include any rental terms, such as length of lease desired, deposit amount, pet policy, and utilities/expenses covered by landlord.

When listing your pricing, particularly in the **rooms/shared** category, remember that you want to compare overall value. When you're reading other listings, it's not only the rent amount that's important, but also any separate charges the landlord has mentioned. To gain more exposure for your listing, you can show a lower rent amount, but make up some or all of it by including a separate utility amount in your listing.

Rooms and shared rental listings should always include mention of common areas. Let your prospects know what parts of the home will be available for them to enjoy. Include a sentence that gives readers an idea about the living arrangements. Are you looking for a true roommate to enjoy and share in the responsibilities of the entire property? Or are you looking for an "on the go" type who needs only a place to sleep at night? Be upfront about any restrictions you impose.

While it's always helpful to mention nearby conveniences, such as malls, restaurants, and theaters, when you're listing a vacation property, this information can be a big selling point. If you can honestly say "within walking distance" of any place a visitor may want or need to go, then do so. If you're uncertain what to include, find the websites of local hotels, particularly any bed-and-breakfast places, and see what places they mention.

Include the names of any local tourist attractions and their general driving times. Many visitors want to use public transportation, so let readers know if your property is near a bus, subway, or train route. Mention any popular events going on during that time. Another selling point is how easily and inexpensively visitors can get from the airport to your property; be sure to mention any low-cost, easily accessible transportation.

Vacation listings should also include available dates. Keep the listing updated as you fill the calendar. Pictures are vital for vacation rentals. Offer as many as you can to let readers get a feel for the property. Another way to entice prospects is to let them see the beauty of the locale during the time of year they are looking to visit.

As with any type of listing, you increase the odds of a successful transaction by concentrating on how you can meet your prospects' needs and do it better than your competition. Let readers know not only what your property has to offer, but also how each thing benefits them and makes their visit more enjoyable.

Office/Commercial Property

Although much of the same information from the preceding sections applies to the **office/commercial** section, for business listings the overall slant is a bit more straightforward. While visuals are still important, comprehensive descriptions are vital.

Understanding the commercial real estate market will make the transaction easier. You'll find information on the residential and commercial real estate industries at LoopNet (www.loopnet.com/xNet/MainSite/News/). This site is a great starting point if you're new to the industry.

Listings in the **office/commercial** category range from small office sublets to entire buildings. Any properties used for business purposes should be listed here. Although you still want to focus on identifying a property's benefits, including detailed specifics is more important here than in other categories.

Know Your Business

Commercial real estate is classified by usage, such as office, warehouse, retail, manufacturing, and storage. And most often quoted by square footage. If you're leasing out a single office, then you'll likely quote a monthly cost, but many times the cost of commercial properties is displayed as price per square foot. This industry standard gives people a way to compare costs. It's particularly useful if you're willing to divide the property into smaller units.

Office space covers a broad category that can include high-rise, executive suites, strip centers, and the like. Include a positive and honest description to save everyone time and trouble. A three-story walk-up is not a high-end high-rise, no matter how many times you call it that. Include a blueprint, sketch, or detailed description of the layout when available.

Although these descriptions are generally subjective, office space can be classified into three different categories:

- Class A are the best of the best. Usually a high-rise, a Class A space offers above-average design, construction, and finish. Easily accessible and in a desirable location, these spaces offer all the amenities and have rental prices to prove it.

- Class B buildings are usually newer wood-frame construction, with good access in a good location. They can also be older Class A buildings that may be showing signs of age. Whereas Class A is most likely located in a downtown office area or the financial district, B properties are often in the suburbs.

- Class C is the last office building type. As you can probably guess, it will likely be the least expensive of the three types. These are sometimes older buildings that are well maintained, but can also be properties that are not well maintained or are in a less desirable area. Besides low-rise office buildings, they can also be offices located in strip centers and walk-up offices located above retail and service stores.

Location, Location, Location

As the heading says, when it comes to commercial property, location is what matters. So, tell readers where it's located, what's nearby, and include any positive information you have about foot and vehicle traffic. You can let them know upfront what the existing businesses are and what types of businesses might be suitable for the property.

Another important factor when it comes to retail space is accessibility. If the space has easy access, let readers know that in the ad. Intersections and entrances with traffic signals add value, as does ample parking. And offer information about the surrounding demographics, if it adds value.

Getting It "Write"

Like the other real estate listings, your ad should be benefit-driven, but with more specifics thrown in. Be certain to point out anything that makes the property unique. At a minimum, your title should cover the type of property, the square footage, and any unique selling points.

Include details about any available amenities, such as secretarial support, equipment/furnishings, restrooms, kitchen/break room, and parking. Other than the base rent, you don't have to list any additional fees; wait and go over those in person.

Commercial rentals are handled differently than residential rentals. Although straightforward leases can apply, there are other types of leases, such as a triple net lease, so it's important to know your options.

After you've researched your market, you'll have a greater understanding of what information you need to include in your listing to be able to grab that readers' attention and have them rushing to contact you.

Parking/Storage Rental

The **parking/storage** category is the easiest one in the **real estate** section. Keep these listings simple and direct. Include the type of storage, square footage, and price. List any benefits the readers gain by renting the unit.

Three things that most people want to know when considering storage is accessibility, environment, and security. People want to know when they can access their property. The more opportunities, the better. Also, mention if the unit has an interior or exterior door.

State in your listing if the readers' items will be protected in a climate-controlled facility. This will often sway people in your direction because it can be a great benefit.

Security is also important to people storing their stuff with you. Mention if they must bring their own lock or if you supply one.

From Here...

Using the strategies discussed in this chapter, you'll have your property off your hands in no time. In the next chapter, you'll find out how to create effective listings in the **for sale** category.

8

Listing in For Sale

Are you ready to sell that antique glass lamp? Do you need to get rid of an old desk and free up some space in your room? Perhaps you want to sell a stack of baby clothes without holding your own rummage sale, or you're tired of tripping over that unused snow blower in the garage. Sell them all on craigslist! With craigslist's free advertising and easy ad posting, it's plain to see why users are flocking there to shop for all kinds of items. craigslist is a giant online marketplace where users can sell localized items. Offering a variety of categories, craigslist enables you to sell everything from books and boats to collectibles and event tickets.

In this chapter, we'll examine how to write ads that sell, how to barter or give away stuff free, how to sell vehicles, and what not to do. When you're creating listings on craigslist, the keys are choosing the correct category, writing an eye-catching title, pricing the item correctly, providing an enticing description, and including photos. This chapter shows you how to do it all.

Looking Through the For Sale Categories

If you have something to sell, chances are someone wants to buy it on craigslist. The **for sale** section on craigslist includes 31 categories, as shown in Figure 8.1, so you're bound to find an area in which to sell your item. You'll save some time later if you figure out what category your item falls under before ever listing your ad. Listing your item under the right category can really speed up your sale, but placing it where potential buyers can't find it won't bring you much success. It's also a good idea to peruse the **for sale** categories to help you determine what sort of price to list for your item. So it's worth your while to educate yourself about what types of items are sold in each of the categories.

for sale	
barter	arts+crafts
bikes	auto parts
boats	baby+kids
books	cars+trucks
business	cds/dvd/vhs
computer	clothes+acc
free	collectibles
furniture	electronics
general	farm+garden
jewelry	games+toys
material	garage sale
rvs	household
sporting	motorcycles
tickets	music instr
tools	photo+video
	wanted

Figure 8.1
The **for sale** section includes 31 subcategories.

Table 8.1 provides a rundown of all 31 categories in the **for sale** section of craigslist.

Table 8.1   The <u>for sale</u> Categories on craigslist

Category	Description
<u>barter</u>	This category is geared toward items people want to swap for other items, no money exchanged. For example, you might want to trade a pair of baseball game tickets for an electronic component you need for your in-home theater system.
<u>bikes</u>	Use this category to sell kids' bicycles, adult bikes, mountain bikes, BMX bikes, antique bikes, bicycle paraphernalia, tandem bikes, and so on.
<u>boats</u>	This category covers everything from rowboats to yachts. Sell your sailboat, pontoon boat, outboard motor, boat trailer, paddle boats, and other seaworthy transportation.
<u>books</u>	Sell your used books, new books, big books, little books, schoolbooks, magazines, and anything else that's printed.
<u>business</u>	This category includes items such as office furniture and supplies, office equipment—even entire businesses for sale.
<u>computer</u>	Sell anything related to computers in this category, including monitors, peripherals, cables, laptops, printer cartridges, video cards, and so on.
<u>free</u>	Need to get rid of something without making a profit? Use this category to list anything you want hauled off free, from mattress sets to swing sets.
<u>furniture</u>	Sell your desk, chairs, tables, cabinets, bed frames, and other furniture in this category.
<u>general</u>	This category is wide open for miscellaneous items that don't fit into other <u>for sale</u> categories.
<u>jewelry</u>	Use this category to sell your gold and silver jewelry, diamond rings and necklaces, watches, antique baubles, and more.
<u>material</u>	This category includes construction and remodeling materials such as bricks, lumber, doors, windows, plumbing items, lighting, countertops, and so on.
<u>rvs</u>	If you want to sell your camper, motor home, recreational vehicle (RV), or related item(s), this category is the place to sell it.
<u>sporting</u>	Use this category to sell sporting accessories and equipment, such as athletic gear, fishing poles, ice skates, and so on.
<u>tickets</u>	Can't make it to the big game or concert? Sell your tickets in this category (no scalping allowed).

Category	Description
tools	If you're not using that table saw you got for Christmas a few years ago, you can sell it in this category, which includes power tools, hand tools, automotive tools, and so on.
arts+crafts	This category offers anything classified as arts and crafts, from oil paintings to needlework, airbrushed t-shirts to handmade dolls.
auto parts	Use this category to sell all things automotive, including tires, car parts, engine parts, equipment, and so on.
baby+kids	Has your child outgrown his stroller? Sell it in this category, along with baby clothes, kids toys, children's furniture, bedding sets, car seats, and more.
cars+trucks	This category is the place to go to sell your car or truck.
cds/dvd/vhs	Need to whittle down your movie or music collection? Sell off your CDs, DVDs, or VHS tapes in this category.
clothes+acc	You can list all kinds of clothing for sale in this category, including coats, accessories, and shoes.
collectibles	Use this category to list your porcelain figurines, comic book collection, autographed baseball cards, and other collectible items you want to sell.
electronics	Sell off your speaker set or stereo equipment in this category, which covers all things electronic.
farm+garden	If it's related to farming, you can sell it in this category. Items can include farming equipment, farm animals, lawnmowers, plows, and so on.
games+toys	Sell your computer games, gaming systems, train sets, Lego sets, and remote-controlled cars in this category, which includes anything related to games and toys.
garage sale	Use this category to list your local garage sale, rummage sale, tag sale, or whatever people call it in your area.
household	This category includes household items, from kitchen gadgets to appliances, to window treatments and vacuums.
motorcycles	Sell your motorcycle, scooter, helmet, or leather chaps in this category.
music instr	Did your kid give up the trombone? Sell it in this category, which lists everything from instruments to studio equipment.
photo+video	You can sell all kinds of cameras, video cameras, light stands, projector screens, camera bags, and anything related to capturing images.

Category	Description
wanted	If you're looking for an item rather than selling one, you can use this category to advertise your needs. If you're selling something unique, this category is worth searching in case a potential customer is ready to buy what you want to sell.

Always list your item in the proper category. Granted, sometimes an item fits more than one category or doesn't fit well into any category at all. If you can't find a category to suit your item, list it in the **general** category. Even if your item fits in more than one category, post only one listing in the most relevant category. Duplicate listings of the same item, even with different wording, is considered spamming.

Whatever you do, don't post an ad in a category it doesn't belong in; that's frowned on and someone will probably flag it for removal. If you're selling a set of golf clubs, for example, don't post the ad in the **tools** category.

Warning 4U The **for sale** section is not for business listings; it is only for individuals wanting to sell their personal belongings. It doesn't matter what size business you are, posting here will get your listings flagged. Even if you are a stay-at-home mom looking to make some extra money selling handmade items, posting them here is prohibited. All business listings must be posted in the **services** section.

Planning Your Ad

The better prepared you are before you start creating your ad, the better your results when you finish. This is certainly true when writing ads for craigslist. Planning a well-made craigslist ad involves the following "ingredients":

- Listing title
- Price
- Location
- Objective
- Specific details
- Terms
- Requirements

- Preferences
- Deal breakers
- Photos

To begin with, decide what item you're selling and which location in craigslist you want to use to post your ad. You probably already have something in mind that you want to sell, such as a piece of furniture, a kid's bicycle, or a household appliance you no longer need. As far as a location goes, list in the community nearest your physical location to follow craigslist's terms of use.

For good planning, take time to answer a few important questions. What's your goal in selling the item? Are you trying to make a certain amount of money from the sale, or are you more interested in just getting rid of the thing? Setting a goal can help you focus your ad before you ever begin writing it. One often-overlooked step that can add loads of value to any used item you are selling is simply to clean it. Removing layers of dust or grime and applying some elbow grease or the right cleaner can take off years of wear and tear from the item. It also can remove spots or stains—perceived damage that can greatly reduce the selling price.

Restore and renew your item early on in the selling process. It will give you a better comparison condition when doing your research and also better pictures for your listing. And all for just a few minutes and little or no money!

One of the main parts of good planning involves figuring out the right price for the item you're selling. Do your research. Start by finding out what similar items sell for elsewhere on craigslist or on other Internet auction sites. Set your price accordingly. If you set too high a price, probably no one will respond to your ad. Although you might want to leave out a price for your item to entice your prospects, listings that do not include a price are often removed by flaggers. People want to know the price you're asking upfront, so put it in your ad. Be reasonable, though. The idea is to get people to look at your ad, not skip it for a better deal elsewhere. Everyone's looking for a bargain online, so keep this in mind when determining a price. If you look too greedy, it's a big turnoff.

You should also be aware that you'll probably receive email from people wanting to buy the item at a lower price than listed. There's nothing wrong with writing something at the end of your ad about the price being non-negotiable.

Another part of planning is taking time to create good photos of the item you're selling. When people say a picture is worth a thousand words, they're right, at least when it comes to online sales. You likely have access to a digital camera. Most digital cameras are easy to operate, and you can easily move the images from the camera to your computer. When the images are stored on your computer, you're ready to go. To keep yourself organized, consider storing your craigslist photos in a particular folder you can easily remember and access. You can read more about the importance of including good pictures in Chapter 5, "Successful Listing Strategies."

craigslist allows up to four pictures with each listing, and it's a good idea to use all four when you can. Clear, crisp images can really give some validity to your listing, showing that you're legitimate and actually have a widget to sell. Many users will skip listings that don't include pictures. People want to see what they're going to buy. Don't use a picture that's not a photo of the actual item. In other words, if you're selling a bicycle, don't use a picture from a catalog. Go outside and take an actual picture of your bicycle. Take several angles and be sure to show any flaws. If you use a stock photo, people are suspicious and wonder what the item really looks like. If the item has a broken piece or missing element, show it. Honesty is the best policy, and trustworthy people are easy to do business with again.

The last element of planning is timing. Believe it or not, posting your listing at the correct time can make a difference in the responses you receive. Who is the target audience for your item? College students? They typically have time for Web surfing in the later hours of the evening. Is your target audience at-home moms? They're probably most available in the morning or early afternoon while the kids are at school or napping. Because listings are posted chronologically, it's in your best interest to make sure your post appears online when your target audience is there.

Tip 4U If you're serious about doing business on craigslist, try doing a Google or Yahoo! search for the keywords *Internet demographics* or *Internet usage*. Online resources can help you to figure out the correct time of day to reach your target buyer.

Writing Great Ads

By now, you've planned the price and location for the item you're selling, and you've already taken several pictures to accompany the ad. It's time to get down to the business of writing. There are two areas to focus on when writing great ads: the posting title and the posting description.

When you start a listing, craigslist presents a simple form (see Figure 8.2). You can use this form to fill in details about the item you're selling and add photos. Oh, sure, you can whip up something in a hurry and throw it online, but if you really want successful, fast sales, put a little more effort into creating your ad. You need to write ads that stand above the rest, ads that are sure to garner interest. Follow the steps in Chapter 5 to create a top-notch listing that gets you the most responses.

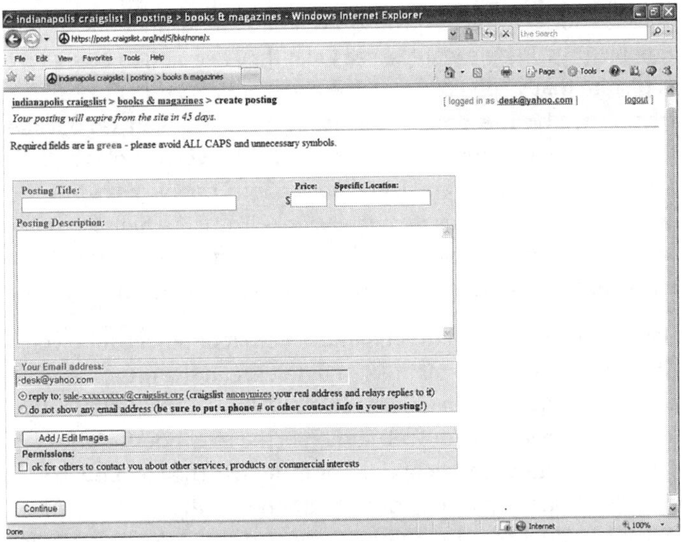

Figure 8.2
craigslist presents a form to capture details about the item you want to sell.

Writing a Great Posting Title

At the top of the form sits the <u>**Posting Title**</u> field. What you enter in this field is very important. It's what people see when they look in the category. If you don't have a good title, people aren't likely to click it and view your ad. The title is the key to making people want to read your ad. Remember, ads are listed in chronological order, with the most recent postings at the top of the pile. Good titles should include something that grabs readers' attention and makes them want to read the ad. Start with a benefit, or include something that is relevant and will pique the reader's curiosity.

The <u>**Posting Title**</u> field allows up to 70 characters, so try to use them all to write a good title. Consider using attention-grabbing phrases you normally see in advertising on TV, the radio, or in newspapers and magazines.

 Tip Never use ALL CAPS in any title or listing description. This format is difficult to read and is considered "shouting" in Internet etiquette.

If you can, include the exact item name and manufacturer name. Users often look for specific items, and you can save time by putting the info up front. Plus, including this information makes you look as though you know exactly what you're selling. Compare these two examples:

Dell Laptop

Dell Inspiron 800m Laptop Get Work Done w/Lightning Speed High RAM

Another helpful tip is to list the benefits of any important features or specs about an item in the title. For example, if you're selling a computer hard drive, state that the user can store lots of pictures. If you're selling a car, talk about enjoying the fast pick-up or jamming to the stereo (if either are noteworthy).

Finally, check your spelling and grammar. Nothing is more questionable than a misspelled ad! Scammers are notorious for poor spelling and grammar. Take time to proofread your work or let someone else check it over for you.

Writing a Great Posting Description

As covered in Chapter 5, writing a great listing makes all the difference between a successful transaction and a frustrating experience. Use the information you gathered during your research to create a listing that has the user eager to contact you.

Start with a few brief sentences to get the reader involved in your listing. You can lead with a story that describes the reader using your item. If you are selling a sofa, it could be "Lean back and relax in luxury on this velvety rich chocolate brown suede sofa with comfy, high back cushions. Rest your weary dogs on one of the 'smooth glide' dual recliners. Imagine all that comfort, right in your own living room."

Then go on to bullet point additional benefits and features. Avoid using long sentences or pointless comments. Keep things positive, short, and to the point.

Your description should also mention the condition of the item. Describe the good and the bad. Neglecting to mention a dent or scratch can come back to haunt you later. Be very forthcoming about any problems with the item and, if possible, include them in a photo. You can certainly focus the reader's attention on the good points first and then mention the bad points. For example:

You'll be making beautiful music with the warm, rich tone of the Bach TR 300 Trumpet. You'll be pleased with the fine crafting and the Bach 5C mouthpiece.

- Bach TR 300 Trumpet
- Bach 5C Mouthpiece
- Beautiful lacquered brass
- Recently serviced
- No scratches
- 1/16" dent near third valve
- Locking hard case included

Repeat the information from the top sentences in the bullet points to catch skimmers who go straight for the list.

Include any specs about the item. For example, if you're selling a computer, mention drive size, monitor size, RAM, processor name, and so on. Don't paste in a giant manufacturer's listing of specs that no one understands. Stick with the important features.

I cannot stress enough how important pictures are in describing an item, but don't rely only on a photo. Mention the color(s) of an item, giving an accurate account of what it looks like.

The description should also mention any sizes or dimensions for the item, especially with larger items that require bigger vehicles to haul away. For example, how big is the dining room table? Can it be disassembled? What are the dimensions of the box containing the plasma TV you're selling? How much does the item weigh?

Be sure to include any statements regarding the terms of the sale. State your price followed by "firm" if you are not willing to negotiate. Mentioning anything about offers or bidding will get your listing flagged off quickly. If you set a deadline, such as a concert date for tickets or a date by which you must sell, mention it.

Tip 4U Some sellers use HTML coding to make their listings stand out. If you know how to write HTML, you can certainly use it to make your ad look nice. However, getting carried away with HTML can end up making your ad look tacky and hard to read. In many cases, the HTML coding is a distraction. "Use sparingly" is the best advice regarding this tactic.

Your description should end with a call to action for the reader to contact you. craigslist provides an anonymous email address for each post, so you don't have to worry about giving out your real email address. If you use a disposable email address as described in Chapter 3, you can also display it within the call to action without compromising your personal information. This makes it easy for readers to contact you, and that's a big selling point. Easy contact—easy sale.

Some users like to put their personal email address or phone number in the listing. Doing that is really not a good idea. Spammers are constantly trolling craigslist looking for information to add to a spam list or call list. You can exchange personal information later when you actually have a potential buyer.

Tips for Category-Specific Listings

Some of the categories in the <u>**for sale**</u> section need a little more explanation when it comes to creating good ads. This section looks at some of those categories.

Bartering

The idea behind the <u>**barter**</u> category is to give people an opportunity to swap stuff without needing to go through a cash transaction. For example, you may be looking for a special bumper for a car you're restoring and want to trade a set of tires or some other classic car part in exchange for the bumper. Or maybe you're a mom looking to trade a crib for a toddler bed. It's quite common to barter services, such as trading house painting for a limited edition collectible or swapping a repair job for a dishwasher.

There are several things to keep in mind when listing in the <u>**barter**</u> category:

- Include as many details as you can in the description, especially if intangibles are involved.
- Be as realistic as possible about the value of what you're trading.
- Outline any process or procedure for the barter, listing any time frames, and so on.

Selling Bikes

Bike descriptions need to include make, model, type, frame type, age, color, size, approximate wear, damage, maintenance record, upgrades, purchase price, and reason for sale. Be sure to mention whether the bike is a mountain bike, street bike, BMX, or whatever. It's not uncommon to stumble upon stolen bikes. Criminals are good at disguising serial numbers and IDs with spray paint or scratching them out, so if you're a seller, be ready to stand behind your bike's authenticity. If you're a buyer in this category, be thorough in your inspection.

Offering Books

When listing books, be sure to include all the pertinent information, such as hardcover or paperback; vintage or new; whether it includes a book jacket, edition name, or number; and overall condition. Include the title, subtitle, author, genre, publication date, ISBN. If it's an old book, describe the condition: stains, brittle pages, water damage, creases, spine damage, cover, binding condition, and so forth.

Listing a Computer

When describing computer items, include important specs and note any documentation or disks included or any hardware included. Be sure to list manufacturer, date of purchase, repair history, upgrades, and so on. If you're selling a hard drive, be sure to erase all personal data. Quite a few secure erase programs are available on the Internet; conduct a search and see what you can download and use to clean the hard drive and any extra storage devices. If the computer came with a manufacturer's "restore" disk, consider using the disk to restore the machine to its original state.

Advertising Furniture

Photos can really help illustrate furniture items for sale, but you should also describe in detail the measurements, color, and any known manufacturer or history about the piece. Potential buyers will need to know the item's condition and size to plan for transportation and for any help needed in loading.

Emptying the Jewelry Box

You probably already guessed this, but the **jewelry** category is a target area for scammers and buyers from other countries. Be cautious and follow the safety tips in Chapter 3. If the jewelry has been appraised, be sure to mention this fact and state the appraised value. You cannot expect to get the full value, but stating the value is helpful if the jewelry has been appraised. Also, when photographing jewelry, consider using a dark background to take close, sharply focused pictures.

Kid Stuff

Be sure to check any items you're selling in the **baby+kids** category against possible recalls, such as defective car seats. Safety is a big issue with children's items, so don't try to sell a car seat that has been in an accident, for example, or toys with missing parts. Anything with a lot of wear will not sell well either, so use good judgment. This is one category where presenting cleaned items isn't only a good idea, it's the law in some states. So be certain to wash clothing and wipe down toys from the start.

Clearing Out Old CDs, DVDs, and VHS Tapes

Buyers expect legitimate items in the **cds/dvd/vhs** category—no bootleg or home video copies. List the genre, release date, and rating for movies. Also be sure to mention whether the movie is widescreen or full screen, if applicable, and it doesn't hurt to give a plot summary.

Selling Cars and Trucks

If you're selling a vehicle in the **cars+trucks** category, there are several key things to mention. First and foremost, what are the model, make, year, color, and mileage of the vehicle? Include information about the vehicle's history, repair history, known problems and flaws, any accidents, maintenance records, or other issues that need full disclosure. What's the condition of the vehicle? Back up your statements with good photos that show the vehicle inside and out. You also can print out free and paid reports about your vehicle at www.carfax.com to give potential buyers the unbiased proof they need to make a decision.

Posting Farm and Garden Items

Strangely, **farm+garden** is the only category on craigslist that allows the sale of animals. The caveat is they must be farm animals, such as horses, cows, pigs, chickens, rabbits, and so on. No pets allowed! Give detailed descriptions about the appearance, health, and history of the animal. Pictures here are a must.

Advertising Your Sale

Are you planning a garage sale? Whether you call it a garage sale, rummage sale, yard sale, or tag sale, you can advertise it on craigslist in the **garage sale** category. When planning to advertise your sale, give enough warning ahead of time regarding the date(s) of the sale. List start and end times, and whether early birds are allowed. Also list what sorts of items you're going to sell. Although I normally advise against listing your address, this is one time where I suggest you include it. Post your listing no sooner than the day before the sale, and be certain to delete the listing as soon as it ends.

Ad Posting Basics

So what's involved with actually posting a sale ad on craigslist? The process really boils down to a few steps. Granted, some of the steps are more tedious than others.

To create an ad listing, follow these steps:

1. Log on to your craigslist account.

2. Click open the **post new ad in:** drop-down list and choose a location, as shown in Figure 8.3.

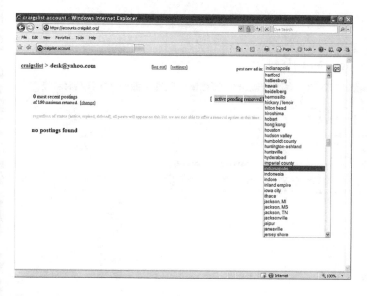

Figure 8.3
Start your ad by first choosing a location for the listing.

3. Click the **go** button to continue.

4. Click the **for sale** link, as shown in Figure 8.4.

5. Click the category under which you want to list the ad, as shown in Figure 8.5.

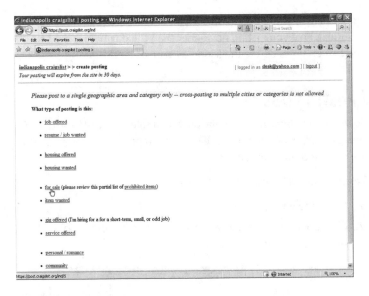

Figure 8.4
Click the **for sale** category link.

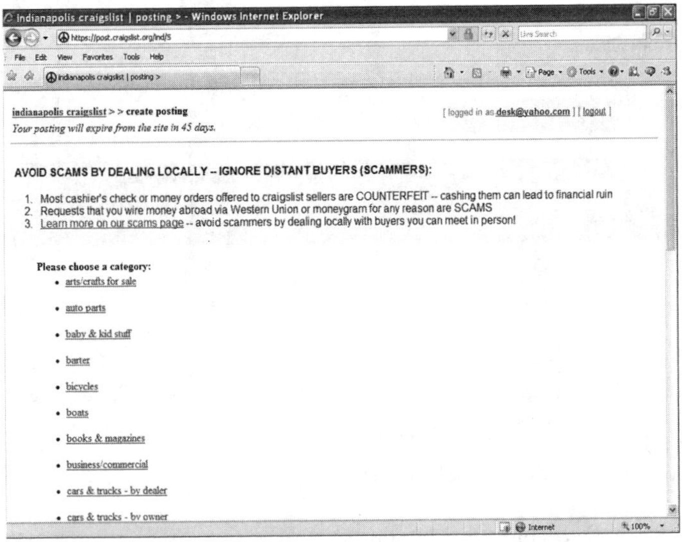

Figure 8.5
Choose a category.

6. Fill in the ad listing form, as shown in Figure 8.6. Enter title, price, and a specific location where the item is located. Use the **Posting Description** field to write up a good description of the item for sale.

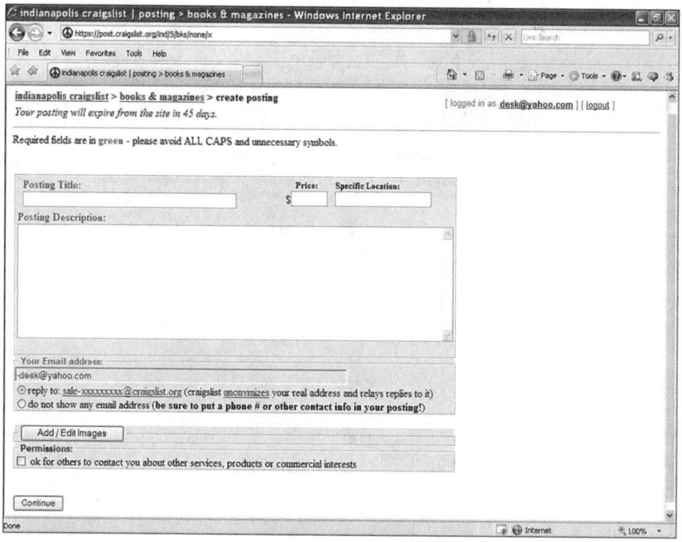

Figure 8.6
Now you're ready to supply the details.

7. In the **Your Email address** area, leave the **reply to:** radio button selected. craigslist creates an anonymous email address for potential buyers to respond to the ad.

   If you want to include your own phone number or contact information in the ad instead and prevent users from contacting you through craigslist, click the **do not show any email address** option.

8. To add photos to the ad, click the **Add/Edit Images** button.

   Optionally, you can allow others to contact you about other services. It's best to leave this option unselected, unless you like a lot of spam.

9. Click the **Continue** button at the bottom of the form.

10. The next screen displays your ad, as shown in Figure 8.7. Review your ad. If you need to go back and edit something, click the **Edit** button; if it's okay, click **Continue**.

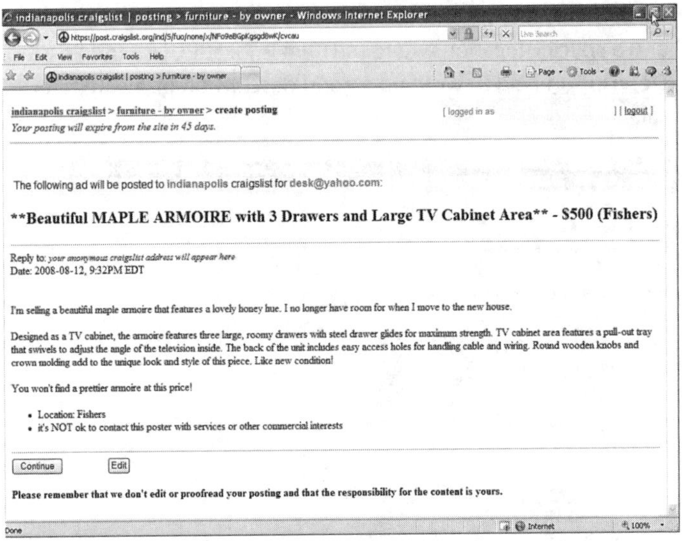

Figure 8.7
You can preview the listing before posting it online.

Within about 15 minutes or so, your ad will appear on craigslist. That wasn't so hard, was it?

If you need to edit a listing at any time, you can do so from your account page. Make any changes; then click the **edit this posting** link. Any changes you make show up immediately in the ad.

If you need to remove the ad entirely, click the **delete this posting** link.

Classified ads appear on craigslist for 7 days in the larger metropolitan areas (Boston, Chicago, Los Angeles, New York, Portland, Sacramento, San Diego, San Francisco area, Seattle, Washington DC), but are online for 45 days in all other cities.

Responding to Contacts

When you post a listing on craigslist, you might receive responses right away, or they might take a while to show up. Be patient. When queries start coming in, respond as fast as you can, and make it very easy for people to continue communicating with you until the deal is done. Timing is everything in a sale. Don't post a listing and then go on a four-day vacation. Be around to respond to contacts, answer questions, and close the deal.

Although it's most fair to consider prospects in the order they contact you, that's not always in your best interest. Consider prioritizing responders based on who is willing to meet your asking price. If you know you have a serious buyer, call that person or allow him to call you. Don't count on wrapping things up with email because email takes a while to bounce back and forth. If you want a faster sale, phone calls are the best way to go. If you do make the first call, be sure to identify yourself and the reason you're calling, being polite and courteous.

Proper etiquette is that the buyer comes to the seller to pick up an item, unless you feel uncomfortable with this arrangement. You can choose a neutral location to exchange the item for money, if the item size allows. And speaking of money, *never* take a personal check. Too many scams happen with check writing. Although PayPal might seem like a good option, craigslist does not promote its use and users will flag listings that mention it. The easiest and most reliable method is cold, hard cash.

Tip 4U As always, safety first! Use good judgment and follow the tips outlined in Chapter 3 to avoid scammers, criminals, and other unsavory types.

Advertising No-No's

There are guidelines regarding what you can say or post in the **for sale** section of craigslist. As mentioned already, you cannot post the same ad that's already up and running. Posting the same item to different categories or communities, even if you reword the listing, is a direct violation of craigslist's terms of use.

Advertising is not allowed, so if you're selling some sort of pyramid scheme or scam, you'll run into all kinds of trouble. The **for sale** section is not for business listings of any kind. If you own a business with products to sell, you must do so in the **services** section only. Also, you cannot include links to commercial sites or services except when listing in the **services** section.

If you violate any rules, your listing will be flagged, and if enough flags are received about a listing, it's pulled. If you're not sure why your listing was pulled, you can always contact the flag help forum (www.craigslist.org/forums/?forumID=3), shown in Figure 8.8. There are lots of people in the forum who can look at your ad and tell you why it was flagged or pulled.

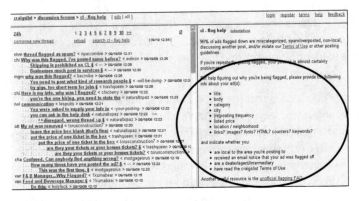

Figure 8.8
The right-side frame of the **flag help** forum lists detailed information about what to include in your forum post to get the fastest response.

From Here...

In this chapter, you learned all about how to post an ad to sell an item on craigslist. You learned about the various categories, how to write an exciting ad, and how to go through the steps for posting it online. Next, you'll learn how to post listings in the **services** section.

9

Listing in Services

The **services** section, shown in Figure 9.1, is the only place on craigslist where businesses can post listings for goods and services. Although it may seem odd to post goods in the **services** section, in keeping with craigslist's terms of use, that is the only place businesses are allowed to advertise. That's not to say that you won't find business listings in other sections, of course; flaggers spend a great deal of time working to take down those listings.

Info 4U Because most of the **services** categories include product ads, this chapter refers to both *services* and *products* (depending on the topic), but most information applies to both.

In this chapter, we'll go through each **services** category and look at ways for you to create effective and interesting advertising for the craigslist market. When you peruse the listings, you'll probably find a wide variety of poorly designed and/or poorly written ads. This is a great opportunity for your business to shine, and the following information will help you get started.

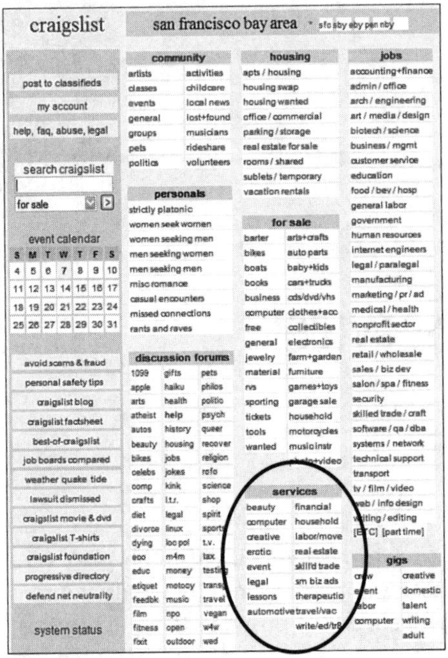

Figure 9.1
Businesses can take advantage of free advertising in the **services** section.

Phone Verification

Before we dive into creating your listing, let's look at a new process that craigslist has put into place to stop spammers in the **services** section. craigslist has been fighting scammers and spammers since they first appeared on the site. But in the last couple of years, Craig has been very vocal about the company's aggressive approach to keeping them at bay.

craigslist is now requiring all posters to the **services** section to post using an account that has passed a phone authentication process. You cannot access the posting pages until you have been verified. A phone number can be associated with only one account. And not just any phone number will do. Most VoIP phone numbers, such as those from Vonage (www.vonage.com) or Skype (www.skype.com)

will not work, nor will many cell phone numbers (although some calls do go through).

Follow these steps to complete the phone verification process so you can start listing in **services**:

1. To begin posting in **services**, while logged in to your account, click the link for the category where you want to post your listing. Then click the **post** link, as shown in Figure 9.2.

Figure 9.2
Clicking the **post** link in your chosen category is the fastest way to begin the phone verification process.

2. When the category links appear, click the correct link, as shown in Figure 9.3.

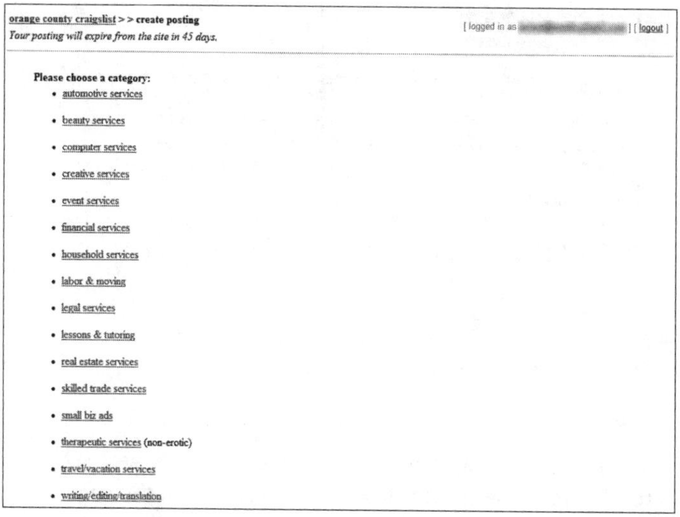

Figure 9.3
Click the correct category link to continue.

3. The phone authentication notification screen will appear, as shown in Figure 9.4. Click either of the authentication links to continue. At this point, you may be asked to log in again. If so, simply log in and the process will continue.

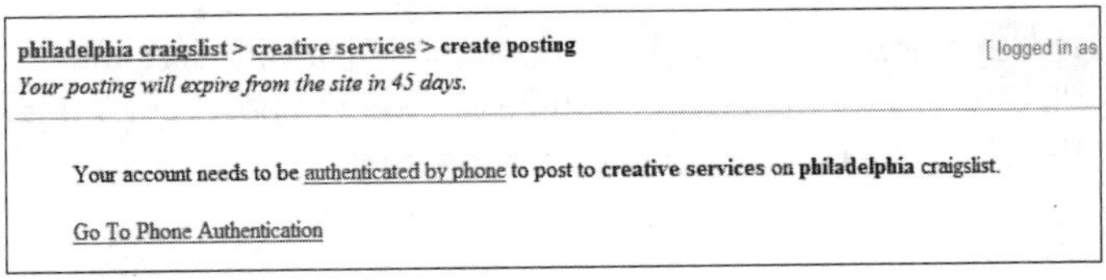

Figure 9.4
Either authentication link will take you to the next step.

4. When the Telephone Account Verification page appears, as shown in Figure 9.5, enter your phone number. Then choose to receive your verification code via text or voice and specify whether you prefer English or French. After you've entered the correct info, click **verify** to go to the next screen.

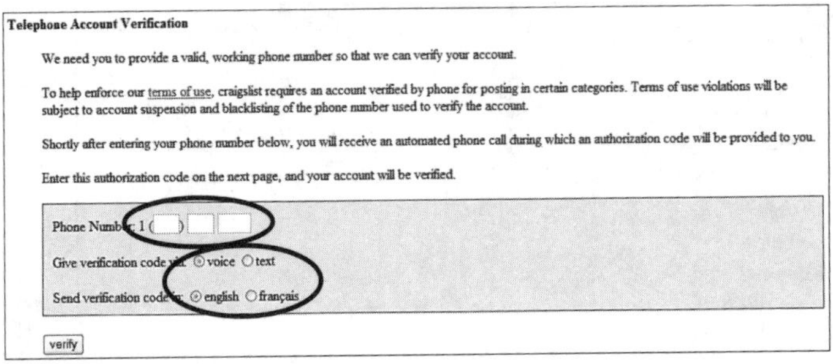

Figure 9.5
Enter your phone number and click **verify**.

5. You can enter the account verification code on the next screen (see Figure 9.6) and then click **verify**. As stated on the page, if you haven't received your verification code after five minutes, refresh the page to see the status.

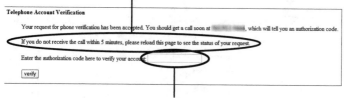

What To Do If Your Phone Doesn't Ring

Telephone Account Verification

Your request for phone verification has been accepted. You should get a call soon at ▓▓▓ ▓▓▓, which will tell you an authorization code.

If you do not receive the call within 5 minutes, please reload this page to see the status of your request.

Enter the authorization code here to verify your account

[verify]

Enter Your Authorization Here

Figure 9.6
Enter the verification code or reload the page after waiting five minutes.

6. If you don't receive a voice or text message and reload the screen, one of the two messages shown in Figures 9.7 and 9.8 will display. The first message indicates that the call is still pending, and the second tells you that craigslist couldn't verify the phone number.

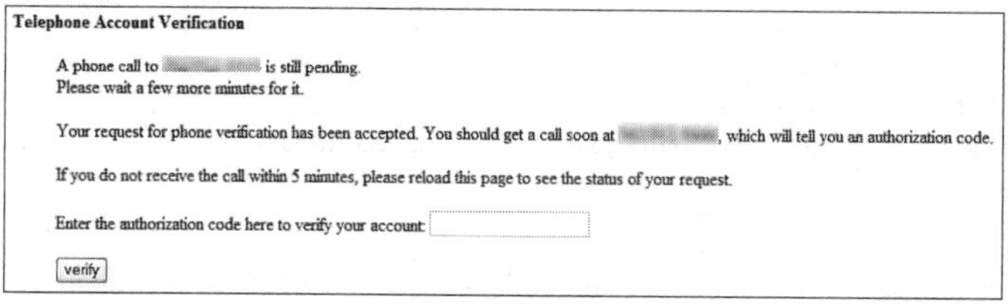

Telephone Account Verification

A phone call to ▓▓▓ ▓▓▓ is still pending.
Please wait a few more minutes for it.

Your request for phone verification has been accepted. You should get a call soon at ▓▓▓ ▓▓▓, which will tell you an authorization code.

If you do not receive the call within 5 minutes, please reload this page to see the status of your request.

Enter the authorization code here to verify your account

[verify]

Figure 9.7
A pending message will appear if the authentication call is still in progress. Wait a few minutes and try again.

7. After you've entered the correct code, you'll see the congratulations page, as shown in Figure 9.9. You can either choose to return to your account or continue with your posting.

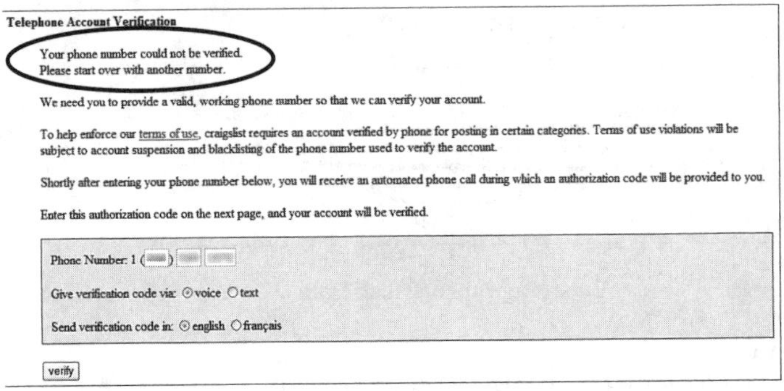

Telephone Account Verification

Your phone number could not be verified.
Please start over with another number.

We need you to provide a valid, working phone number so that we can verify your account.

To help enforce our terms of use, craigslist requires an account verified by phone for posting in certain categories. Terms of use violations will be subject to account suspension and blacklisting of the phone number used to verify the account.

Shortly after entering your phone number below, you will receive an automated phone call during which an authorization code will be provided to you.

Enter this authorization code on the next page, and your account will be verified.

Phone Number: 1 (▭) ▭ ▭

Give verification code via: ⊙ voice ○ text

Send verification code in: ⊙ english ○ français

verify

Figure 9.8
If craigslist is unable to verify your number, this page will let you know so that you can try again.

Telephone Account Verification

Congratulations!

Your account ▬▬▬▬▬▬▬▬ has been verified.

go to my account | continue posting

Figure 9.9
The congratulations page lets you know that your verification code was accepted.

This phone authentication process is likely the first of ongoing security measures that craigslist implements to fight spammers and scammers. Now that you're able to post, let's move on to the good stuff—marketing strategy.

Planning Your Marketing

Following are five simple rules that can help you do better marketing:

▪ **Take your advertising seriously.** Put the same time and effort into your free craigslist listing as you would if you were paying to run an ad in a newspaper, the Yellow Pages, or on TV. Remember that all advertising is a reflection of you or your company.

- **Study some basic advertising principles.** If you read and follow the recommendations in this book, you'll be able to write better ads than 99% of the people out there. Because most people are not in advertising, they have no clue how to speak to their prospects. There's no substitute for understanding the basic concepts of marketing.

- **Find your USP.** A unique selling proposition (USP) is critical for any business. It makes you stand out from your competition. It brands you and quickly tells your prospects why they should choose your solution over the hundreds of other solutions.

  Ideally, your USP should be something that's unique to you or something that you do or provide better than anyone else does. Don't fall into the trap of making price your USP. Unless you're Wal-Mart, that's a no-win position for your business. Think of the five basics (who, what, where, when, and how) when deciding what sets you apart from the competition. Consider your offering and how it's made, packaged, and distributed. And look at your company—is there something that would resonate with your customers?

- **Sell the benefits.** Ultimately, you're not selling a product; you're selling a solution to your customers' problems. Tell them about the benefits of your solution. If you're advertising a restaurant, mention enjoying a delicious, no-work meal. A hair salon's ad should get prospects imagining better-looking hair, increased self-confidence, and even a whole new look. When you sell with benefits, you reach more people where it counts: their emotional hot buttons.

- **Create a targeted ad.** A well-designed and targeted ad is your goal. First, your advertising layout should match the venue. With its minimalist design, craigslist is not the place for slick ads loaded with graphics. Second, your ad should focus on a specific customer base. While your service may have very broad appeal, a single ad should target only one demographic group. If you try to write for all genders, ages, and your market in general, you'll likely lose everyone. The most effective ads zero in on a very precise customer profile.

Now that you know those five important rules, let's go over one of the biggest marketing mistakes that businesses make: reinventing the wheel.

Don't Keep Reinventing the Wheel

If you own a widget store (online or offline), it's easy to see why you would be focused on selling a widget. This way of thinking turns every sale into an unrelated event; after someone has purchased from you, you go back to the beginning of the selling cycle to find a new prospect.

The problem with thinking only in terms of sales is that it takes more time, effort, and money to acquire a new customer than to keep an existing one. To convince a cold prospect to buy, you generally have to get the prospect's attention, establish rapport, spark interest, build credibility, generate desire, and get him to act, all through some combination of advertising and one-on-one sales. By the time that person has become a satisfied customer, you've most likely accomplished all these things already. So, on average, leading that customer back through the selling cycle will take less time, effort, and expense than reaching new customers would.

If you change your focus from looking at each sale as an unrelated event and every contact with a customer as an isolated incident to building long-term relationships with your customers, you can increase your sales while reducing your customer acquisition costs. Offering a small discount or freebie can help to get both customers and prospects to give you their contact information, which you can record for use in future marketing campaigns.

Info 4U   When collecting your customers' contact information, clearly state that you would like to include them on your offline and online mailing lists to receive your newsletter or occasional mailing, which includes sales and discount offers.

You must also clearly state that their information will be kept private and you promise never to share, sell, or rent their information to anyone.

Now, you can start gathering info to design a successful advertisement.

Before You Do Anything Else

The following steps are crucial to creating the most effective advertising possible. You can read about them in greater detail in Chapter 5, "Successful Listing Strategies."

1. **Educate yourself.** Write down all the features your product or service offers. Then translate each of those features into benefits.

   Next, know your market. Some important demographics to note are age ranges, location, gender, education, income, hobbies, employment status, and so on.

   Finally, research the competition. Search the relevant categories to see where competitors are posting. This will give you an idea of what your competitors are offering, where they're listing, and how you can beat the competition.

2. **Set a specific and detailed goal for your ad.** Whether your goal is to make sales or generate leads, write down some concrete numbers you're looking to hit and a date to achieve them.

3. **Gather images.** Whether you're selling a tangible item or promoting a service, take pictures to use in your ad. Product images, your storefront, and happy customers (with their permission, of course) are great shots to include.

Put On Your Advertising Exec Hat

Before you begin to write your ad, organize your information using the following list. To start, you can type the information on separate lines.

- State your goal for this listing. Do you want to generate sales or leads?

- Describe your target market for this listing. Be very specific.

- Describe the offer you want to promote. Is there a certain product or service that you want to move or that's more likely to sell? Are you running a special?

- List the benefits. How is this target market better off when they do business with you? How does your product or service improve their life?
- Describe your service or product and its features. What about your product or service will appeal to this market?
- List any valuable information you can share with your prospects.
- State any proof. Do you have some testimonials? Certifications? Can you include research?
- Include your contact information.

Ready to Write!

When you have all your information together, begin writing your ad. Sell the readers on the benefits. The ad doesn't have to be long, but you'll have the most success if you build credibility and provide proof before you lead into your actual offer and call to action.

As with all advertising, use punctuation, follow the rules of grammar, and avoid slang and insider terminology. Hold the readers' attention by keeping sentences and paragraphs short, to the point, and easy to read. Don't use all caps in your title or listing.

Offering Free Content

A good way to build credibility is to give readers some valuable information free. You can use this information as a way to demonstrate your knowledge and develop trust with your prospects. You don't have to give away the farm, only enough information to build rapport.

A simple way to build rapport in your listing is to open by sharing some valuable industry insights or "content" with your prospects. In the Internet marketing world, this technique is a well-tested way to build a customer list and create an ongoing relationship.

There are two ways to use this content:

- Provide all of it in your listing, in hopes of the readers' following your call to action.

- Include a portion of it in your listing and let the readers know that they can receive the rest in a report by providing you with their contact information.

Now that you can construct an effective listing, let's go over each category. I'll cover some of the types of businesses that list in each one. There are also ideas for free content that you can offer your prospect. A simple way to provide the information is in a numbered or bulleted report form with a title such as "5 Things You Need to Know Before You Choose a _____" or "11 Mistakes Every _____ Buyer Should Avoid." I've included actual title examples from craigslist postings to show you the do's and don'ts of writing attention-grabbing headlines.

Automotive Services

The **automotive** category is a huge catchall in many communities. You'll find ads for anything having to do with vehicles, from buying new ones, to repairing them, to financing and insurance.

Suggestions for Free Content

- What to look out for when buying a used car
- How to spot the best deal on new car loans
- What to look for when choosing an insurance company or agent

Examples of Do's and Don'ts

Example: "Don't get taken...call me!"

Don't be too cryptic. Curiosity can get people to click your headline, but in a category like **automotive** where competition is high and so many different products and services are covered, being vague will get your ad passed over.

Do play the curiosity card if you have something juicy to back it up. This headline was actually the lead for a listing for an independent mechanic. The ad gave three reasons you should never take your vehicle to a dealer for repair. "Three Things to Know Before Choosing a Repair Shop" is a better title for this ad. It makes people want to read more, and the free information included in the listing makes people more educated consumers.

Example: "[[[[[[[[[[[[NEED IT TOWED OR TRANSPORTED???????]]]]]]]]]]"

Don't try to stand out by using unusual characters or all caps. To say this title is hard to read is an understatement. At most, you should initial cap each word.

Do ask a question that qualifies the prospect. "Need Your Vehicle Towed or Transported Today?" This tow truck listing was offering immediate service. If this business can live up to its claim, its unique selling proposition could be offering "no-wait" service.

Example: "brakes"

Don't make it too short. Even if what you're advertising is obvious. It doesn't matter what your listing says or even if you do the best work in the world; if people aren't enticed by the title, they won't click through to your listing.

Do use the title to highlight a benefit. This brake repair person offered convenient on-site service. You can have up to 70 characters to grab your readers. "Brakes Fixed at Your Location - Skip the Rental, the Ride, and the Wait" tells the readers what's different about this business and points out the benefit of not having to leave your car somewhere.

Beauty Services

As you might guess, the most common services covered in the **beauty** category are hair salons/stylists, nail salons, skincare, waxing, tanning, and makeup. You'll also find fitness trainers and workout gym listings, but some communities prefer those to be in the **therapeutic** category.

Suggestions for Free Content

- How to choose the best haircut for you
- What are the different types of artificial nails?
- How to select the right personal trainer
- What to know before you go to a tanning salon

Examples of Do's and Don'ts

Example: "FREE HAIR FREE HAIR FREE HAIR FREE HAIR"

Don't confuse the reader. The vision of someone running around throwing handfuls of "FREE HAIR" is almost frightening. Plus, others might skim the ad and see "HAIR FREE." This person was actually advertising one free hair salon service with the purchase of another service. And all caps is a big no-no.

Do use familiar sayings when possible. This stylist could use "Find Out for Yourself If Blondes Have More Fun" to advertise her free cut-with-color promotion. A play on the well-known saying can trigger interest in those familiar with it.

Example: "I'm sooo Bored!! come see me for a great summer discount"

Don't give prospects the idea that no one is interested in your business. And I suggest that you do not make your unique selling proposition the fact that *you have no customers*, especially when it comes to a beauty service.

Do give your prospect a call to action. This nail salon needs clients right away. "Bad Day? Let Us Pamper You Right Now and Make It All Better" gives readers a reason to call at that very moment.

Example: "* FREE Acne Pimple Kit *"

Don't give the prospect an unpleasant visual. More proof that some people don't stop to imagine what image their words may be putting in the readers' minds.

Do create a positive promise. "Have Beautiful Blemish-Free Skin Naturally in 10 Days" has the readers imagining themselves after using this list's skin care products.

Computer Services

Many of the listings in the __computer__ category are for computer repair or maintenance, and most of them try to stand out by advertising that they offer the cheapest service. That's a no-win situation because it often ignites a pricing war.

Website design and hosting services are also top advertisers in this category, although some designers list in the **creative** section also. Either way, in this highly competitive market, you'll stand out among the noise with a strong USP. You'll also want to advertise here if you sell computers or offer any type of training.

Suggestions for Free Content

- What to do first if you're having computer problems
- How to protect your computer from viruses, spyware, and hackers
- What to consider before choosing a hosting company

Examples of Do's and Don'ts

Example: "Network Cabling,"

Don't forget to double-check your work. Given the comma at the end of the title, I think this person meant to write more. This title will likely get lost among all the more descriptive headlines.

Do proofread your ad before you submit it. The associated listing talks about other types of work the company does. "Have Your Network, Phone, or TV Up and Running Today" gives people a better idea of the broad range of services this company offers.

Example: "online advertising"

Don't forget to capitalize. Your goal is to capture people's attention, so your headline needs to stand out while being easy to read. Use initial caps, but don't go overboard. Typing in all caps is considered yelling and is a turnoff for most people,

Do use proper punctuation. This listing for an inexpensive and simple-to-use Internet website solution would do better highlighting its offering with the title "Bring in Customers with Your Own Internet Site Today."

Creative Services

In most communities, **creative** is a melting pot category for industries that require even the smallest amount of creativity. It also gets a lot of crossover from the **event** category. Businesses that list in this category include photographers, videographers, landscapers, artists, musicians/singers/music teachers, graphic/website designers, chefs, silkscreen printers, entertainers, and printers, among others.

Suggestions for Free Content

- What to consider when choosing a wedding photographer or videographer
- Why a logo is important to your business
- What to look for when choosing a music teacher

Examples of Do's and Don'ts

Example: "Princess Parties"

Don't miss an excellent opportunity to create desire. Children's parties, and special events as a whole, are very big business. People spend billions of dollars annually to create the party everyone will remember. Don't miss an opportunity to press some emotional hot buttons.

Do play on emotional cues. "Make Your Princess' Birthday Wish Come True" goes right to the heart of what most parents want—to give our kids memories of their special day that will last a lifetime.

Example: "Personalized Cheff"

Don't design your ad on the posting page. People are put off by typos. They can be viewed as carelessness or a lack of attention to details.

Do use a word processing program when writing your ad. Check spelling and grammar. An error-free ad tells readers you take pride in your work and treat it seriously. This listing talks about being a food coach in the kitchen and could generate interest with the headline "International Chef Shows You How to Take Control of Your Kitchen."

Example: "Photography"

Don't forget that the title is also the headline. It's your only chance to grab your prospects' attention and get them to click on your ad. Don't use a generic keyword.

Do jump on the chance to get readers thinking. This one-word descriptive was actually the headline for a well-written ad for a commercial photographer. "Capture the Heart of Your Business with Custom Images" will touch business owners. This photographer also mentioned doing other types of photography. A brief mention is fine near the end of a listing, but the majority of the copy should be aimed at your target niche.

Erotic Services

Despite the efforts of craigslist's management, the **erotic** category is generally loaded with clandestine—and not so clandestine—illegal activity. And it has been publicized as of late that the police monitor the category for sting operations.

If you're running a respectable business, I suggest skipping this category and finding another way to advertise. If you aren't, you probably don't need my help anyway.

Event Services

The **event** category includes many of the same businesses that post in the **creative** category, but with a specific focus on special events. Businesses that list in this category include photographers, videographers, artists, musicians/singers/music teachers, graphic/website designers, chefs, deejays, bakers, silkscreen printers, entertainers, bartenders, and more.

Suggestions for Free Content

- How to have a stress-free event
- What to ask when choosing a DJ
- How to save money on your special event

Examples of Do's and Don'ts

Example: "Need help planning a menu"

Don't be ambiguous. This person needs help planning a menu, right? Actually, he's asking a question, but without the right punctuation, readers are left wondering.

Do eliminate confusing wording or imagery from your headline.
This is a chef for hire who will help plan the menu and execute it. This person could lead with "Entertain Your Guests and Leave the Kitchen Duty to Me" to tell readers the real benefit they'll experience by having someone else deal with the food responsibilities.

Example: "HIRE an EXPERIENCED FORMER RADIO DJ FOR YOUR NEXT EVENT!!"

Don't scream at the reader. Words in all capitals are harder to read. And many readers consider it impolite to YELL.

Do connect your headline with your ad copy. This headline was the lead to a long and thoroughly written ad that included great information about what to consider when hiring a DJ. This person covered nine reasons that offered proof why he was the best man for the job. "Nine Important Points to Consider When Choosing a DJ" would have had just about everyone clicking on it to learn his secrets.

Financial Services

Anything to do with money falls into the __financial__ category. Common businesses include consumer loans, mortgage/refinance, commercial loans, credit repair, accounting/bookkeeping, tax preparation, insurance, foreclosure help, and more.

Suggestions for Free Content

- Understanding your credit
- What to consider when choosing a tax preparer
- The importance of keeping good financial records

Examples of Do's and Don'ts

Example: "MT760.MT799.BLOCKED FUNDS"

Don't use industry terminology in headlines. Some people will know what they're looking for and understand exactly what you mean. However, plenty of other people can benefit from what you offer but won't know what you can do for them if you talk in terms they don't understand.

Do keep things simple. You'll connect with your prospects better if you keep your copy easy to understand and make it a quick read. Reach the greatest number of people by eliminating technical terms and industry slang.

Example: "Basic QuickBooks Bookkeeping"

Don't sell yourself short. Qualifying bookkeeping with a term such as "basic" downplays the importance of what this person has to offer. If you're worried about getting in over your head, ask some questions during your initial contact and decide at that point if it's a good match.

Do tell readers what you can do for them. This bookkeeper had a solid ad that covered the importance of keeping track of the day-to-day financial details. She could lead into the ad with "Are You Keeping Records When You Need to Be Making Money? Let Me Help!"

Household Services

Another high-volume category with lots of variety is **household**. This category includes anything and everything having to do with your home—inside and out—such as house cleaning, appliance installation/repair, heating and cooling installation/repair, landscaping/lawn care, handyman services, construction/remodeling, electricians, concrete work, plumbers, pet sitting, homeowners/renters insurance, and more.

Suggestions for Free Content

- What to know when hiring a contractor
- How to choose the right house cleaning service
- What to ask a lawn care professional

Examples of Do's and Don'ts

Example: "$60 AN HOUR OR $250 FLAT RATE TO CLEAN YOUR ENTIRE HOUSE!"

Don't try to sell on price. Never include the price of your service in your headline or your listing. You've qualified readers by price before you've even had a chance to tell them what they're purchasing.

Do sell them on savings. If you want to run a special, include it as a percent off or discount amount. You'll let people know that they're getting a good deal and have them curious about the cost. A headline like "You'll Love Our Sparkle-and-Shine House Cleaning Special" gets the readers picturing their clean house. In the listing you can offer up a percentage off or offer five hours for the price of four.

Example: "Hauling R' us!"

Don't go for humor or bad puns. Making a play on words is okay, but if it doesn't work, it doesn't work. Avoiding humor in a headline is usually best, as it rarely motivates a reader.

Do stay relevant. This demolition and removal service should try "You Got a Problem? We'll Make It Go Away for Good!" if it wants to pique readers' curiosity with a smile.

Labor and Moving Services

The **labor/move** category is mainly filled with ads for moving and transport companies, truck rentals and general labor, but you can also find listings for trash removal or lawn care in most communities.

Suggestions for Free Content

- How to avoid being scammed by moving companies
- What to look for when comparing moving companies
- Steps to a stress-free move

Examples of Do's and Don'ts

Example: "FEMALE---NO JOB IS TOO BIG OR SMALL"

Don't put obstacles on the path to calling you. Leading with this title is not a good choice. If this "Jill of all trades" cannot or will not do some tasks, best to do the qualifying during the initial contact. You never know what opportunity might come up once the lines of communication are open.

Do give the prospect a call to action. "Stop Putting It Off! Call Today and Have It Done Tomorrow!" invites readers to contact you to get work done. It also leads them to imagining the relief of having a task completed that's been hanging over their head.

Legal Services

The <u>legal</u> category contains listings for all types of legal representation, as well as paralegal services, notary publics, and credit repair listings.

Suggestions for Free Content

- How to save money by using a paralegal
- How to protect yourself from lawsuits
- What to look for when choosing an attorney

Examples of Do's and Don'ts

Example: "Cheaper Lawyer, Criminal/DWI"

Don't use words with negative impact. Words with negative meanings or connotations give readers the wrong idea. "Cheap" can describe cost—or quality. Don't associate your business with poor quality.

Do choose words that give your prospect a clear, positive image. "You Can Afford Honest, Effective Legal Representation" gives readers hope and a positive visual.

Example: "social security income benefits"

Don't stay neutral. This headline gives readers very little to go on. People are in need and are impatient.

Do give your prospects a clear understanding of the topic. A company offering information about Social Security disability benefits would do good to lead with "What You Must Know Before You Apply for Disability Benefits."

Example: "Wanted training"

Don't try to play the curiosity factor when you post a wanted ad. If you're looking for something, include specifics in your headline. This law office is in need of software training.

Do give as much information as possible when placing a wanted ad. "Wanted: Setup and Training on ProLaw Software" gives readers enough information to know whether they can help.

Lessons and Training

If you're offering any type of lesson or class, the **lessons** category is the place to go. Although you can list any types of lessons you offer, you'll find a fair amount of competition if you offer lessons for piano, math, fitness, dance, tennis, swimming, guitar, or singing.

Suggestions for Free Content

- What to look for when comparing fitness centers
- How to help your child get the most out of tutoring
- How to choose beginning instruments for young musicians

Examples of Do's and Don'ts

Example: "Music Lessons - 20 Yrs. Exp. - Excellent References"

Don't forget what's most important to your prospects. Although the preceding headline covers the quality of the teacher, what's most important to readers is what your offer will do for them.

Do give a clear picture of the benefits they'll get. This experienced piano teacher for adults would do better to save her qualifications for her listing and offer a headline like "Amaze Your Family and Friends When You Sit Down to Play."

Example: "Certified Teacher Avaliable For Tutoring"

Don't let carelessness ruin your credibility. You have only a few seconds to grab the readers' attention, build trust, and create credibility. Even small mistakes like the misspelling of *Available* add up to lost sales and a damaged reputation.

Do pay attention to details. Put time and effort into creating an error-free listing. Use spell check and have someone else give you feedback if you're uncertain about anything.

Example: "Great/Friendly Tutor"

Don't think in the abstract. Words like "great," "friendly," or "incredible" offer vague descriptions. They're best saved for testimonials from your customers.

Do choose relevant words that pack a punch. "Is Your Child Struggling in Math? Two Hours a Week Will Help" is a great lead. This title covers the problem and gives a quantifiable solution.

Real Estate Services

If you're an agent, mortgage broker, title company, or property manager, list in the **real estate** category. Depending on the community, you may also be able to list here if you provide services related to real estate.

Suggestions for Free Content

- How to get the best deal on a mortgage
- Mistakes that first-time buyers make
- What to look for when choosing a real estate agent
- How to decide between listing your home and FSBO

Examples of Do's and Don'ts

Example: "Staging Just Like A Model Home"

Don't use industry terms that might be lost on your target market. Although many people may know the term "staging" or can figure it out from the context, you can miss a large market segment if you don't connect with inexperienced consumers.

Do write for beginners if they're part of your target market. If your target market includes people who are unfamiliar with your product or services, use wording that bridges the gap between them and you. "Set the Stage to Make Your Home More Desirable in Today's Market" gives readers a benefit and introduces them to what you can do for them.

Skilled Trade Services

Although the extent varies by community, there tends to be a lot of crossover between the **skill'd trade** category, **household**, and **real estate**. If you offer construction, remodeling, or landscaping services, you should list in **skill'd trade**. If you're going to list in more than one category, remember to cover different services or take different approaches to avoid having your listings flagged.

Suggestions for Free Content

- What to look out for when choosing a remodeling company
- How to keep your lawn and garden healthy and thriving
- What to consider when planning a kitchen or bath makeover

Examples of Do's and Don'ts

Example: "Finish Carpenter fully licensed and bonded"

Don't settle for getting lost in the crowd. In a high-volume category, a boring listing will get lost in the crush. While the title may be accurate, it does little to stick out to skimmers.

Do be bold to catch readers' eyes. This title does little to convey the amazing work the carpenter is capable of doing. His listing included a link to his website with images of a few of his cabinetry, stairway, and fireplace mantel masterpieces. He would do well to use a headline like "Give Your Kitchen the Beauty and Warmth of Custom Master Cabinetry" and add pictures from his website to his listing.

Example: "FENCES,DECKS,ARBORS,PARIO COVERS,REPAIRS, (BBB MEMBER) FAMILY OPPERATED"

Don't cram everything into the title. Readers will get lost on an unreadable laundry list while trying to figure out what you really do. And again, I point out the importance of proofreading and spell check.

Do make the title as long as necessary. Make the headline as long as you need to get your point across, but make certain that it's readable. "Enjoy More Outdoor Living with Our Custom-Built Fences and Decks" will target a large market and get them picturing their new backyard.

Small Business Ads

The <u>sm biz ads</u> category is a catchall in most communities. If what you offer doesn't fit in another category or you're looking to sell a local small business, this is the place to list, but you'll find your ad surrounded by business opportunity listings, many of which are prohibited on craigslist.

Suggestions for Free Content

- What to consider when buying an existing business
- How to avoid work-at-home scams
- How to make money online

Examples of Do's and Don'ts

Example: "Clean Supreme, LLC"

Don't lead with only your business name. Although using your name may give readers an idea of what you're offering, it's not likely to generate emotion, which is really what causes people to act.

Do push an emotional hot button whenever possible. This commercial cleaning company can strike a chord with "Give Your Customers a Great First Impression with a Spotless Office."

Example: "^^^^^^^^^^^ Winner, Winner, Chicken Dinner! ^^^^^^^^^^"

Don't be ridiculous. This title has nothing to do with the business opportunity listing it led to. People may click out of curiosity, but most will be annoyed at such a tactic.

Do stay within the terms of service. If your ad isn't allowed on craigslist, consider finding another way to advertise.

Therapeutic Services

The **therapeutic** category is largely filled with listings for massages. You should also list here if you offer other types of therapeutic services such as Reiki, hypnosis, and acupuncture.

Suggestions for Free Content

- Which type of massage is best
- What are the different types of alternative therapies?
- How to stay healthy naturally

Examples of Do's and Don'ts

Example: "YOUR PLACE OR MINE"

Don't be misleading. Many of the massage listings cover erotic massages and possibly more. However, this listing appeared to be for a licensed professional. The title makes it sound borderline and may be misleading to the wrong person.

Do create a professional image. If your business is strictly professional (and anything else is prohibited on craigslist), then your ad should be too. "Release Stress and Relax Your Muscles with Deep Tissue Massage" keeps it business-like yet enticing.

Example: ">>> ACUPUNCTURE/ALLERGY HELP >>> SERIOUS ONLY INQUIRE >>"

Don't be negative. Part of running a business is dealing with shoppers and tire kickers. Accept that it comes with the territory.

Do stay positive. You never know who might end up being your best customer. This listing for an acupuncture specialist could lead with "All Natural Help for Chronic Pain Suffers - Feel Better Today" and accept that not everyone who contacts her will end up being a customer.

Travel and Vacation Services

List in the **travel/vac** category if you offer any products or services related to traveling and tourism. Many craigslist communities hold mass transportation and hotel discount listings in this category, but you'll also find services such as taxi, house sitting and pet sitting, and local hot spots.

Suggestions for Free Content

- Unusual things to enjoy when you're visiting a specific area
- Tips to have better family vacations
- How to get the best deals on travel arrangements

Examples of Do's and Don'ts

Example: "Bed and Breakfast"

Don't overlook important details. For a travel or vacation listing, location is critical. Many consumers are easily annoyed when a title doesn't include commonsense information.

Do include highly relevant information. Be considerate of your prospects and make it easy for them to be interested in your offer. Your hotel advertising should include a location in the title such as "Enjoy a Relaxing Getaway at One of Portland's Best Bed and Breakfasts."

Writing, Editing, and Translating Services

If you're offering any of these services, the **write/ed/tr8** category is the place to list. You'll be listing alongside all types of writers and editors, as well as transcriptionists and publicity specialists.

Suggestions for Free Content

- Interview tips
- What to consider when choosing an editor
- The importance of a well-written business plan

Examples of Do's and Don'ts

Example: "FREELANCE WRITER"

Don't try to be everything to everyone. The most successful advertising targets a very specific market with a very specific offer. If you try to emphasize everything, you end up featuring nothing.

Do focus on one goal per listing. Decide what market you want to target and create an offer tailored to their wants and needs. The creator of this title talks about helping people record their memoirs, so a better lead would be "Have People Told You to Write a Book About Your Life? Let Me Help!"

Example: "WWW.*servicename*.COM #1 Resume Service"

Don't lead with your website. In keeping with Craig's vision, most users want local service and are leery of anyone who's in a hurry to drive people to an unknown website.

Do stay local. Follow the terms of use and advertise locally. You can include a link to your website in your listing, but you'll have greater success with craigslist if you remember to stay close to home.

From Here...

Now that you know the ins and outs of the <u>services</u> section, move on to the next chapter, where you can learn how to list in the <u>jobs</u> and <u>gigs</u> categories when you need to hire more employees!

Listing in Jobs and Gigs

The advent of the Internet has really given employers and employees an excellent tool to find each other. In days gone by, you had to rely on newspaper advertising, job postings on bulletin boards, employment agencies, word of mouth, recruiters, or just hoofing it on foot from one office to another to find a job. Today, the Internet has opened up all kinds of avenues to finding employment, and craigslist is part of a vast online resource for job opportunities.

This chapter covers how to write job listings that bring in qualified candidates, how to fill small or odd jobs, how to respond to potential applicants, and how craigslist compares to other online job sites.

Comparing Online Job Resources

What's so different about job listings on craigslist versus job listings on other sites, like Monster.com or CareerBuilder.com? Employers wanting to hire all types of workers find that craigslist's **jobs** and **gigs** sections offer a far better value than other employment sites on the Internet. In a few craigslist communities, you have to pay a small fee to post job ads, but in most places, posting is still free. On sites like Monster.com,

HotJobs.com, and CareerBuilder.com, employers pay hundreds of dollars per ad.

craigslist didn't start out as a job-hunting site, but users are flocking there to look for the next great opportunity. craigslist and other networking sites are quickly becoming the place to go to find targeted candidates and positions. Many of the other online job-posting sites encourage boilerplate want ads that generally don't target the skill sets needed for the position available. With craigslist, jobs are categorized, with the most recent listings posted at the top of the page. Smaller businesses can find better responses for locally available opportunities and more esoteric jobs on craigslist as opposed to the mega job sites. Users complain that too many temporary agencies and recruiters post jobs on the mega sites, and it's too easy to get lost in the crowd. You might find it useful to survey the larger job sites to see what's out there, and then put to use what you find there in your own postings on craigslist.

Because craigslist is generating phenomenal growth and interest, you may be amazed at how quickly you start receiving responses to your ad. Experts report that for serious, focused job hunts, niche sites are the way to go.

Looking Through Job Categories

Before you start creating a job listing ad on craigslist, take time to learn a little about the various categories. In Indianapolis, for example, the craigslist **jobs** section includes 33 categories, as shown in Figure 10.1, so you're bound to find a category that fits the type of job opening you have available. You'll save some time later if you figure out first what category your job listing falls under. Listing your item under the right category can really speed up your job-filling process, but placing it where potential applicants can't find it won't bring you much success.

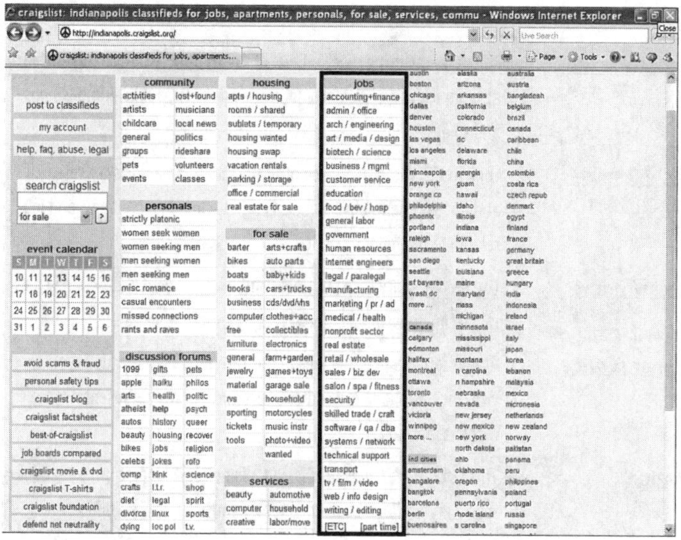

Figure 10.1
The **jobs** section includes 33 categories.

Table 10.1 shows a rundown of all 33 categories in the **jobs** section of craigslist.

Table 10.1   Categories in the craigslist jobs Section

Category	Description
accounting+finance	This category lists jobs like bookkeeping, stockbroker, certified public accountant, financial analyst, controller, tax accounts clerk, loan officer, and accounts payable specialist.
admin/office	You'll find all kinds of administrative and office positions in this category, such as assistant, receptionist, office manager, and so on.
arch/engineering	This category covers anything related to the fields of architecture, engineering, and computer-aided design (CAD). Listings include all kinds of engineering positions, design architect, AutoCAD draftsman, and other related jobs.

Category	Description
art/media/design	This category is the place where all the creative listings hang out, such as graphic design, Web design, freelance artist, publishing positions, and so on.
biotech/science	Look to this category for scientific positions, lab associates, research and development jobs, chemical engineering, microbiology, and jobs related to the field of science.
business/mgmt	Use this category to list business and management positions, such as marketing jobs, management jobs, sales jobs, and more.
customer service	As you can imagine, the jobs in this category focus on customer service, such as phone call centers, customer service representatives, cashiers, and so on.
education	This category features teachers of all ages and types, from preschool teachers to college educators, tutors, music teachers, and instructors of all subjects.
food/bev/hospitality	This category lists restaurant jobs, hotel employment, cooks and chefs, laundry attendants, and everything related to the food and hospitality services.
general labor	List any kind of general labor job in this category, including cleaning, laborers, automotive, landscape help, janitorial jobs, and more.
government	This category focuses on a wide range of government jobs, anything from clerical workers to field officers.
human resources	This category covers anything related to human resources, such as recruiters, assistants, directors, auditors, and so on.
internet engineers	Anything involving Internet development and programming falls in this category.
legal/paralegal	Law office jobs, attorneys, and paralegal positions are found in this category.
manufacturing	This category includes anything revolving around manufacturing, from working on a production line to managing production, automotive industries, and so on.

Category	Description
marketing/pr/ad	This category lists jobs that fall into marketing, public relations, and advertising. Expect to see listings like copywriters, account representative, and marketing positions. Watch out for scams in this category, such as get-rich schemes, work-from-home schemes, and Internet schemes.
medical/health	Job seekers will find all kinds of employment opportunities in this category surrounding the medical and health fields, such as nursing jobs, dental assistants, clerks, and so on.
nonprofit sector	Look for campaign positions, fundraiser jobs, nonprofit coordinators, and directors in this category.
real estate	Real estate agent jobs appear in this category, along with property managers, loan officers, assessors, and more.
retail/wholesale	Anything related to selling retail or wholesale can be found here, including store sales and management positions, cashiers, trainees, and so on.
sales/biz dev	This category lists sales jobs of all kinds; however, the category is also full of scams and schemes, so be forewarned.
salon/spa/fitness	Look in this category for listings for personal trainers, beauticians, salon specialists, nail technicians, stylists, and massage therapists.
security	This category includes security positions, night watchmen, guards, private security jobs, and other related positions.
skilled trade/craft	This category lists jobs for tile and carpet installers, painters, carpentry and woodcraft, plumbers, heating and cooling technicians, and other skilled trade positions. Anything involving a skilled trade or craft can be listed here.
software/qa/dba	You'll find listings in this category for quality assurance (QA) specialists, database administrators (DBAs), software technicians, software developers, and other computer-related jobs.
systems/network	This category includes jobs such as UNIX/LINUX administrators, programmers, IT managers, network technicians and analysts, and so on.
technical support	This category includes computer technicians, computer support staff, field service technicians, help desk positions, and all manner of support jobs.

Category	Description
<u>transport</u>	If it involves wheels, this is the category: post driver, delivery, and other transportation jobs.
<u>tv/film/video</u>	This category covers television, radio, film and video production, from talent to camera operators and editors.
<u>web/info design</u>	Look in this category for Web designers and developers, programmers, and anything related to the Internet.
<u>writing/editing</u>	This category includes technical writers, magazine and newspaper jobs, editorial positions, copy writers, and jobs related to publishing.
<u>ETC</u>	Jobs that don't fall easily into any of the other categories are listed here.
<u>part time</u>	This category isn't a separate category. It displays any job listing marked as part time, regardless of the chosen category.

Always list your job ad in the proper category. If you can't find a category to suit your item, list it in the <u>ETC</u> category.

Another good idea is to peruse the job categories to help you see what other employers are doing with their listings. This can give you some good ideas about well-written ads versus lousy ads. Scanning through some of these ads can quickly tell you what kinds of applicants may apply and why. If you're targeting certain skills and experience, you'll see how important it is to be specific in your own listings.

Employers and job seekers alike should always be on the lookout for scams in the <u>jobs</u> section on craigslist. Some areas are fraught with ads for get-rich schemes, work-at-home propositions, and other scams. Although craigslist tries to monitor and control such listings, so many of them spring up so fast that it's hard to regulate them. If the <u>jobs</u> category you've chosen is swamped with scams and get-rich-quick schemes, and you're listing your ad for free, consider pulling the ad every two days, waiting 30 minutes, and reposting it to keep your ad at the top of the stack. Follow the guidelines explained in Chapter 5, "Successful Listing Strategies." Of course, this technique isn't appropriate for paid ads because you'd have to pay again every time you list the ad.

Writing a Successful Job Listing

When you're writing a job listing, your goal is to attract the right kinds of candidates for the job. You want to find people possessing the skill sets you need. For starters, it's not always a good idea to hand off the job description task to someone who's unfamiliar with the position. For example, the folks in human resources can't really explain in detail what's required—only the people who have performed or managed the job can do that. Make sure that the description is written by someone who knows the job well. You'll find better-suited applicants if your ad expresses the true requirements of the position.

Listing Basics

So what's in a good job posting on craigslist? How do you write an ad that finds the applicants you want? Glad you asked. Table 10.2 lists some important areas to cover in a job listing.

Table 10.2   Parts of a Good Job Listing

Item	Description
Listing title	This is the attention-grabbing text that potential job applicants read when searching through craigslist. Make your listing title count and stand out from all the rest.
Company info	Include a brief description about your company, including the general location and benefits of working there. It doesn't have to be very long, just enough to define who you are as an employer.
Job title	Clarify the exact job title, even if it's not glamorous.
Job summary	Briefly describe the job, including how it fits into the rest of the company. You might also mention why there's an opening, such as new growth, previous employee moved away, and so on.
Job duties	Clearly define the scope of work, what specific tasks the job entails, and include how much traveling (if any) is involved with the position.
Requirements	List all the requirements and qualifications needed to do the job. Be sure to include what sort of experience you expect or how much education is needed. List any technical or software skills required and anything else that's crucial to performing the job successfully.

Item	Description
Schedule	Clarify the expected work schedule, such as Monday through Friday, 8–5. If you offer a flexible schedule, mention it in this category.
Job type	List the type of employment, such as full-time, part-time, or contract. If it's a project-based position, be sure to state the approximate time length of the project.
Location	Clarify where the majority of work takes place. Is it in an office building onsite, or is telecommuting allowed? If you don't clearly state this info, you'll be swamped with email from people wanting to work from home.
Compensation/benefits	Explain what sort of compensation or benefits are involved. Is it an hourly or salary position? If you don't want to mention pay, can you specify a range? List any benefits, such as health insurance, onsite amenities, vacation, and so on.
Response instructions	Clearly state how you want people to respond to the ad. Do you want them to email a resume as an attachment or in an email message? Should they include a cover letter? Do you want work samples or salary requirements? You might include a phone number, but as we've covered elsewhere, listing phone numbers and addresses on craigslist can lead to unwanted solicitations. Save the phone number and personal information exchange for when you know you have a good candidate.
Hiring process	To be really professional and save yourself some headaches later, give a brief description of the hiring process. How long will you be taking applications? How will you contact qualified applicants? What sort of references are you looking for? Providing this information is a courtesy to the applicant, and good customer service, too. If you don't intend to reply to each applicant, include a statement such as "will contact qualified applicants for interview" or something similar.

When you're writing a job posting ad, always write in specifics; don't be vague or obscure. If you can quantify any of the requirements, do so. For example, state that the applicant needs to type 60 words per minute or possess at least three years of experience. "Fast typist" can mean anything, but "must type 60 wpm" is very clear about what skill set is needed.

Keywords are essential with craigslist advertising, whether it's in job postings or **for sale** postings. Use a variety of keywords that users would most likely type to search for the position. If you're looking for an administrative assistant, by all means, use the keywords *administrative assistant* in the title and description. But you might also include other words normally associated with the job, such as *secretary*, *administration*, *executive assistant*, and so on.

Try to be conscious about the design of your ad. Big blocks of text are uninviting and hard to read on a computer, so consider breaking the text into short paragraphs and bulleted lists, or even apply some frugal HTML coding to make your ad attractive. You don't need to make it look too slick, but make your listing content look good and well laid out. Use the space wisely, don't ramble, but be precise and professional.

Make sure you proofread your listing very carefully before posting or hand it to someone else to read over. A second set of eyes can catch any glaring errors.

Remember, a poorly written ad can expose disorganized hiring personnel or a potentially bad boss. Nothing frightens away good candidates more than a poor job ad that succumbs to any of the following:

- Vague descriptions
- Incomplete listing information
- Too many requirements or impossible requirements
- You might or might not want to ask about salary requirements in your ad; sometimes asking for salary requirements is a sign of a company with a limited budget or on the verge of bankruptcy
- Illegally asking for personal information
- No compelling reason to respond to the ad

If you really want to write a better than average listing, check out the tips in the next section.

Beyond Basics

If you want to stand out from the crowd, write from the perspective of what's in it for the applicant: What would make the qualified candidate apply for the position? Is there room to grow and learn? Are there incentives? With this approach, you're selling the job, making it a desirable position. Take a look at the following two job listing examples. Example A is good, fairly traditional. Example B does a much better job selling the position.

Example A:

Our company is looking for an experienced public relations associate who is excited about promoting our company and spreading the word about our products. We're an award-winning company offering lots of growth opportunities.

Job responsibilities include writing news releases, Web bulletins, newsletters, marketing materials, and presentations.

Requirements: Candidate must have a background in public relations or business communications, possess a strong grasp of writing and editing fundamentals, strong design skills, and be able to juggle deadlines. Candidate should also be familiar with Web page basics, including working with HTML, Flash, and related software. Hours vary; some weekends likely.

Example B:

Are you looking for more than just a "regular job"? Are you ready to start utilizing your PR skills and invest your time in a company that wants to succeed and encourages you to succeed also? Isn't it about time you found an ideal position that recognizes your talents and makes you feel like you made a contribution at the end of each day?

Look no further! Acme Industries is a fast-growing company with a commitment to quality products that make a difference in our community. We're excited about our impact, integrity, and growth, and we want a public relations associate to join us and be a valuable part of our mission.

We'll reward your passion and skills, along with a strong understanding of these basics:

- *Excellent writing and copyediting skills*
- *Strong design sensibilities*
- *Experience meeting tight deadlines and schedules*

■ *Strong commitment to making a difference in the community*

■ *Experience with HTML, Flash, and Adobe Photoshop*

This job could be the best career move you'll ever make! We're a top-rated employer in the Metropolis area, known for our tranquil setting, great benefits, excellent compensation packages, and unique work amenities. We can't wait to talk to you, so respond now!

If you want the best candidates, you need to be prepared to market your ad to your target audience. Ads like that shown in Example B are typically viewed nearly three times as much as those like Example A.

Posting a Job Listing

Before you post your ad, you need to know about the guidelines. craigslist reminds you when you're about to post a job offer to follow these rules:

■ Every job must offer monetary compensation. Unpaid positions such as internships, deferred pay, and so on, are not allowed in the **jobs** section. Unpaid positions are a better fit in the **volunteers** category of the **community** section.

■ You're not allowed to post the same job in more than one category or city.

■ The **jobs** section doesn't allow business opportunities requiring upfront fees, multilevel marketing, referral marketing, or positions involving nudity (save that type of listing for the **erotic** category of the **services** section, as explained in Chapter 15, "Win-Win Results in Listings").

■ Although this point is not listed in the guidelines, if you're a recruiter, be sure to mention this fact in your ad. craigslist doesn't allow "resume fishing," bait-and-switch tactics, or other misleading promises in the job listings.

■ craigslist doesn't allow postings about job fairs or open houses.

■ You cannot link to a job website or a Web page listing jobs in your company.

Job postings in San Francisco cost $75. Postings in Boston, Chicago, Los Angeles, New York, Orange County, Portland, Sacramento, San Diego, Seattle, and Washington DC cost $25. According to the craigslist help pages, job postings appear for 30 days in all these cities. All other areas are free at the time of writing, and postings appear online for 45 days.

When you're ready to post a job listing, follow these steps:

1. Log on to your craigslist account.

2. Click to open the **post new ad in** pop-up menu and choose a location, as shown in Figure 10.2.

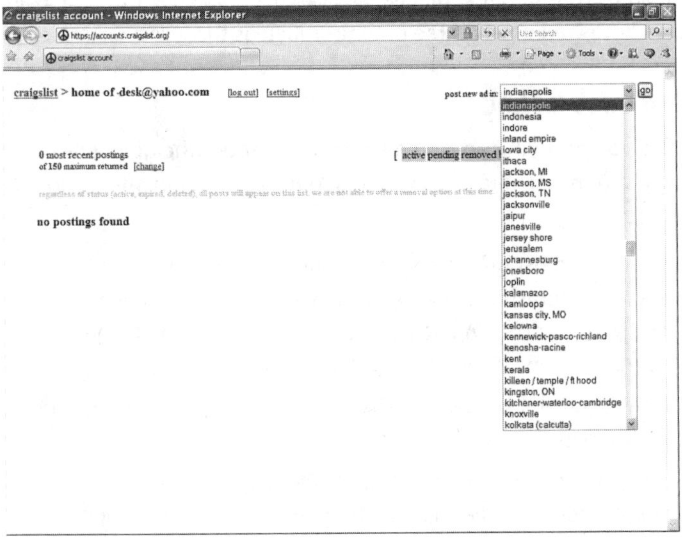

Figure 10.2
The first thing you must do is choose a location.

3. Click the **go** button to continue.

4. Click the **job offered** link, as shown in Figure 10.3. If you're posting in an area that requires a fee, the fee amount is listed next to the link.

5. The posting guidelines appear, as shown in Figure 10.4. Click the **I will abide by these guidelines** button to continue.

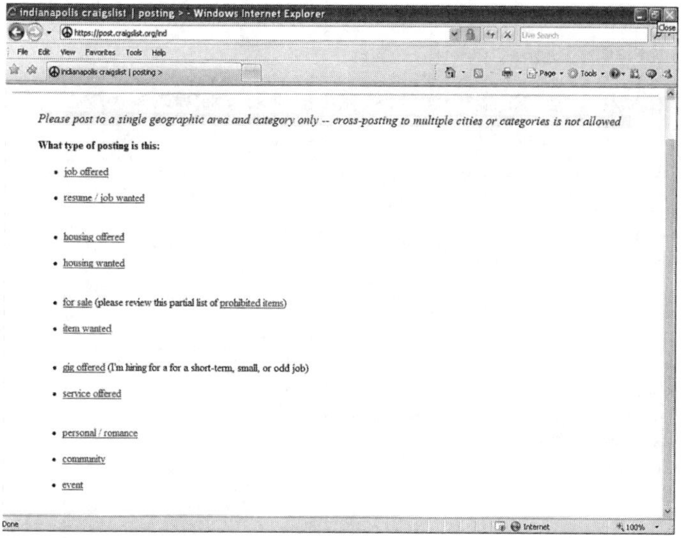

Figure 10.3
Click the **job offered** link.

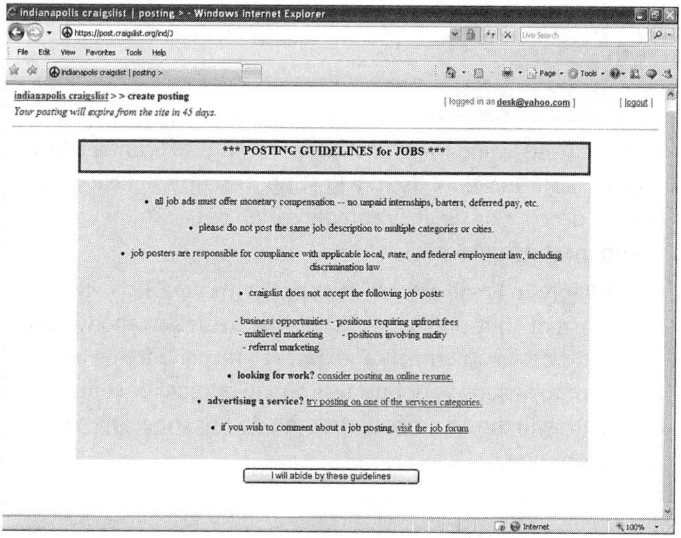

Figure 10.4
Click the button at the bottom to continue.

6. Click the category under which you want to list the job, as shown in Figure 10.5.

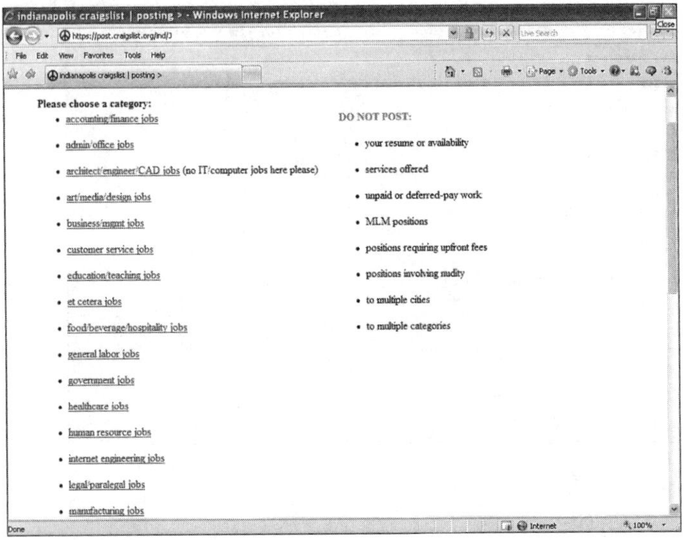

Figure 10.5
Choose a category.

7. Fill out the ad listing form, as shown in Figure 10.6. Enter a title and a specific location. Use the **Posting Description** field to write the job description. Specify compensation details in the **Compensation** field.

8. In the **Reply-to Email address for applicants** area, leave the **reply to:** radio button selected. craigslist creates an anonymous email address for potential candidates to respond to the ad. If you want to include your business phone number or contact information in the ad instead, click the **do not show any email address** option.

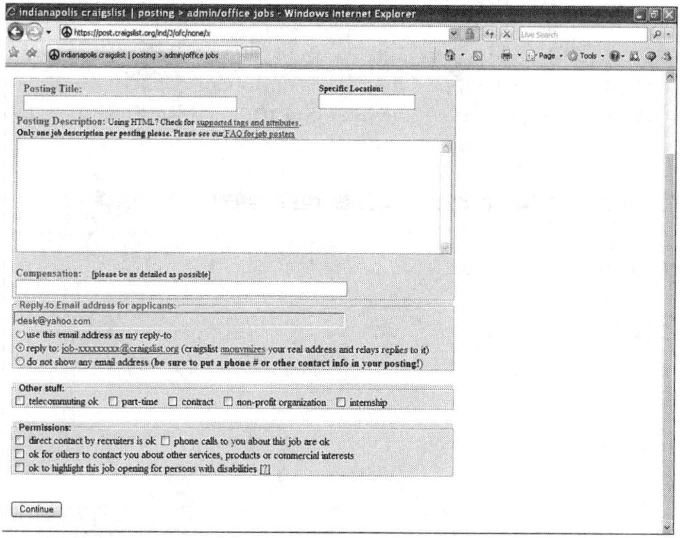

Figure 10.6
Fill out the form, including title, location, description, and compensation.

9. Use the check boxes under the **Other stuff** heading to specify telecommuting, part-time, contract, non-profit, or internship status.

> **Tip 4U** Be sure to indicate whether the job is open to telecommuting. If not, add a statement that says working from home is not an option. If you don't clearly state this, you'll get lots of inquiries asking about it from people desperate to find work-at-home jobs.

10. Use the check boxes under the **Permissions** heading to specify how you want to be contacted.

11. Click the **Continue** button at the bottom of the form.

12. The next screen displays your ad for review. Read over the ad, and if it's okay, click **Continue**. If you need to go back and edit something, click the **Edit** button.

Within about 10 to 20 minutes, your ad will appear on craigslist.

If you're posting in an area that requires a fee for listing an ad, you have an opportunity to select the categories in which to post before you actually fill out the job title and description form. Each category you select incurs a fee, as shown in Figure 10.7. craigslist will then invoice you for the cost of the ad.

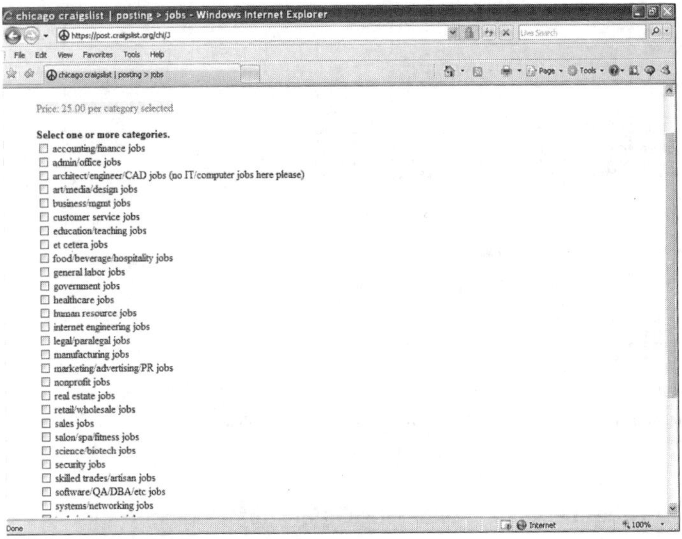

Figure 10.7
If you're posting in a city requiring a fee for advertising on craigslist, you can choose one or more categories for your paid ad. Keep in mind that each category incurs a fee.

You can also create a block ad account on craigslist, which lets you post frequent job listings and get a price break. In other words, you pay a discount price for a block of ad listings. Purchasing a block might be a good idea if your company or organization lists a lot of job postings each month. Visit the craigslist help page and click the **about paid posting accounts** link to learn more. You'll have to fill out an online application form to start the process.

Posting Gigs

The **gigs** section on craigslist mainly lists short-term jobs, odd jobs, or just plain small jobs—basically, any job that's not considered a permanent position. Gigs can be paid jobs or unpaid jobs. Divided into nine categories, shown in Figure 10.8, gigs can be anything from a one-time task or project to a short-term job, or even a traditional gig involving a band. For example, are you looking for a Web page designer to set up your small company with a simple website? Post an ad in the **gigs** section under the **computer** category. Need a one-time cleaning lady to tidy up the house before a move? Post an ad in the **domestic** category. Looking for a DJ to play at your wedding? Try the **talent** category.

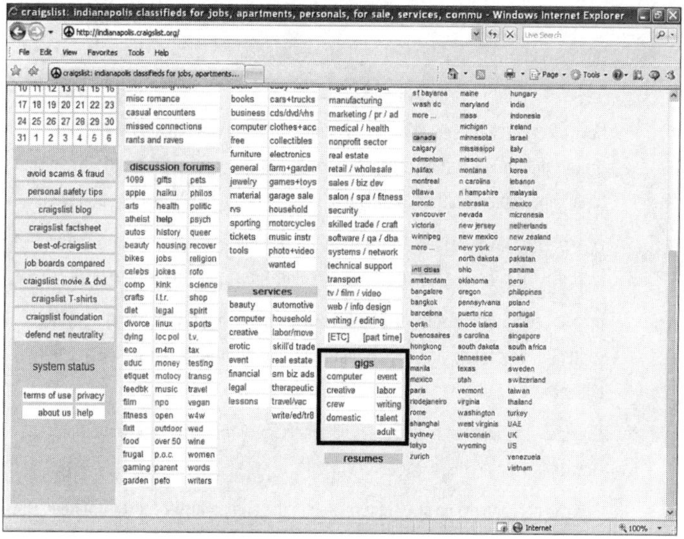

Figure 10.8
The **gigs** section covers short-term, small, or odd jobs.

Table 10.3 shows a rundown of the nine **gigs** categories.

Table 10.3   gigs Categories on craigslist

Category	Description
computer	Post computer-related gigs in this category, including Web page design, tech help for a new office computer system, data entry projects, and so on.
creative	The gigs in this category include graphic design, videography, interior decorating, photography, illustration, and anything revolving around creative arts and crafts.
crew	Are you looking for short-term crew member for a video or film production, a concert production, or a sound editor? This category includes any sort of crew-related position, with the exception of acting (which goes under the **talent** category).
domestic	Need a cleaner for a day or a handyman for a project? Advertise in this category, which includes everything from short-term childcare situations to dog walking. Domestic gigs can include anything home-related or lift-related, such as a personal trainer or tutoring.
event	Have an event that needs some extra hands? Post it in this category. Events include concert promotion or staff, convention marketers, short-term chefs and kitchen staff, trade show representatives, wedding catering or photography, parties, and so on.
labor	Post any gigs involving physical labor in this category, such as lawn work, remodeling help, electrical work, mechanical help, moving, house painting, and so on.
writing	Do you need a writer? Advertise in this category, which lists everything from Web content to brochures, magazine submissions to copy writing, translation to editing, and more.
talent	Looking for a singer or dancer? Post in this category, which includes everything from clowns and magicians to singers and actors.
adult	This category mainly involves gigs related to the porn industry, mostly amateur. This category includes modeling, talent, film "stars," and so on.

The last category in Table 10.3 probably needs a bit more explanation. When most people think of gigs, small jobs, and odd jobs, porn doesn't immediately come to mind, or at least to most people's minds. But the old saying "sex sells" is really apropos in the **adult** category. According to craigslist, you must be 18 to enter this area, but they can't check IDs or anything. You should probably be forewarned that there's adult content in this category, which quite simply means lots of innuendo and graphic advertisements. The listings here solicit everything from "new video stars" and lingerie models to strippers and amateur photo shoots. Many of the ads found here are simply listings looking for paid sex. Before you jump in, just know that these areas are policed—literally—so you might find more than you bargained for in responding to any of these gigs. On the other hand, if you aspire to star in a sex video, then this just might be your special category and the grand start to your award-winning career.

When you're posting a gig, one of the screens before the listing form asks you to specify whether you want to hire someone or offer a service. Choose the **I want to hire someone** link to continue to the listing form. As with the regular job listings described earlier in this chapter, you're presented with a form for filling out a title, description, and payment amount. Be precise about what you're looking for; clearly state what your expectations are about the project. Vague ads result in vague queries, while well-written ads result in qualified candidates ready to do the job.

Be sure to use an anonymous craigslist email address to allow prospective gig fillers to contact you. This will help you avoid spam and scams on the site.

Responding to Applicants

After you post a job listing, you may see responses immediately, or it may take awhile for candidates to find you. Don't be surprised to see the majority of responses within the first day or so of posting. Be prepared to handle the influx of inquiries based on the contact information you included in the ad. Handle the inquiries professionally and in a timely manner. Diplomacy is always the best plan, even if the candidate isn't qualified.

Take time to send an email message stating you received the submission. You can respond in any of these ways, as appropriate:

- A thank you and a notification that you will contact the candidates if their qualifications match those required
- Notification that you will contact them shortly with additional information

- Rejection and encouragement to reapply later
- Rejection without any additional information

Not responding at all makes you look terribly unprofessional. Also, avoid any detailed information or negative feedback in your response. That kind of response will only cause headaches or trouble later.

As you weed through the applications, it's a good idea to keep the "near misses" in a database for future jobs they may be better suited for in your company.

Tip 4U
Be careful! I know we keep saying this over and over again, but it's only because we care about you and don't want to see you mixed up in some sort of online scam or criminal activity. Use caution when posting ads on craigslist, even job listings. Use good judgment and follow the tips in Chapter 3, "Safety First," to protect your personal information. Be wary of schemes and scams because they do seem to lurk around every corner of craigslist.

From Here...

Now that you've learned how to post a job listing on craigslist, we hope that you'll find many suitable candidates to choose from for the position. If you're looking for a job, rather than looking to fill a job, check out the next chapter to learn how to post a resume in craigslist's **resumes** section.

Listing in Resumes

Responding to jobs listings isn't the only way that craigslist can help you in your quest for career advancement. The **resumes** section, as shown in Figure 11.1, is a popular stop for recruiters, human resource staff, and anyone looking to fill a position.

	discussion forums		general	farm+garden	retail / wholesale
avoid scams & fraud	1099	gifts	pets	jewelry	games+toys	sales / biz dev
personal safety tips	apple	haiku	philos	material	garage sale	salon / spa / fitness
craigslist blog	arts	health	politic	rvs	household	security
craigslist factsheet	atheist	help	psych	sporting	motorcycles	skilled trade / craft
best-of-craigslist	autos	history	queer	tickets	music instr	software / qa / dba
job boards compared	beauty	housing	recover	tools	photo+video	systems / network
craigslist movie & dvd	bikes	jobs	religion		wanted	technical support
craigslist T-shirts	celebs	jokes	rofo			transport
craigslist foundation	comp	kink	science		services	tv / film / video
defend net neutrality	crafts	l.t.r.	shop	beauty	automotive	web / info design
	diet	legal	spirit	computer	household	writing / editing
	divorce	linux	sports	creative	labor/move	[ETC] [part time]
system status	dying	loc pol	t.v.	erotic	skill'd trade	
	eco	m4m	tax	event	real estate	gigs
terms of use privacy	educ	money	testing	financial	sm biz ads	computer event
about us help	etiquet	motocy	transg	legal	therapeutic	creative labor
	feedbk	music	travel	lessons	travel/vac	crew writing
	film	npo	vegan		write/ed/tr8	domestic talent
	fitness	open	w4w			adult
	fixit	outdoor	wed			
	food	over 50	wine		resumes	
	frugal	p.o.c.	women			
	gaming	parent	words			
	garden	pefo	writers			

Figure 11.1
The **resumes** section on craigslist is the only section that doesn't contain categories.

Using the information in this chapter, you can avoid common resume mistakes, market yourself effectively, and create a resume that shows companies how your talent and experience will benefit their business.

Knowledge Is Power

As always, research is the best place to start, and the Internet offers a wealth of information to help you in your job search. There are three areas to explore:

- Industries
- Jobs
- You

Wait—study *yourself*? As strange as it might sound, you are no different from any other product. A great salesperson has an in-depth understanding of his or her target market and product offering. Because understanding your strengths, weaknesses, likes, and dislikes will help you form the best plan of attack to come out on top of your job search quest, we'll start there.

Your Most Important Sale

A quick look at a few of the resumes posted on craigslist makes it clear that many people don't understand the true purpose of a resume. A resume is an advertisement for your #1 product—YOU! A good resume showcases what you have to offer and explains how you obtained and applied your knowledge and skills. No one knows your benefits and features better than you do. Although you should never lie on your resume, you do have to promote yourself and blow your own horn.

You might want to rush through the resume-writing process because of circumstances or to get past the discomfort, but you give yourself an advantage over your competition by investing the time to do the job right. Each of the following steps will expand your knowledge, increase your self-confidence, and improve the outcome of your job search. This chapter breaks down the job-hunting process into manageable steps that you can follow to build a winning employment search campaign.

Dealing with Job Search Jitters

Are you overwhelmed just thinking about writing your resume? Do you dread drafting a cover letter? Do you panic at the idea of an interview? Relax—you're not alone. Most people experience some level of anxiety during their job search.

When the goal of any task is literally *life-changing*, the stakes seem very high, so it's easy to see how fear of failure can keep you from moving toward that goal. Here are several important tips to help you move past the fear:

- **Expect a learning curve.** Job search skills—including writing, marketing, interviewing, and negotiating—are learned. Keep studying and improving by practicing and fine-tuning as you go. Schedule some "throwaway" interviews, especially in the beginning, so you gain confidence and experience without feeling pressured about the outcome.

- **Keep moving.** Do at least five things every day to keep the momentum going. Make a call, follow up with someone, send out a resume, read an article, attend a networking meeting or trade group, research industry trends, brush up on a skill, listen to a motivational speaker. In addition to keeping you moving forward, all the seeds you plant in this process will increase your garden of opportunities.

- **Expect to make mistakes.** My friend and mentor, marketing guru Anthony Coyne, put it best during one of his sales coaching speeches: "You are going to make mistakes, and that's okay. When you realize that you are going to screw up, you can start to have fun with the process and accept it. Making mistakes means you are 'taking action'…moving forward…learning…getting better."

- **Remember that employment is a win-win situation.** If you lack self-confidence, that fact will come across during the interview. Work on having faith in yourself and your abilities, without being arrogant. A company isn't doing you a favor by hiring you; it's a *mutually beneficial arrangement*.

- **It's all about the best match.** While it's easy to feel rejected when you aren't offered a job, note that a rejection is not a reflection of your worth. The employment process is about matching the needs, atmosphere, and benefits of a company with the abilities, personality, and wants of an individual. This involves many factors and can be very subjective. It has nothing to do with your value as a human being.

What to Look For

Although you want to keep a file about specific job openings that interest you, the purpose of this research is to learn about what's happening in the various industries and job markets, what and where the opportunities are, how you can take advantage of them, and how you can gain a competitive edge. A good mind-mapping software such as Mindjet MindManager (www.mindjet.com) can make this data much easier to understand.

The following list gives you some information to look for:

- **Locations.** First, decide on cities, states, regions, and so on, where you want to work. Knowing these areas first is important because you want to research local market conditions.

- **Industries.** List industries that interest you and what's interesting about them. Search for information about hiring trends and job outlook on both a national and local level.

- **Jobs.** Include all relevant job titles with a list of their skills and responsibilities. Job titles can vary greatly for similar positions, so group like jobs together. Besides gathering this information from the "help wanted" ads, you'll also find job descriptions while researching trade publications, industry insights, and other people's resumes. Note job locations to help you identify regional hiring patterns.

- **Skills.** Make a list of all skills included in job descriptions that interest you. Note any skills that you see again and again. *Hard skills* (sometimes called *technical skills*) are those specifically related to a job's duties—for example, accounting, software programming, or machine operation. *Soft skills*, such as customer service, problem-solving, and team building, may be equally important, but much harder to quantify.

- **Requirements.** Note the requirements for various positions, including desired length of experience.

- **Keywords.** Specific words and phrases often are used to describe duties, skills, and experience. You want to use these keywords on your resume, so list skills and responsibilities, as well as industry terminology and acronyms.

- **Companies.** Create your own database, listing any companies you consider potential employers. Include name, address, contact information, website, industry information, and any other pertinent data.

- **Compensation.** Keep track of salaries and wages by job, industry, and location. Few "help wanted" ads list compensation, but trade organizations, trade publications, and job banks often publish job earnings information on an annual basis.

- **Benefits.** Write down any benefits being offered. This lets you know what the possibilities are, so you can decide what benefits are important to you when evaluating job offers. Benefits must also be considered as part of the compensation package.

- **Resources.** When you find a valuable source of information, write it down, so you can easily refer to it.

Where to Look

Now that you know what to look for, let's cover where you should look. You can review resumes and job listings in the various craigslist communities. You'll find a good cross-section of job listings in the larger craigslist communities, such as San Francisco, New York, Los Angeles, and Chicago, which charge companies a fee to list. Your local newspaper's website is another good quality source of information on both local industries and job information.

Obviously, the Internet is overflowing with sites offering advice on finding and landing your dream job. Searching on terms such as *sample resume, interview skills*, or *hiring trends* will bring you millions of results. Narrow your results by targeting your search terms. Try *sales resume sample* or *IT hiring trends* to find the most relevant sites.

Use a critical eye when researching on the Internet. Whereas education (.edu) and organization (.org) sites usually offer the most unbiased information, commercial (.com) sites that include lots of free information can be a goldmine as well. Regardless of the type of site, look for current information. Globalization and digital connectivity can shorten business cycles. Standards and trends change faster than ever before. Look for information covering the most recent 3–6 months. Table 11.1 lists a variety of websites offering quality information.

Table 11.1   Online Career Resources

Title	Website
Industry Info	
AllBusiness.com	www.allbusiness.com
Job Search Info	
About.com	www.about.com/careers
CareerBuilder.com	www.careerbuilder.com
JobHuntersBible.com	www.jobhuntersbible.com
Hire Intelligence	www.integrablog.com
JobStar Central	www.jobstar.org
JobWeb	www.jobweb.com
Monster.com	www.monster.com
Quintessential Careers	www.quintcareers.com
Resume-Help.org	www.resume-help.org
Salary.com	www.salary.com
Simply Hired	www.simplyhired.com
The Riley Guide	www.rileyguide.com
The Wall Street Journal CareerJournal	online.wsj.com/careers/main
Recruiters' Portal	
Recruiting.com	www.recruiting.com
Resume Info	
Guaranteed Resumes	www.gresumes.com
Resumania	www.resumania.com

Title	Website
Trade Publications	
TechExpo Directory of Engineering and Scientific Trade Technical Magazines	www.techexpo.com/tech_mag.html
Directory of Open Access Journals	www.doaj.org
Wikipedia	wikipedia.org/wiki/ Category:Trade_magazines
Website Directory	
Open Directory Project	www.dmoz.org

Don't forget to utilize any existing networking resources you have. People love to think of themselves as authorities, and most will be happy to share their insights with someone who is appreciative. You'll often receive valuable information to help in your job search.

If you know people who are already employed in an industry or job you're targeting, contact them and let them know you're considering a job or career change. Tell them you're looking for an "expert" in their field and ask if they would give you a few minutes of their time to share their knowledge. They may even offer to refer you to a hiring source or another company insider. Some companies offer recruiting bonuses to their employees for referring qualified applicants that fill specific positions, so it could even put money in their pocket, too.

What to Do with the Information

Now that you have some information, start analyzing your data. Even as you complete your research, you may recognize industry and hiring trends on a national or regional level. Because job titles can vary greatly, compare job descriptions to find crossover positions between companies and industries. A cluster of similar job openings in one location can indicate a demand at a local level that may not be present across the United States.

You might find that a company that interests you is on a hiring spree. To better understand the opportunity, look for recent media coverage and financial disclosures that indicate whether the company is experiencing high growth or high turnover, and why. If the company still interests you, scan any job postings and visit the company's website to find keywords and phrases used, and then include those words when you're targeting that company.

As you learn more about the various options, note which look most promising and why. Be open to discovering new opportunities and letting go of outdated beliefs and strategies. Prioritize industries, companies, and jobs in order of opportunity and by their appeal to you, to make the best use of your time and energy.

Your Features and Benefits

Now that you know more about the industries you're targeting, it's time to learn more about yourself and what you have to offer for those specific industries. Start by taking an inventory of your personal work history. Compile lists of your skills, experience, and accomplishments, which you can truthfully include on your resume by using popular keywords. Create a separate list for each job you've held that includes the length of experience you have for each item. Create a summary list that groups similar skills, experiences, and accomplishments.

You have the obvious items written down, but let me add that rarely do a job title and description fully cover the list of tasks people perform in the course of a workday. Look for ways that your experience translates into hidden skills and abilities. Often this is where previously overlooked soft skills successes can be identified.

For example, while your job title may have been "software programmer" for the last three years, you probably did more than sit at a computer and write lines of code day after day. Did you speak directly with clients on a regular basis? That demonstrates verbal communication and customer service skills. Were those clients upper management? That's executive-level communication skills. Did you use project management skills by successfully coordinating or running coding projects from beginning to end? Look for other ways you've demonstrated valuable skills while performing your regular job functions.

Another case in point would be an administrative assistant who lists data entry, word processing, filing, and phone skills as her regular duties, along with competencies in Microsoft Word and Excel. But by exploring different facets of her job, she can demonstrate successful event-planning skills by staging company-wide, quarterly offsite sales meetings, purchasing experience by locating and negotiating with office supply vendors, and Microsoft PowerPoint experience by creating presentations for her boss.

Take time to evaluate all the different areas of your current and previous jobs. Go over the list of requirements created from job postings and watch for overlooked experiences that are hidden gems on your resume. Document your skills and duties using power words.

It's All in the Numbers

Many job applicants think of a resume as a simple fact sheet, listing their work history, skills, training, and education. But in today's competitive job market, your resume needs to quickly show prospective employers what value you can bring to the company. One of the best ways to do this is to highlight your accomplishments and successes with numbers. If this is something you aren't used to doing (many of us aren't), now is the time to start.

As you look over your work history, document ways that you made a positive impact at your job. Common ways to show this include statements about increased revenue, sales, or customer satisfaction; reduced costs, expenses, or man-hours; or improved processes. Your changes can be documented in facts, figures, or statistics. Include any problems you solved or larger issues you were able to resolve.

For example, if one of your regular tasks required four hours of your time, but you improved the process and cut it down to three hours, then you reduced man-hours or improved efficiency by 25%. If you negotiated a vendor contract that brought your purchase cost of a component from $8.00 to $6.55 each, you reduced materials cost by 18% or increased profits by $1.45 a unit.

You should also include specific data on your resume whenever possible. It adds credibility and has a greater impact. Read the difference between the general and specific statements in Table 11.2.

Table 11.2 Sample Resume Descriptions

General	Specific
Produced monthly customer newsletter.	Produced 28 issues of monthly newsletter distributed to over 7,000 customers.
Administrative support to sales staff.	Administrative support to 11 salespeople.
Interviewed, hired, trained, and supervised warehouse employees.	Interviewed, hired, trained, and supervised 14 warehouse employees.
Exceeded quarterly sales quota.	Exceeded quarterly sales quota by at least 10% for eight consecutive quarters.

Define Your Marketing Strategy

The most successful advertising campaigns start with a solid marketing strategy. In creating this strategy, you put to good use all the information you've gathered. Four factors are important when planning your strategy: The first two factors are the job market and your skills and abilities. The third factor is what types of work appeal to you, and the fourth is how quickly you must find a job. Correctly balancing these variables will show you where to focus your efforts and help you create a solid plan for finding a new job.

Target your efforts by writing down your goal. Be as specific and detailed as possible regarding the job description, location, hours, pay, benefits, and even how quickly you want/need to find a position. This is the most important step on your roadmap to success. When you have your goal on paper, you're ready to jump into action.

Create a Killer Resume

There was a time when writing your resume meant typing up a paper with your contact information, followed by a brief description of your work history and education, that you could hand out to anyone. Today, that resume wouldn't get you a second look. Now, employers expect custom resumes targeted to specific positions that quickly show how a prospect's abilities meet the company's needs. Although writing numerous resumes may sound time-consuming, with the information you've compiled, you can create a master resume and quickly tweak it for whatever job you target.

When posting to craigslist, gear your resume toward your goals and include all additional skills and accomplishments. Because you won't have an exact target in mind, write your resume to play to your overall strengths. Use a simple, text-based layout and avoid any flashy or HTML-laden gimmickry. With any resume submission, never try to be cute or funny. In a sea of mediocre—or worse, horribly written— resumes, let yours stand out for the quality of product and the strength of presentation. Using tricks to get attention tells an employer that you don't have another way to stand out.

To increase the importance of submitting a well-written resume, many companies are now using resume-scanning software. These programs scan your resume into a database and allow the employer to search resumes using keywords they select. This can work in your favor, if your resume is a match for a job you didn't even know was available. However, the use of such software makes it vital that resumes use a standard format, including well-defined job descriptions, and utilize relevant nouns and active words that employers are likely to search for.

Start putting together your resume by writing descriptions for each of your jobs. Whenever possible, include numbers to quantify and power words to add energy. *Power words* are active descriptors that put energy into your accomplishments and skills. They paint a vivid picture and capture the readers' attention. The following list of power words will get you started:

accelerated	acted	adjusted	advocated
accomplished	activated	administered	analyzed
achieved	adapted	advertised	applied
acquired	addressed	advised	appraised

approved	conceptualized	determined	examined
arbitrated	concluded	developed	exceeded
arranged	conducted	devised	exchanged
ascertained	conserved	diagnosed	executed
assembled	consolidated	directed	expanded
assessed	constructed	discovered	expedited
attained	consulted	dispatched	experimented
audited	contacted	displayed	explained
augmented	contracted	dissected	expressed
authored	controlled	distributed	extracted
balanced	converted	diverted	extended
billed	coordinated	documented	facilitated
bound	copyrighted	drew up	fashioned
briefed	corrected	earned	filed
budgeted	corresponded	edited	financed
built	counseled	educated	flagged
calculated	created	effected	followed
carried out	cultivated	elicited	formed
catalogued	curtailed	eliminated	formulated
charted	cut	empowered	found
clarified	debugged	enabled	founded
closed	decided	encouraged	gathered
coached	decreased	endorsed	generated
collaborated	defined	enforced	governed
collected	delegated	engaged	guided
communicated	delivered	engineered	handled
compared	demonstrated	enhanced	headed
compiled	derived	enlarged	hired
completed	designated	entertained	hypothesized
composed	designed	established	identified
computed	detailed	estimated	illustrated
conceived	detected	evaluated	implemented

improved	mastered	pinpointed	recommended
improvised	maximized	placed	reconciled
increased	measured	planned	recorded
influenced	mediated	posted	recruited
informed	mentored	predicted	reduced
initiated	merged	prepared	referred
innovated	minimized	presented	refined
inspected	modeled	presided	regulated
inspired	modernized	problem-solved	rehabilitated
installed	modified	processed	reinforced
instituted	monitored	procured	rendered
instructed	motivated	produced	renewed
interpreted	navigated	proficient	reorganized
intervened	negotiated	programmed	repaired
interviewed	notified	projected	replaced
introduced	observed	promoted	reported
invented	obtained	proofread	represented
inventoried	opened	proposed	rescued
invested	operated	proved	researched
investigated	optimized	provided	resolved
judged	ordered	publicized	responded
justified	organized	published	restored
kept	originated	purchased	restructured
launched	overhauled	qualified	retrieved
lectured	oversaw	quantified	revamped
led	packed	questioned	reviewed
lobbied	participated	queried	revised
logged	patented	quizzed	revitalized
maintained	perceived	raised	risked
managed	performed	reasoned	safeguarded
manipulated	persuaded	received	scheduled
manufactured	piloted	recognized	screened

selected	strengthened	team-built	undertook
served	structured	teamed with	unified
serviced	studied	tested	united
set up	suggested	traced	updated
shaped	summarized	tracked	upgraded
shipped	supervised	trained	used
simplified	supplemented	transcribed	utilized
sold	supplied	translated	verbalized
solved	surpassed	troubleshot	won
sponsored	surveyed	tuned	wrote
started	synthesized	tutored	
steered	systematized	typed	
streamlined	taught	understudied	

From the Top

Now that you have the pieces of the puzzle done, start putting them together. Use a word processing program to produce your resume so that you can take advantage of spell check and the thesaurus. Although Microsoft Word (www.microsoft.com/word) is the most common, the freeware program OpenOffice.org (www.openoffice. org) has received very positive reviews.

Again, a simple text-based layout is the best way to post your resume. Avoid any complicated or unusual formatting. Use a common simple font, such as Arial 11 point. Use asterisks or bullets to highlight key points, as shown in Figure 11.2.

Unlike printed resumes or other digital versions, your online resume shouldn't include your direct contact information. Don't leave yourself open to identity theft by publishing your personal information and career path on the Internet! Although I normally recommend using craigslist's anonymous email system, when it comes to your resume, you should use a real email address. To maintain your privacy and protect your regular email address from spam, use a free Gmail address (www.gmail.com). Gmail has a great spam filter, and you can set up the account to forward to your primary email address. When selecting your new email account, don't use any identifying information, but be sure to choose a name that reflects a professional image.

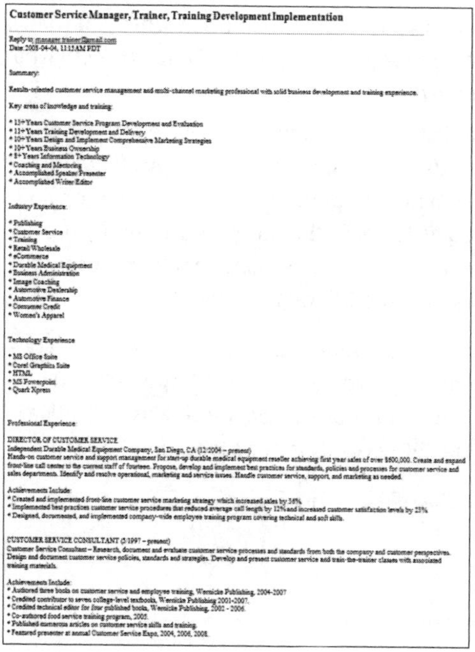

Figure 11.2
A clean, well-defined resume will make the information easier to read.

You can also replace company names on your resume with descriptions. Besides keeping your personal life off the Internet, using descriptions rather than names reduces the chance that your current employer will find out that you're looking for work elsewhere.

Getting It All Down

In recent years, resume experts have promoted using an objective at the top of all resumes. Unfortunately, many objectives read something like this: "Hardworking, motivated people person seeks a career with advancement potential in a well-established company." Objectives fail for two reasons:

  ▪ Most objectives simply state the obvious—this person is looking for a good job. There aren't many ways to say this without sounding redundant, trite, or outright silly.

■ The person isn't reading your resume to find out what you want or what he or she can do for you; this person wants to know what *you* can do for *him or her*!

Research has shown that initially, a screener scans each resume only between 10 and 20 seconds before deciding who moves forward. You have well under one minute to grab that person's attention and show him or her how you will benefit the business. Do this by replacing an objective statement with a targeted summary that presents the reader with a clear list of benefits you have to offer.

A strong summary, as shown in Figure 11.3, includes one or two concise sentences that describe who you are, followed by a bulleted list of your experience and another list of any technical skills and affiliations you have. Remember, 20 seconds is not a long time to read.

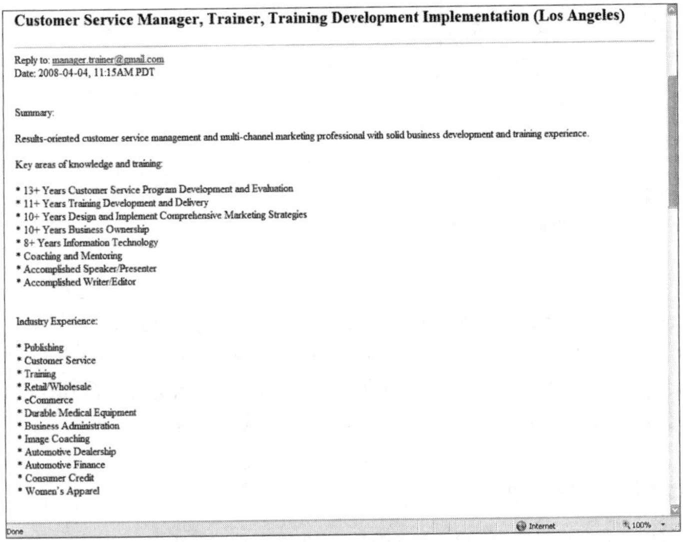

Customer Service Manager, Trainer, Training Development Implementation (Los Angeles)

Reply to: manager.trainer@gmail.com
Date: 2008-04-04, 11:15AM PDT

Summary:

Results-oriented customer service management and multi-channel marketing professional with solid business development and training experience.

Key areas of knowledge and training:

* 13+ Years Customer Service Program Development and Evaluation
* 11+ Years Training Development and Delivery
* 10+ Years Design and Implement Comprehensive Marketing Strategies
* 10+ Years Business Ownership
* 8+ Years Information Technology
* Coaching and Mentoring
* Accomplished Speaker/Presenter
* Accomplished Writer/Editor

Industry Experience:

* Publishing
* Customer Service
* Training
* Retail/Wholesale
* eCommerce
* Durable Medical Equipment
* Business Administration
* Image Coaching
* Automotive Dealership
* Automotive Finance
* Consumer Credit
* Women's Apparel

Figure 11.3
A good summary makes it easy for anyone to find out where your strengths are.

Below the summary, list your work history with your current or most recent position at the top, as shown in Figure 11.4. In most cases, your job titles say more about what you have to offer than any business name, so make them easy to spot. After each job description, list all your accomplishments while in that position. The final section of your resume includes a list of all college-level or higher education, and any other special training you've completed.

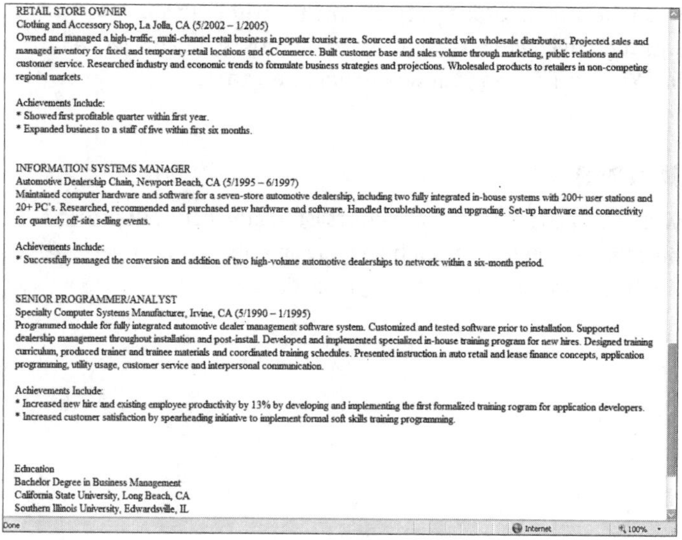

RETAIL STORE OWNER
Clothing and Accessory Shop, La Jolla, CA (5/2002 – 1/2005)
Owned and managed a high-traffic, multi-channel retail business in popular tourist area. Sourced and contracted with wholesale distributors. Projected sales and managed inventory for fixed and temporary retail locations and eCommerce. Built customer base and sales volume through marketing, public relations and customer service. Researched industry and economic trends to formulate business strategies and projections. Wholesaled products to retailers in non-competing regional markets.

Achievements Include:
* Showed first profitable quarter within first year.
* Expanded business to a staff of five within first six months.

INFORMATION SYSTEMS MANAGER
Automotive Dealership Chain, Newport Beach, CA (5/1995 – 6/1997)
Maintained computer hardware and software for a seven-store automotive dealership, including two fully integrated in-house systems with 200+ user stations and 20+ PC's. Researched, recommended and purchased new hardware and software. Handled troubleshooting and upgrading. Set-up hardware and connectivity for quarterly off-site selling events.

Achievements Include:
* Successfully managed the conversion and addition of two high-volume automotive dealerships to network within a six-month period.

SENIOR PROGRAMMER/ANALYST
Specialty Computer Systems Manufacturer, Irvine, CA (5/1990 – 1/1995)
Programmed module for fully integrated automotive dealer management software system. Customized and tested software prior to installation. Supported dealership management throughout installation and post-install. Developed and implemented specialized in-house training program for new hires. Designed training curriculum, produced trainer and trainee materials and coordinated training schedules. Presented instruction in auto retail and lease finance concepts, application programming, utility usage, customer service and interpersonal communication.

Achievements Include:
* Increased new hire and existing employee productivity by 13% by developing and implementing the first formalized training rogram for application developers.
* Increased customer satisfaction by spearheading initiative to implement formal soft skills training programming.

Education
Bachelor Degree in Business Management
California State University, Long Beach, CA
Southern Illinois University, Edwardsville, IL

Figure 11.4
Successful resumes are designed so screeners quickly see the benefits the applicant can offer the company.

Leave off information such as "References upon request" because people know to ask if they want them. Never include information about your gender, age, marital status, health, hobbies, transportation, or if you have children. Discussion of many of those topics by a potential employer is considered a discriminatory practice. Also, although you may see it done, never include pictures or a video with a resume.

By working through this chapter, you now have a completed resume that needs to be proofread, then proofread, and proofread again. Ideally, after you think you have corrected everything, have two more people read it. If no one else is available, try printing it out and reading it upside down. That forces you to focus on each word, so you might catch a mistake you overlooked before.

When the resume is free of errors, follow the listing steps, cut and paste your resume into the text box, and submit it. After 20 minutes or so, check to be certain that it has posted. To keep your listing as high on the search results page as possible without violating craigslist guidelines, you can delete and repost your ad every 48 hours. You are now on your way to your new career.

From Here...

Now that you know how to use craigslist to advance your professional life, read on to find out how you can enhance your personal life in the "anything goes" **personals** section.

Listing in Personals

At one time, running an ad in the personals was someone's dirty little secret. The Internet reinvented personal classifieds as "online dating," gave it a shiny new image, and even made a movie about it. Remember *You've Got Mail*?

Warning 4U	Before you even think about advertising for a date, a rendezvous, or even a movie buddy, go to Chapter 3, "Safety First," and read "Safe and Sound Online Dating."
	On *any* online personals site, please put *safety first!*

The craigslist **personals** section (see Figure 12.1) is a world unto itself, frequented by a wide variety of interesting people. It's one of the more popular sections in just about every craigslist community.

One important point to remember—unlike sites such as Match.com (www.match.com), Yahoo! Personals (personals.yahoo.com), or eHarmony (www.eHarmony.com), craigslist has no gatekeepers, no moderators, and no fees or questionnaires to answer in the personals. Anyone on craigslist can post and/or respond to a listing.

Figure 12.1
The craigslist **personals** section can be a very entertaining read.

Even if the only checkpoint is a small listing fee or an identity verification process, that would be at least somewhat effective in deterring those people who have either malicious intent or just too much time on their hands. However, you don't have those options on craigslist, so you must be a bit more discerning when trying your luck in **personals**.

Categories include the standard dating types, more adventurous categories such as **misc romance** and **casual encounters**, and a friendship category called **strictly platonic**. Whatever your goals for your personal life, you can probably pursue them in one of the **personals** categories.

Research has shown that, when it comes to mainstream online dating sites, ads that include pictures get a much higher response rate than ads that don't. *However, I don't recommend posting your picture in a **personals** ad on craigslist.* Save that for paid sites or more formal, moderated dating sites. You can let the reader know that you will send a picture in return for a picture or after you have exchanged email addresses.

Deciphering the Code

Personal ads are riddled with abbreviations and acronyms, a common practice for reducing word costs in paid ads. It's hard to set yourself apart from the pack and express your personality if you're using Morse code to tell your story. Using these abbreviations can also label you as a personals junkie, even if you've only researched the terms to do it right.

That said, understanding how to use the terms will at least be less confusing. A three-letter abbreviation is commonly used to describe yourself or the person you hope will respond. The format for the three-letter acronym is generally marital status/race/gender. For example, SBF is short for "single black female" and DHM stands for "divorced Hispanic male." Some people will substitute sexual preference for marital status.

As you read the personals, you'll see other letter combinations, since some people include whatever information they feel is most important. Use Table 12.1 to get an idea of what it's all about. *I warn you in advance that some terms are sexually explicit.*

Table 12.1—Abbreviations, Acronyms, and Slang

Term	Meaning
A	Asian
ASL or A/S/L	Age, sex, location
B	Black
B&D (BD)	Bondage and discipline
Bareback (BB)	Sex without a condom
BBW	Big beautiful woman
BDSM	Bondage and discipline, dominance and submission, and sadism and masochism
Bear	Man with a hairy body
BF	Boyfriend

Term	Meaning
Bi	Bisexual
Bi Curious	Interested in bisexual activities
C	Christian
CD or C/D	Cross-dress or cross-dresser
CE	Casual encounters
D	Divorced
DDF	Disease and drug free
DS	Dominance and submission
F	Female
FTA	Fun, travel, adventure
FtM or F2M	Female-to-male transgendered
FWB	Friends with benefits (friends who are intimate without emotional attachment)
G	Gay
GF	Girlfriend
GL	Good-looking
H	Hispanic
Host	Have someone come to your home
HWP	Height/weight proportionate
I	Indian
ISO	In search of
J	Jewish
K	Kids
L	Lesbian
LD	Light drinker
LDR	Long-distance relationship
LS	Legally separated or light smoker
LTR	Long-term relationship
M	Male or married

Term	Meaning
MBA	Married but available
MtF or M2F	Male-to-female transgendered
M4M	Men seeking men
M4W	Men seeking women
MC	Missed connections
NA	Native American
NBM	Never been married
ND or N/D	No drinking, no drugs
NK or N/K	No kids
NS or N/S	Non-smoker
NSA	No strings attached
OP	Original poster
P	Professional
POV	Point of view
POZ	HIV-positive
PSE	Porn star experience
R&R	Rants and raves
Roses	Dollars—used to quote prices for prostitution (200 roses = $200)
S	Single
SM	Sadomasochism
SO	Significant other
SP	Strictly platonic
TG	Transgendered
TS	Transsexual
TV	Transvestite
VGL	Very good looking
W	White
WAA	Will answer all

Term	Meaning
Wi	Widowed (first position of three- or four-letter acronym)
WTR	Willing to relocate
W4M	Women seeking men
W4W	Women seeking women
YO	Year old (for example, "24yo" means "24-year-old")
420	Marijuana

There are probably other, less commonly used terms, and occasionally a new one pops up along the way. But with craigslist, you don't have to worry about cost, so go ahead and spell it out (correctly, of course).

What Do You Really Want?

As with any other listing on craigslist, figuring out beforehand what you want and what's important to you will make the experience less frustrating and improve your chance of a successful outcome. Start by being honest with yourself about what you want, and you'll save everyone time, trouble, and heartache.

In business the best outcomes are winning situations for both parties. And those win-win deals are usually achieved through negotiations. It's the same with relationships. If you come to the table with clear goals but willing to address the wants and needs of the other person, you can both come out ahead.

Before you jump into the online dating scene, take some time to answer the following questions. Thinking about each of these important points will help you better understand yourself and your intentions. Write down everything you can think of so you can use the information in creating your ad.

What are you really looking for? Take some time to reflect on this question. If you're honestly looking for that one special someone to spend the rest of your life with, then the "seeking" categories are for you. If you're looking for something less committed, be clear about that in your listing and decide which of the other categories is more appropriate.

Looking for a casual encounter isn't a crime, but it's wrong to do it by claiming you're marriage-minded. If you aren't certain what you want, try picturing yourself in the future. What feels right? Do you see yourself happily single or joyfully married? Does a life of first dates sound good? Or maybe more of a companion who maintains his or her own personal identity?

What's your timeline? While you shouldn't put a wedding date in your listing, don't leave the results completely open-ended in your mind. Even if both of you have the same goal in mind, if you see yourself married in a year and the other person is on a five-year plan, neither of you will be happy with the pacing. Be reasonable and be honest. While you could meet your true love and be married in a week, it isn't likely.

What do you enjoy doing? Although people like to say "opposites attract," in reality being with someone who shares your likes and dislikes is a lot more fun. Make a list of things you really enjoy. Highlight the ones that you do the most. Do you play sports or watch them? Is a good time closing out the dance club, or dinner and a movie? Is your ideal vacation roughing it in the wilderness or a week at the Ritz-Carlton? Are you more extreme geek or X-Games? Finding someone who enjoys the same activity level and types of activities that you do is more important than finding someone who does *exactly* what you do. Not that a homebody and a world traveler can't work it out, but that kind of relationship takes more effort to succeed and the odds are not in their favor.

Take a personal inventory. Make a list that tells all about you. Start with your physical attributes; then move on to your personality traits, likes, dislikes, hobbies, talents, and anything else you can think to include. Although you aren't going to throw in more than necessary in your ad, write as much as you can. You can use your notes to try out additional ads later (if you want to), and it will serve as a resource for creating a successful ad and for a list of traits you'd appreciate in a partner.

What works for you and what doesn't? Make a list of personality traits and physical attributes that appeal to you. While they certainly aren't all deal breakers, a few probably are—and you might as well be honest about them. Some experts recommend casting a wide net with a personal ad by being as generic as possible. But when it comes to attraction, there isn't always rhyme or reason to what catches our eye or what just doesn't "do it" for us.

Will you go the distance? Knowing and accepting your limits will save time and frustration. Long-distance romances—and short-distance ones—take work. If you tend to work long hours, enjoy an active social life, or have many responsibilities, be honest with yourself about how much time you're willing to spend for a commuter relationship. On the other hand, if your schedule is extremely busy, being involved with someone you see only a couple of times a month may be the perfect arrangement.

Nine Secrets for Successful Online Relationships

As people read your ad, most are going to create some sort of mental picture of you. One of your goals is to create as accurate, positive, and interesting a visual image as possible. Readers create this image not only from what you say, but also how you say it. The same is true of the communication that takes place after the listing. Before we get into the nitty-gritty of personal ad writing, read through this list and write down what comes to mind. You can use these secrets for better experiences in all your relationships and interpersonal communication.

Secret 1: The Truth Will Set You Free

Being honest is important for a successful online dating experience. Don't shave 20 years or 40 pounds off your profile. Why set both of you up for disappointment? The other person may be perfectly content with the truth but will never get over being deceived. Be upfront about your looks, and also about habits such as exercise, smoking, and drinking. Otherwise, you'll exhaust yourself trying to hide the "real" you, and sooner or later your date will find out the truth anyhow.

You don't have to rifle through all your baggage in your listing, or even on the first couple of dates, but don't try to be someone you're not. Unless they're intrusive or offensive, answer questions openly and honestly. If a topic comes up that you're uncomfortable discussing, tell the other person that and offer to discuss it when you're ready.

Secret 2: Don't Worry, Be Happy

Most of us are naturally attracted to people who are positive and upbeat. Your ad—and as often as possible, you—should be positive and upbeat too. You can show your cheerful side in your ad and in person by avoiding negative writing or talk. Gear your listing to what you enjoy, what you have to offer, and what you hope to find in a match. Skip explaining what you dislike, any faults you might have, and what turns you off, until you know each other better.

Secret 3: Be Uniquely You

Although putting your finger on it may be difficult at first, focus on what makes you unique. There is no one else in the world like you. Look at the personal inventory you completed earlier in the chapter. Ask some of your friends what they think of when they think of you. Asking them may feel a little silly at first, but it's a great way to find out what other people feel makes you special.

That combination of traits—both the ones your friends see and those that you see in yourself—give you your uniqueness. When you are communicating with someone, in your ad, by email, or in person, you can spotlight those positives by sharing stories or comments that reflect them. For example, to convey your love of sailing, start your ad—or your conversation—by mentioning that you're looking for someone to sail off into the sunset with. Or, if you're a homebody, comment that you would love to have someone to help turn your house into a home. There are many ways you can let people in on who you are and how unique you are without simply giving them a list of likes and dislikes.

Secret 4: You're So Funny

Used wisely, humor can spark some real interest in the reader and a date. Who doesn't love to laugh, right? But, knowing the right kind of humor and using it in moderation are the keys. Don't play the class clown by trying to turn everything into a joke or making yourself or another person the subject of your punch lines. Avoid sensitive issues such as religion and politics. Go for warm, friendly humor that brings out a smile or a quiet laugh. Save off-color humor for when you know the person better.

Secret 5: It's a Good Value

Whether you're looking for friendship, casual dating, or happily ever after, the best match for you will likely be someone who shares your values and overall outlook on life. So, it's good to mention those values early on. One way you can tell people what matters most in life to you is by sharing stories, quotations, or sayings that you hold dear. If they resonate with the other person, you'll start out on common ground.

Secret 6: It's Not About the Toys

Don't try to sell yourself by your job, your car, your home, or your high-end stereo system. Those are all bonuses (let's be honest), but no one worth spending time with becomes your friend or dates you because of your earthly possessions. The same thing goes for appendages. You may be proud because you're well-endowed, but let the other person see for themselves—when the time is right for both of you.

In your listing and always, let your qualities shine. Describe your activities and hobbies that reflect those qualities. Dog lovers often take their pets to the dog park or for a long run. Compassionate people sometimes volunteer their time and energy to help others. Outdoor types usually spend a fair amount of free time hiking, camping, fishing, and so on. Paint an active picture of doing something you would enjoy doing with the other person. That way, you tell people about things you enjoy and, directly or indirectly, what motivates you to do them.

Secret 7: You're All That

Seriously, you are—but so is the other person! Although a quiet self-confidence is appealing to most people, bragging, boasting, or talking endlessly about yourself is a big turn-off. In your listing, tell the readers enough to get them imagining you, but don't turn it into your biography. Include positive details about what you're looking for in the other person. The same goes for any interaction you have with someone. You both want to find out if there's a connection, and much of that can happen through the give-and-take of conversation.

Tell a story or answer a question and then invite the other person to share. Doing this tells that person you're interested in what she has to say and in learning more about her.

Secret 8: Be in the Moment

Whether you're writing your personal ad, reading a response, or sitting across the table during a first date, pay attention and put some thought into the moment. Write your listing in a word processing program and put it away for a day or two. A fresh set of eyes may show you what you need to edit or add. As eager as you may be to get started, waiting an extra day or two can give you better results.

When corresponding by instant message or email, don't dash off a response. Be certain you understand what the other person wrote and respond to any questions or comments.

When you're with someone, actively listen to what he's saying. Although you can easily get in the habit of thinking about what you're going to say next rather than listening to what the other person is saying, it won't score any points with your date. Lean toward him slightly and focus on what his words and his body language are telling you.

Secret 9: Embrace the Process

An unavoidable situation in my life once left me frustrated and edgy a good deal of the time. A dear friend explained that, although I had no control over the situation, I could decide whether I was going to accept the situation and make it my ally or fight it tooth and nail as my enemy. He was right. I chose to accept the situation and find joy in it whenever I could. I made the best of it, and it no longer had a negative influence on me. Now, anytime people tell me that they don't enjoy dating, I share with them my friend's advice and gently remind them that dating is supposed to be fun. It is certainly unavoidable if you want to be in a long-term relationship. Make the most of it and choose to enjoy the process.

Igniting Sparks

Six categories in the craigslist **personals** section deal with dating, romance, or casual sex (see Figure 12.2). Whether you're straight, gay, or lesbian, the four "seeking" categories (and their short forms, w4w, w4m, m4w, and m4m) are best for conventional dating and relationship ads.

Even if you're looking for an ongoing relationship, if you want to express any "kink," post to the **misc romance** category to avoid having your ad flagged. Depending on your community, the **misc romance** category is for ads that are more than "one night stands" but fall outside the more traditional dating categories.

The **casual encounters** category is the place to post for all forms of "no strings attached" (NSA) sex and "friends with benefits" (FWB) hookups. This category is usually filled with posts for same-day adventures of all kinds.

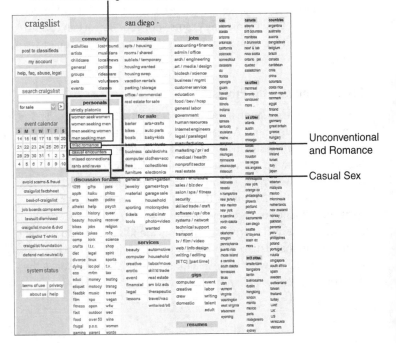

Figure 12.2
The **personals** section includes multiple dating categories.

Thinking Long-Term

Whether you're marriage-minded or not, if a conventional LTR (long-term relationship) is your goal, the seeking categories are probably the best place to go, but LTRs in the **misc romance** category may work, too. Start by using the same steps that you do when promoting anything else:

- **Do your research.** Read posts from the same category. Are you a man in search of a woman? Read the **men seeking women** category. Write down what appeals to you. Notice how things come across in the listing. Try to avoid common phrasing; use new and interesting ways to tell your story.

- **Define your goal.** Imagine that your listing is up and running; then write down how you see the process playing out. Among the flurry of responses, one or two pique your interest. What do they say? What's the tone? What kinds of things do you write about when you respond?

  You start exchanging email. How many messages and how often? What's the next step and who takes it? When do you finally meet face-to-face, and how does that happen? What does the other person look like? How is she dressed? Keep this up until you reach "the end." Is it long-term dating, or do you see yourself happily married to someone?

  Although answering all those questions might sound silly, being able to visualize what you want isn't silly at all. It's much more likely that you will achieve a clearly defined goal.

Thinking Short-Term

What if you're not really interested in dating but still want to have some fun? The **casual encounters** category may be for you. This isn't a category for the faint at heart; it's a no-holds-barred, free-for-all of sexual hookups. While spontaneity tends to be the rule here, knowing what you want and don't want is a good thing. You can refer to Table 12.1 to figure out your requirements, preferences, and deal breakers.

Like to live in the "here and now"? Great, but even so—or even more so—you need a plan, or at least an exit strategy. If you start seeing little red flags, don't ignore them for the sake of short-term pleasure. Those flags are waving for a reason.

Warning 4U Seriously, if you're going to disregard all the safe and sound advice I offer in Chapter 3, please at least let someone you can confide in know where you're going and when to expect you back, or write down the information somewhere that will be easily found.

Strictly Platonic: Making New Friends

There's no reason to sit at home bored to tears! Throw a listing into the **strictly platonic** category, and you can become a social butterfly in no time. If you're new to an area, traveling, or just need to get out of your rut, you've found the right place. If you invest a few minutes before you post, you can easily make your listing stand out in a sea of sameness:

- **Do your research.** If you don't have a specific activity in mind, make a list of things to do that sound interesting. This list is especially helpful if you're not familiar with the area and want some great ideas. The more successful ads come across as lighthearted and easygoing.

- **Define your goal.** Are you looking to make a new best friend or simply someone to see a show with because you have an extra ticket? Are you thinking male or female, or does it matter? Are you looking for friendship that leads to more? Include that info in your goal because it will play a big part not only in how you write your ad, but in the outcome.

Because friendship can mean so many different things to each individual, I've included an additional list to help you better define what you're looking for. If you're looking for someone for a particular activity, such as a partner for dancing lessons, things such as height or fitness level can make a difference.

1. Do you live here or are you visiting?
2. Single outing, more than once, ongoing friendship?
3. One activity or a variety?
4. A new friend or someone to do a particular activity?
5. Specific location or area, days or times?
6. Local only, or for trips too?
7. Someone to pay her own way or will you cover it?
8. Particular background?
9. Special personality traits or physical attributes?
10. Specific interests, preferences, requirements?

Now you should be able to define a clear, concise, detailed goal to get you started with your listing.

Missed Connections: Finding Someone Who Caught Your Eye

More than one person has gained media attention by being the subject of a post in the **missed connections** category. A gentleman in San Francisco was featured in the press because of a series of posts from a woman who became smitten with him from seeing him at the bus stop each day. Because the posts included the time and bus stop, people began to show up each day to see this mystery dream date. Eventually, the news picked up the story and contacted the man. He was clueless but had wondered about the growing crowds. Alas, there was no match because he was happily married.

Search the Internet and you'll find anecdotal stories of connections found. And the category is so popular in some craigslist communities that it has become the subject of songs, comic strips, and standup routines. Browse the category listings, as shown in Figure 12.3, and you'll be amazed at the number of people and the interesting stories.

On the off chance that the planets align and fate intervenes, hope for the best and prepare for the worst. Realize that the other person might not have felt the same spark that you did. If he did, that's awesome!

Jul 25 - Costa Mesa Silver Toyota Truck Victoria/Victoria Place - m4w - 48 - (Costa Mesa) pic

Jul 25 - you know we would be good for each other - m4w - 39 - (costa mesa/huntington harbor)

Jul 25 - Foxfire Club (Anaheim) - Thursday night - m4w - 49 - (Foxfire Bar & club)

Jul 25 - Dave and Busters! - m4w - 23 - (Irvine Spectrum)

Jul 25 - Bye my sweet sober one - m4w - 42 - (Costa Mesa)

Jul 25 - looking for Sandy Darling, went to Tustin High in '77 - m4w - 50 - (Orange Co.)

Jul 25 - starbucks tustin and 17th - m4w - 41 - (tustin santa ana)

Jul 25 - Marie Calenders - m4w - (fountain valley)

Jul 24 - Jennifer in Seal beach with Black dog - m4w - 35 - (seal beach)

Jul 24 - in front of planet beauty - m4w - (rsm)

Jul 24 - white honda civic - m4w - 28 - (placentia)

Jul 24 - Albertsons Laguna Niguel - m4w - 33 - (LN)

Jul 24 - bummer - m4w - 35 - (lake forest)

Jul 24 - Corrie Floris, I've been looking everywhere! - m4w - 32 -

Jul 24 - Irasse Sushi Wednesday night? - m4w - 38 - (HB)

Jul 24 - what would it take to have you give up on me? - m4w - (Somewhere in the OC) pic

Jul 24 - Hot Blonde College Professor - m4w - 50 - (Walnut)

Jul 24 - you make me weak in the knees - m4w - 26 - (oc)

Jul 24 - Looking for Marisa Felker - m4w - (OC)

Figure 12.3
Perusing the **missed connections** category can be very entertaining.

Rants and Raves: Expressing Yourself

The **rants and raves** category is the Internet equivalent of writing on the bathroom wall or screaming into a pillow. Enter at your own risk. Some of the posts can be highly entertaining and extremely witty, but some are filled with intense anger, profanity, and graphic commentary. Posts are not moderated, and I doubt that flaggers even bother to leave their mark.

I do realize that this category serves a purpose, as we all need to vent at times—me included. But, I don't like to think of that much negativity and anger being out there in the world. If you feel the urge to give someone or something a piece of your mind, then go for it. I hope that, when all is said and done, you can put your anger behind you and move on.

Put It in Writing

Time to put those thoughts into words. Depending on your goal and which category you've chosen, not all the information that follows may apply. And, of course, if you're going to post in **rants and raves**, just do it.

For purposes of clarity, I'll use the terms *reader, potential match,* or *match* to refer to craigslist readers. Since this chapter covers dating and more—and less—consider *match* to mean the person you're trying to meet. Most examples will cover the dating categories, but some may also apply to the other categories.

Before you begin writing the ad, create a picture in your mind of your potential match. Keep that image in your mind while you craft your listing.

For a personal ad, starting with a title in mind seems to set the tone for many people. Most of us can quote a line or two from a song that holds special meaning to us. Using a song lyric in a title works especially well if you don't know what to say. The lyric will likely hold meaning to others, so you'll catch their attention and share some insights that may get them interested enough to click on your listing.

Another interesting option if you have favorite park, beach, or other hangout is to ask, "Who else enjoys spending time at *fill-in-the-blank*?" Other possible approaches are describing your ideal Saturday night, a special place that's important to you, or anything else that brings you joy. Whatever you say, be creative, positive, and warm.

Now you can move on to the ad. It can be as long or short as you want, but longer ads should contain short paragraphs. There's a fine line between enticing the reader with your thoughts and droning on and on. If you can't tell the difference, have someone read over your listing before you post.

The body of your posting should begin where your headline left off. If your title asks about a favorite park, open the listing by briefly describing how and why you enjoy it. For instance, "After an hour or so of walking the trails, I enjoy relaxing by the lake and listening to the peace and quiet. It would be great to have someone to share the day with." Now you've given your potential date a vivid picture of a familiar and well-liked place—assuming he clicked on it because he agreed with the title. You associated yourself with a positive event and shared a little bit about who you are. The reader would likely assume that you enjoy nature and the outdoors. You enjoy moderate exercise and quiet relaxation too.

Using a positive and sincere short story—usually no more than four lines—to start is a great way to connect with your potential match. Don't use this as an opportunity to vent, complain, or bash your ex. If you share something that has meaning to you and the other person relates to that, you're already forming a bond.

Then you can tell more about yourself and what you hope to find. You don't have to post a resume, but some basic statistics are good. Let the reader get to know the "inner you" first. A good place to start is telling why you're posting. Phrase things as benefits or use action words. Finish by asking the potential reader to contact you. Write in a casual, cheerful tone. Make certain your message is clear. Avoid negative words and phrases. Have a few friends read your ad and get their feedback before posting it.

Although *I strongly advise against it*, if you're comfortable doing so, include a picture. Clothed! Really, no woman I know has ever been impressed by a guy who posted naked pictures on the Internet.

From Here...

You've learned about the **personals** category, how to create a compelling listing, and how to have a better experience. Next, you'll take a trip to the other side and learn how to respond to listings.

The Other Side of craigslist

13 Responding to Listings 245

14 Keeping Busy with Listings 253

15 Win-Win Results in Listings 277

Responding to Listings

One reason craigslist has so many rabid fans is that it's fast and easy to use. The search function is straightforward and uncomplicated, yet flexible enough to cover an entire section or to target a particular category. In this chapter, you'll learn the fastest way to find what you want.

Locating What You Want

One way to find what you're seeking is to browse the listings. With the exception of the **personals** section heading, you can click any section or category link (see Figure 13.1) to scan a list of recent posts (see Figure 13.2).

Click the listing to display the ad, and then click your browser's Back button when you're finished reading.

Tip 4U If your browser offers tabbed viewing, you might find it more effective to right-click the title and select Open in New Tab. Doing so displays the listing on a new tab in your browser. Alternatively, you can choose Open in New Window to display the listing in a separate window. If you decide the listing isn't for you, simply close that tab or window by clicking the Close (x) button, and you won't have to wait for the previous page to reload.

Category Link Example

Section Link Example

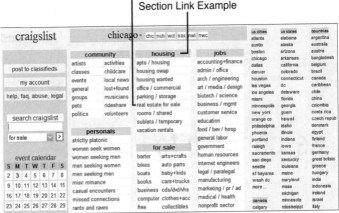

Figure 13.1
Clicking a section or category link will let you browse current listings.

| search for: | | in: real estate for sale ⌄ | Search | ☐ only search titles |
| price: | min | max | | ☐ has image |

[Mon, 03 Mar 14:18:48]   ["foreclosure rescue" fraud alert] [stating a discriminatory preference in a housing post is illegal]
[housing forum] [success story?] [AVOIDING SCAMS & FRAUD] [PERSONAL SAFETY TIPS]

Mon Mar 03

$774900 ELK GROVE HALF ACRE CUSTOM BUILT ALL BRICK HOME! - img

BOONE COUNTY LOTS FOR SALE - (Poplar Grove, IL.)

$325000 -----All Brick Ranch - 3BR,2BA - Full Finished Basement AWESOME----- - (Palanois Park) img

$1200000 Steps from Beach - This Home is Hidden Gem - (Winnetka) pic

$746500 BARRINGTON HILLS 3 BEDROOM, 2.5 BATH CAPE COD ON 5 ACRES! - img

Figure 13.2
Clicking the **real estate for sale** category displays titles for all current listings.

Browsing is a great way to see what's out there, but you can use the search function to find exactly what you need, and quickly! Let's say you want a nursing job in the Winston-Salem area. Follow these steps and you'll find all the relevant listings in no time:

1. From the Winston-Salem home page (see Figure 13.3), click the **medical/health** category in the **jobs** section.

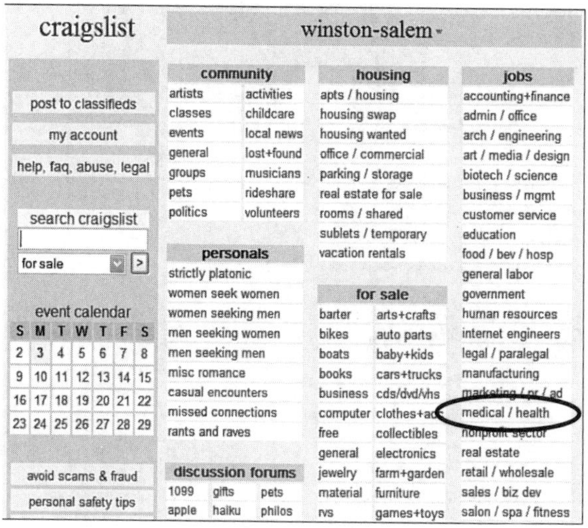

Figure 13.3
Click the **medical/health** link in the **jobs** section to display all related listings.

2. When the healthcare jobs page appears (see Figure 13.4), enter your keyword in the **search for** box. Check any additional criteria and then click on the **Search** button.

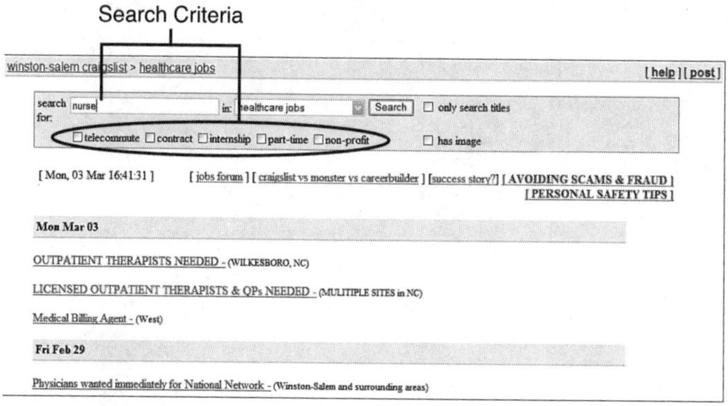

Figure 13.4
Enter your search terms and select your criteria; then click on the **Search** button for a list of matching ads.

3. The search results display a list of all active postings (see Figure 13.5).

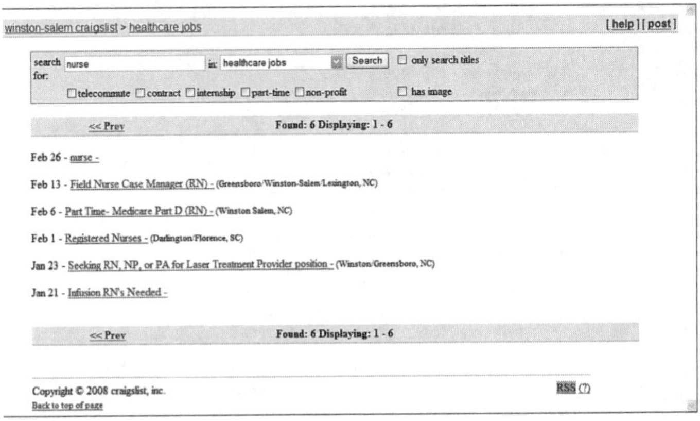

Figure 13.5
You can browse the search results for interesting titles.

If you want to search multiple categories, the search box on the home page is the fastest place to start. For example, suppose you collect Harry Potter treasures. Enter **harry potter** in the <u>**search craigslist**</u> box (see Figure 13.6). The drop-down menu defaults to the <u>**for sale**</u> section, so click the right-arrow (>) button to display a page with all listings in the <u>**for sale**</u> section that include your keywords, as shown in Figure 13.7.

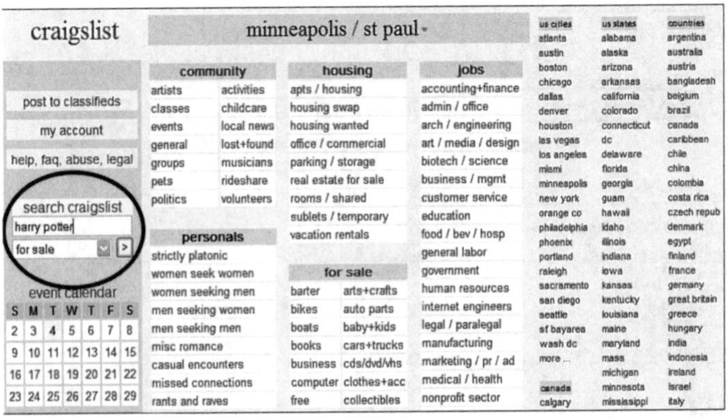

Figure 13.6
Use the search box on the home page to search entire sections.

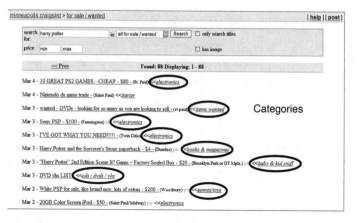

Figure 13.7
Each listing's category follows the title when you're searching whole sections.

If you see a listing that interests you, you can comparison shop by selecting that category from the drop-down menu at the top and clicking the **Search** button (see Figure 13.8). This gives you a fast way to compare prices, features, and locations, as shown in Figure 13.9.

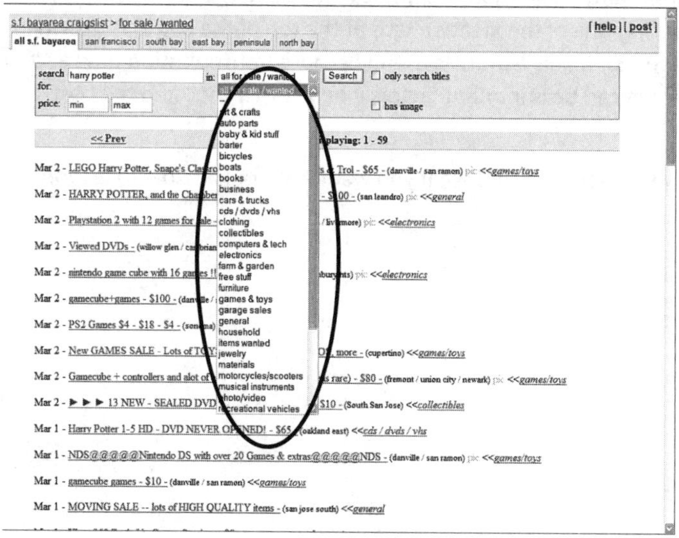

Figure 13.8
Select a category from the drop-down menu and click **Search**.

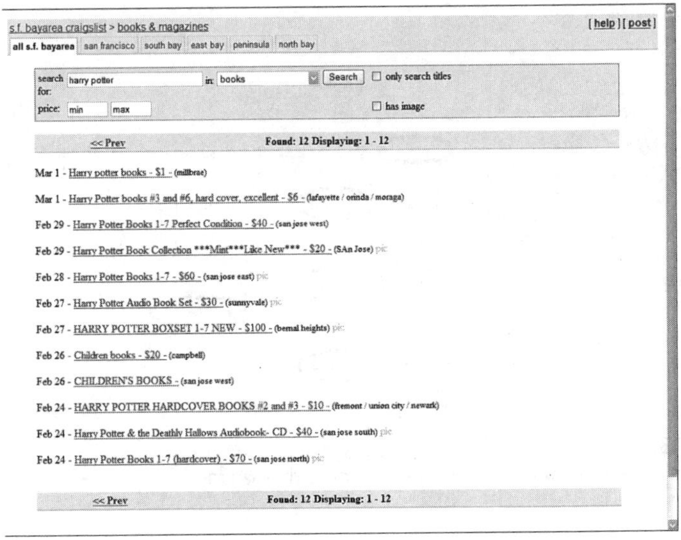

Figure 13.9
Scan the listings for a quick comparison of price, title, and location.

In some larger communities, you can further target your listings by choosing one of the location tabs at the top of the page, as shown in Figure 13.10. This feature is useful because transportation time and expense can be important factors when you're choosing the best deal.

Now that you've found what you want, let's look at how to respond to a post.

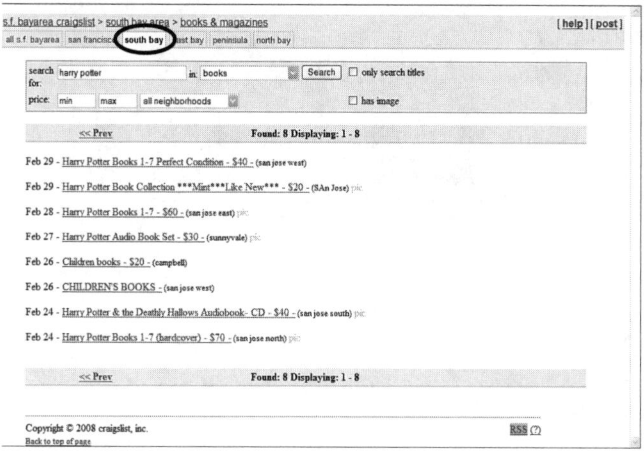

Figure 13.10
Click on an area tab to find the listings closest to you.

How to Reply

Like almost everything else on craigslist, replying to a post is simple. Most craigslist ads include a mailto link, as shown in Figure 13.11. When clicked, the link opens an email message in your default email program, as shown in Figure 13.12. The message has the reply address in the **To** field and the listing title in the **Subject** line, making it a snap to shoot off a message to the other party.

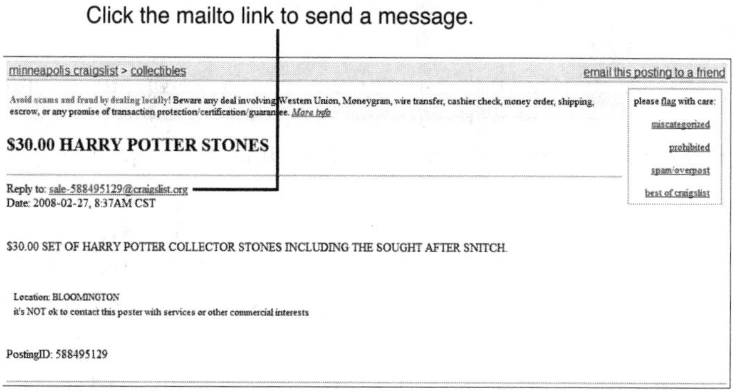

Figure 13.11
Click the email address to reply to a listing.

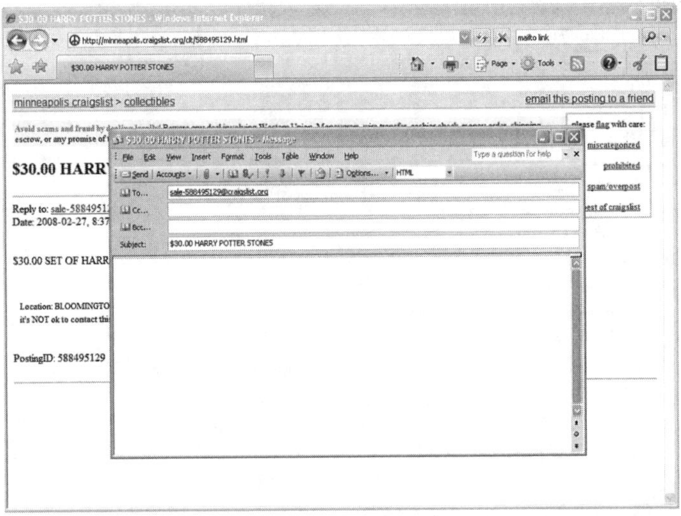

Figure 13.12
A blank email message to the reply address will open with the listing title in the **Subject** line.

If you haven't specified a default email client, your computer's operating system may display an error message. Consult your manual or your favorite technical pal for assistance. If all else fails, you can type or copy and paste the information from the post that interests you into a blank email message in your email software.

From Here...

The technical steps to finding what you want and replying to a listing are easy. Let's move on to the fun part of using knowledge and strategies to meet your goal in every transaction.

Keeping Busy with Listings

Whether you're looking for a new job, new romance, or new adventure, craigslist is a great place to start. When you visit your local craigslist community, you'll probably feel like the proverbial kid in a candy store; there's so much to see that it's a bit overwhelming at times. Among the various sections craigslist devotees successfully follow the site's mission of being a website created to bring people together in the real world.

In this chapter, we'll explore the **community**, **personals**, **jobs**, and **gigs** sections in some detail. You'll find a wide range of listings in each of the craigslist categories—especially in the more established craigslist communities. So dive in, start searching, and get busy!

Enriching Your Life with the Community

The craigslist **community** section is a good place to find a new pet, check the lost and found, hire a nanny, or locate a carpool companion. Featuring 14 unique categories, the **community** section is geared toward social interaction in some form or fashion: it's the place to find events, announce events, look for volunteer opportunities, and much more. The following sections give you a rundown of what each **community** section offers and how to apply search techniques to find what you need.

When searching through the **community** listings, simply click in the **search for:** field at the top of the listing page and type your keyword(s); then select the appropriate category in the **in:** drop-down list next to the search field (see Figure 14.1). If you prefer to search the entire community section, choose the **all community** option. Finally, press Enter or click the **Search** button to start the search.

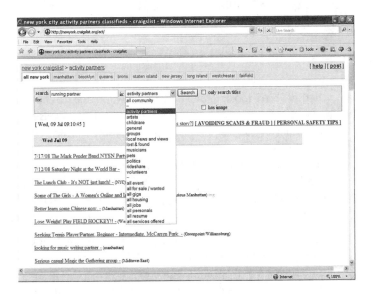

Figure 14.1
Use the search fields to narrow your search through the listings.

If you're searching listings in a large metropolitan area, you can narrow your search by clicking an area tab at the top of the page and then entering your keyword(s).

Tip 4U   You can also click the **community** link on the main page to view a screen full of recent listings among all the **community** categories.

Activities

As mentioned in Chapter 6, "Listing in the Community," the true name of the <u>**activities**</u> category is "<u>**activity partners**</u>," and its goal is to help people with similar interests meet one another. The <u>**activities**</u> category lists all kinds of get-up-and-do-something opportunities, from sports to card clubs to workout buddies. Under this category, you'll find all kinds of listings for activities that require partners.

The <u>**activities**</u> category is ideal for sports enthusiasts of all skill levels to connect. For example, if you're an avid basketball player looking for a team, you're bound to find teams looking for players. The same holds true for volleyball, softball, soccer, and any other kind of team. You can also use this category to find a tennis or golf partner.

In addition to athletic pursuits, the <u>**activities**</u> category helps connect people to card clubs, bowling leagues, fishing groups, bike riders, dance partners, and study buddies. This category is truly useful for connecting people with similar competitive goals and passions, whether it's becoming a better poker player or finding someone to get in shape with.

Before you begin your search through the available activities, start by asking yourself a few questions to narrow down what you're looking for:

- What do you want to get out of any activity connections you make?
- How often are you available to pursue the activity, and what does your schedule allow?
- How far are you willing to travel to connect with the activity?

When you're armed with those answers, it will be easier to scan for the listings that match your needs. Figure 14.2 shows an example of activities listed in the New York City area.

When searching for an activities partner or group, use general search terms, such as **tennis**, **exercise**, **music**, or **dancing**. For certain larger cities, you can search listings in a specific area of the city; this is a great way to cut down on travel time and expense. For example, if you're located in the Chicago area, you can look for activities north, west, or south of the city, as well as in the heart of the city.

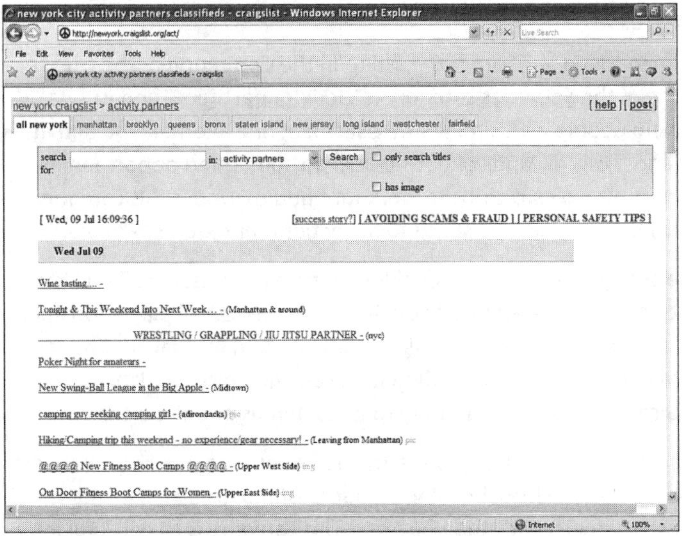

Figure 14.2
The **activities** category is full of listings for participating, meeting people, and expanding your network.

Don't forget to search for activity partners under other areas, such as **groups**, **events**, and **classes**. Some people post similar-type listings to the **general** category, too. When you find a listing that sounds interesting, reply and ask any questions. If a phone number is listed, call ahead to confirm the details.

Artists

The **artists** category is the place to go to connect with painters, photographers, writers, art teachers, art studios, and fine craftspeople. If you're looking for a work of art, stop by this category to peruse paintings of all kinds and styles. You'll also find artists to help you with home projects, such as murals or stencils. Need a portrait? Check out the photographers available in your area.

Large portions of the **artists** and **musicians** categories are about self-promotion, but many times you'll find information about upcoming events, such as gallery showings or musical gigs. When searching through the artists category, type in keywords pertaining to what you're looking for, such as **modern art**, **abstract art**, **murals for children's rooms**, **faux painting**, and **portrait photography**. Many artists include links to examples of their works, so check them out when applicable to learn more about the artists and their art.

In some communities, the **artists** and **musicians** categories are also great places to find unique entertainment for children's parties, such as clowns, superheroes, and so on.

Childcare

The **childcare** category lists all kinds of babysitting and childcare opportunities for both those looking for care and those supplying it. You'll find listings for nannies, home daycare, babysitters, or part-time and full-time help. Childcare is one of the busier topics on craigslist, regardless of location. Figure 14.3 shows a sample of listing titles in the Los Angeles area.

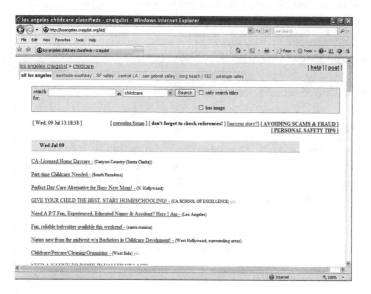

Figure 14.3
The **childcare** category is one of the busiest categories on craigslist.

If you're searching for childcare, apply very rigid standards as you're scanning through the listings. First and foremost, be sure to check references when hiring any childcare help. Ask lots of questions, especially pertaining to background and experience.

To help make your search easier, start by making a list of your needs, and be specific. Here are a few questions to get you started:

- How often do you require childcare? List days, hours, time frames, and so on.
- Is childcare needed at home or another location?
- What sorts of activities do you expect from childcare providers? Will they oversee naptimes, playtime, snack times, transport for your kids, craft time?
- What other duties do you expect? If care is provided in your own home, will you assign cleaning tasks, laundry, dishes, or errands?
- What sorts of preferences do you have regarding the provider? Age, experience, health status, certifications?

Another helpful tip may be to opt for a trial period in which you and the childcare service or provider make sure that everyone's compatible, child to caretaker and caretaker to child. You also can check with your state's licensing board to see whether daycares are licensed.

General

The **general** category, also called **general community**, is sort of a catchall for listings that don't necessarily fit anywhere else on craigslist. You can expect to find a wide variety of listings and topics here, from the mundane to the unusual to the downright quirky—everything from advice to sales pitches. Because the field is wide open, apply some pointed keywords to find what you're looking for in this category. Figure 14.4 shows a sample of listings from the Miami area.

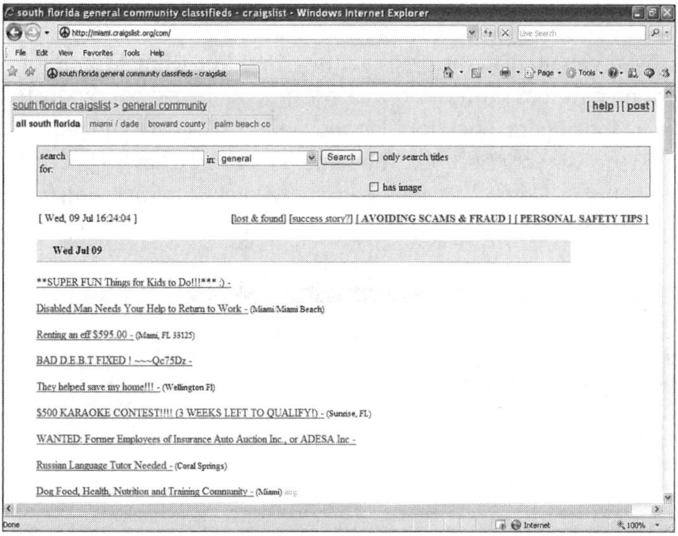

Figure 14.4
The **general** category holds a potpourri of listings.

Groups

The **groups** category is tailored to all sorts of groups. If you want to join a group, or if you're a group looking for more members, this is your category. Groups can include book clubs, movie fan groups, playgroups, automobile clubs, support groups, business profession-als, social networking groups, dinner clubs—and that's just the tip of the iceberg. Spend enough time here, and it's likely that you'll even-tually find a group that suits your interests.

When searching the **groups** category, type in specific keywords, such as **book club** or **play group**. When contacting a group, be sure to inquire about the group's goals, function, meeting schedule, and location. It's also a good idea to find out if the group meets regularly, such as a class, or is a one-time event.

Pets

Pet lovers can unite in the **pets** category. Here you'll find listings for adopting pets, pet sitting, dog walking, grooming, and pet products. If you're looking for a pet (four-legged, finned, scaled, or winged), this category is your best bet. The same is true if you have a pet that needs a home. Figure 14.5 shows an example of a typical listing in the **pets** category.

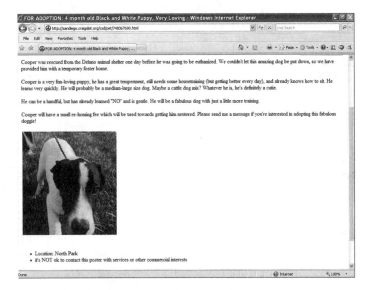

Figure 14.5
The **pets** category offers a variety of pets and listings similar to this one.

As mentioned in Chapter 6, pet sales are not allowed on craigslist. With that in mind, you'll see adoption fees or rehoming fees listed instead. These fees are supposed to be no more than the costs incurred to prepare the animal for a new home. They also are not supposed to recover original costs for the animal or its supplies.

Because this category is fraught with controversy, as explained in Chapter 6, proceed with caution when searching and replying to listings. Be aware that this particular category's listings are subject to a lot of flagging. As you look for a particular pet, keep the following questions in mind:

- Does the listing tell you everything you need to know about the animal, such as gender, special needs, housebroken or not?
- Are pictures available? Pictures can really help to convey the adoptability of a pet.
- What's the animal's history, if known?
- Why is the owner rehoming the animal?
- What is the pet's medical history (shots, vaccines, treatments, and so on)?
- What is the pet's activity level? Is it hyperactive, relaxed, active and playful, scared of other animals or humans, quiet and sedate?

People who list animals for adoption are always advised to screen potential owners carefully. The same is true for people looking to adopt; you should be equally careful in screening the pet. For example, if you have young children in the house, steer away from pets that come from unknown origins or have a background of abuse. As with anything on craigslist, ask lots of questions up front to avoid any potential problems.

Events

The **events** category, also known as the **event calendar**, is the place to find announcements about upcoming events. You'll find everything from free events to paid events among these listings. Figure 14.6 shows an example of event listings in the New York City area. Notice that a lot of classes are listed.

Watch out for multilevel marketing events in this category. They're prohibited on craigslist but sometimes slip through masked as something else. Although such events aren't inherently bad, it's always better to know what you're getting into.

To search for an event, simply type in keywords describing what sort of event you're looking for, such as **wine tasting**, **art gallery**, or **concert**.

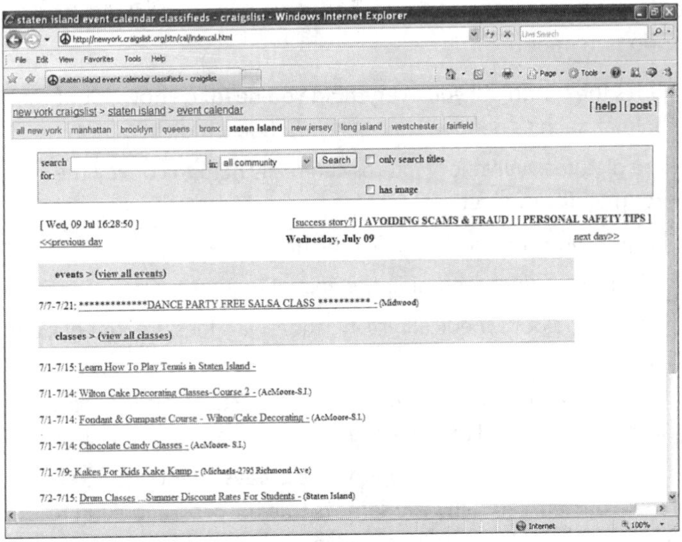

![staten island event calendar classifieds - craigslist - Windows Internet Explorer screenshot showing the craigslist event calendar page for new york > staten island > event calendar, with search box and listings for events and classes.]

Figure 14.6
The **events** category is the place to go to find things to do.

 Tip 4U   If you're looking for something to do on a specific date, use the **event calendar** on the area home page. Click on any date on the calendar to see what events and classes are being offered locally.

Lost and Found

The **lost+found** category includes listings for lost pets, lost objects, and even missing people. In most areas, the category is filled with lost or found pets and personal items. If you're combing the lost and found for your missing pet, use generic keywords when searching the category. Although you may know that you have a brown dog, others may call it a tan or chocolate dog. Take the time to browse all relevant listings posted since your pet went missing, so you don't overlook anything.

If you're searching for a lost item, take time to write down any pertinent information you can remember about the item, to help you during your search. Use the following questions to assemble a list:

- Where did you lose the item?
- What time of day or hour did you lose the item?
- Are there any distinguishing marks on the item, or is a name written on the item?
- What are some generic terms you might use to describe the item?

Armed with some details, you can use the answers you came up with to help you scour the listings for your missing item.

Musicians

The **musicians** category caters to the musically inclined. Need a place to express your musical aspirations? Hook up with individuals and bands in need of your talent. You also can search the category to get in touch with vocal coaches, music teachers, and rehearsal and recording studios. You can find listings for music lessons, voice lessons, instrument repair, and musician and vocalist positions. You'll also find musical events listed here, such as "open mic" nights or band gigs.

Both the **artists** category, covered earlier in this chapter, and the **musicians** category are great places to connect with other creative types. You can find out about local gallery showings, concerts, and other places to express your creativity.

The best advice for searching through these listings is to browse the titles in these categories at first to get a feel for your local community. If you know what you're looking for already, such as music lessons for a particular instrument or rehearsal space, you can type in those keywords and quickly narrow your search.

Local News

The full title of the **local news** category is **local news and views**, and you can expect to find an eclectic mix of listings here. The idea behind this category is to provide a place for local businesses to promote events, news items, press releases, and other information. You'll also find a great deal of advertising, so when scanning this category, keep in mind that much of it is about promoting products and marketing events.

Politics

The **politics** category generally is a discussion forum or a place to vent about politics, candidates, policies, and related topics, rather than a source of information. You might visit this area to view various opinions, rants, and ravings. As you search this category, just remember that although you're in the **politics** category, some of the postings are not what you'd call "politically correct." This category is especially active during major election years.

Rideshare

The **rideshare** category is a place to connect with fellow commuters and share a ride. Whether you need a daily carpool partner or someone to share a ride across the country, visit this category to see what's in the works. Figure 14.7 shows a typical listing from the Dallas area.

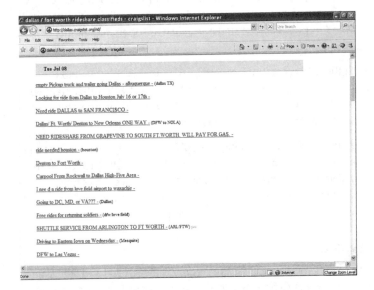

Figure 14.7
The **rideshare** category is the place to go if you want to share a ride or commute.

As for search words, try using specific starting and destination cities and date of trip as keywords. For best results, search through this category ahead of time so you'll have plenty of opportunity to contact others and ask questions.

When inquiring about rides, you should consider a couple of issues:

- Personality types
- Music tastes
- Conversation preferences
- Personal hygiene/habits (smoking, use of perfume, and so on)
- Neatness expectations (eating in the car allowed/prohibited, and so on)

When responding to listings in this category, be as flexible as possible. If you agree to a long-term carpool situation, for example, set a trial period of a couple of weeks to give either of you an out if it isn't working. If you're planning a cross-country trip, it may be a good idea to meet the person first and spend some time together to find out whether you'd be compatible for the extended ride.

Volunteers

The **volunteers** category is an excellent spot for finding volunteer opportunities throughout your community. You'll find listings for everything from pet foster homes to volunteer positions with community groups. If you enjoy donating your time to a worthy cause, scan through the listings in this category and see whether your interests match any of the many needs. Be sure to check back often; many of the listings change seasonally or change based on community needs that arise. Figure 14.8 shows some sample listings from the **volunteers** category in the Chicago area.

Before responding to a volunteer listing, take a moment and make a list regarding how much time you have to give, the days or hours you can volunteer, and what your expectations are. Knowing the answers to these basics can help as you search through the listings for a good match.

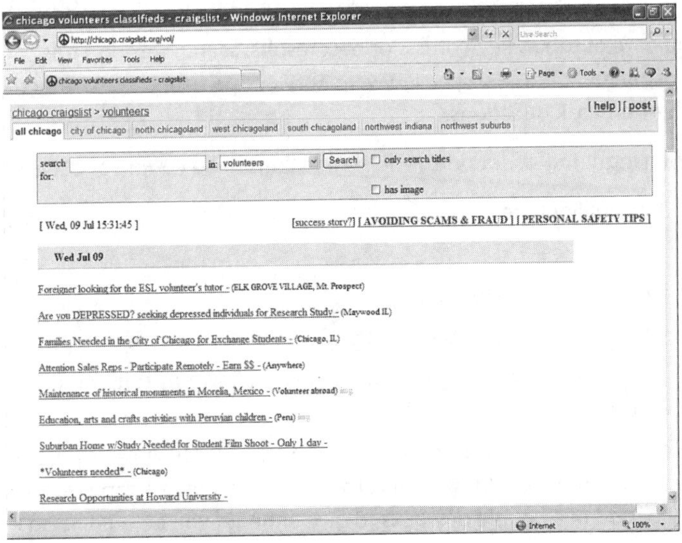

Figure 14.8
The **volunteers** category is the place to look for ways to donate your time to a good cause.

Always be mindful of online scams and links that send you to unauthorized sites or attempt to collect money from you.

Classes

Are you interested in learning something new? In the **classes** category, you'll find listings for all kinds of classes, teaching foreign languages, financial matters, real estate, dance, adult education, and so on. Most of the listings in this category are time-sensitive and require reservations. Some classes are free; others require a fee. If you're looking for a new adventure, classes are a good way to explore and build a new hobby or interest and meet new people along the way. If you don't find a class that sparks your curiosity, revisit the category in another month to see what new classes are coming up.

Catapult Your Career in Jobs and Gigs

Why look for a job on craigslist? There are lots of reasons! For starters, the site is expanding quickly and is fast becoming a great source for job prospects around the globe. A growing community of employers and job seekers flock to craigslist, and with increased traffic comes increased opportunities. With this rising community, you can find jobs not usually listed on other job sites, including lots of part-time and job-flex positions. craigslist also offers a secure and convenient way to search for job listings. Anonymous email addresses protect both the employer and the job seeker until further contact is agreed upon. Those are just a few of the reasons for job searching on craigslist.

You can find job opportunities in both the **jobs** category and the **gigs** category. This section shows you what you can anticipate finding in each area. Although you had a bit of an introduction to these categories in Chapters 10, "Listing in Jobs and Gigs," and 11, "Listing in Resumes," on how to add a job listing or post a resume, this section will tell you a little more about what you can expect to find in these categories and how to search through the listings for potential jobs.

Job Search Tips

When searching for a job, whether temporary, part-time, or full-time, expect to spend a lot of time scanning through craigslist job categories. Looking through listings and trying various search techniques is a time-consuming process.

Try to use specific terms in your searches. For example, start by typing job titles like **sales manager** or **data entry clerk** in the **search for:** field. Remember, newer listings are added to the top of the page, while older listings move down to make room for newer ads. If your search results still aren't displaying the listings you want, you might search only the listing titles. Check the **only search titles** check box in the search field area.

Unfortunately, craigslist might not allow you to use wildcards (*), such as **librar*** to search for **librarian, library**, or **libraries**. (This restriction doesn't seem to apply to all areas of the country, though, so give it a try.) craigslist also doesn't support conventional Boolean searches. But you can place an apostrophe (') just before each search term, which acts as an OR to help narrow results. You also can put terms in parentheses, separated by commas, to perform an OR search. To exclude a term in the search results, precede it with a minus sign in the **search for:** field.

 If you're trying to be very precise with your searches, consider using a site like Yahoo Pipes (http://pipes.yahoo.com/pipes/) to combine craigslist RSS feeds and filter out unwanted listing titles.

Some shady companies and individuals post illegitimate jobs online, so watch out. Following these tips should help you to sort the real jobs from the shady ones:

- Job ads should include some actual details about the job itself, such as a job description. Because most employers don't want to be bombarded with questions, they try to write ads that address questions up front.

- If the ad lists a website, check it out. If the site's legitimate, you know you're looking at a real job listing instead of a scam. Also, checking out the company's website can give you some insight as to what it is and what it does.

- Job ads that advertise "no experience necessary" are sometimes shady. Most jobs require skills of some kind, so approach any that state otherwise with caution.

- If a job ad rolls several different job descriptions into one, such as marketing, sales, and advertising, the job may be impossible to fill. Most of these areas require completely different skill sets or personality types.

Now that you know what to look for, you're ready to jump into the job section.

Perusing the Job Listings

One look at the **jobs** category on the main craigslist page will tell you that there are a lot of areas to search, as shown in Figure 14.9. Depending on what metropolitan area or region of the country you're searching, the number of listings within each category will vary.

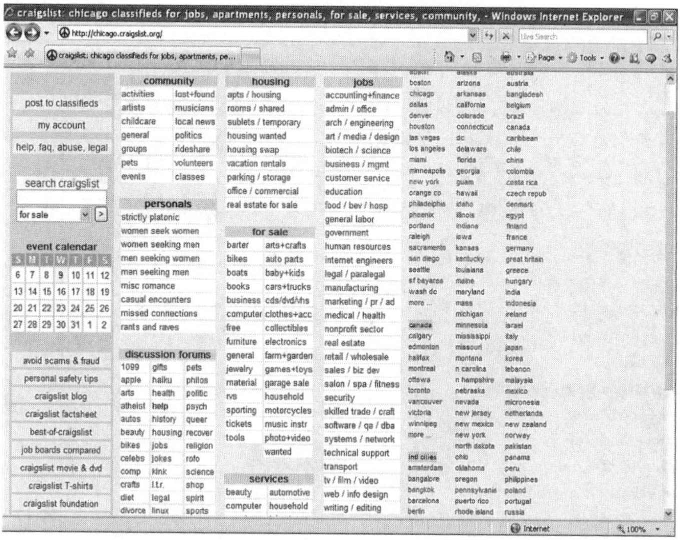

Figure 14.9
The **jobs** section is vast and full of listings.

Each category targets a specific job area, such as **accounting+finance** or **customer service**. So if you're looking for a job as a teacher, your best bet is to start looking in the **education** category.

The **[ETC]** category in the list includes jobs that don't necessarily fit into other categories, as well as listings for paid focus groups and research studies. The **[part time]** category is actually made up of listings from the other job categories. If a poster indicates that a job they are listing is part time, that listing is automatically cross-posted to the **[part time]** category.

To start searching through jobs, simply choose a category; then enter the keyword(s) you want to search for, such as **receptionist** or **analyst**. It's also a good idea to browse through the list of titles and see what's available. Figure 14.10 shows an example of typical listings found on any given day in the Chicago area.

How fresh are the job listings on craigslist? If the job posting is from a large metropolitan area, such as Chicago or Los Angeles, listings are kept online for 30 days. In all other smaller areas, job listings appear online for 45 days.

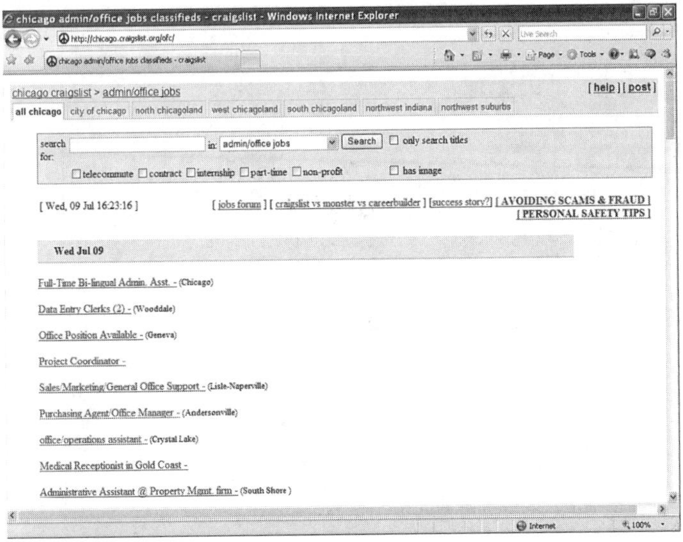

Figure 14.10
Peruse the **jobs** categories regularly to keep abreast of what's available.

Perusing the Gigs

The **gigs** section of craigslist is a compendium of job listings for independent contractors. These jobs are not permanent in-house positions, but rather positions that need temporary filling or one-time projects. For example, a company may need a special brochure written and is looking for a self-employed writer to tackle the project, or someone may be looking for help with a yard cleanup project that's only expected to take a couple of days. The **gigs** section is the place to look for short-term, long-term, internships, and other types of independent contractor jobs. The section offers nine categories, as described in Table 14.1.

Table 14.1 Categories in the gigs Section

Gigs	Categories
computer	All facets of IT-type jobs, programming, Internet research, computer installation and maintenance, and so on

Gigs	Categories
<u>creative</u>	Creative arts, such as photography, graphic design, writing, modeling, editing, and so on
<u>crew</u>	Different types of production work: production designers, makeup artists, producers, film editors, and so on
<u>domestic</u>	Housekeeping, cooking, personal assistants.
<u>event</u>	Event-related positions: bartenders, caterers, servers, greeters, promotions, modeling, and so on
<u>labor</u>	Manual and physical labor positions: building and contracting, yard work, home remodeling, and so on
<u>writing</u>	All facets of writing: technical writing, advertising copy, blogging, grant writing, Web writing, translating, editing, and so on
<u>talent</u>	Models, actors, singers, dancers.
<u>adult</u>	Modeling and acting for the adult entertainment industry, escort agencies, and so on

Responding to Job Listings

Finding a job listing is half the battle; responding to it is the other half. When you find a listing you want to respond to, simply click the link supplied in the ad. Some ads offer links to their own websites for contacting them regarding a job; others use their own email addresses.

Many ads utilize the craigslist email system. You'll know it's a craigslist email address if the end of the link includes *@craigslist.org*. When you click the **Reply to** link, it opens an email message in your default email program. The message has the reply address in the **to** field and the listing title in the **subject** line, making it a breeze to send off a message to the person listing the job.

When applying for a job, follow these four surefire tips:

- **Write a cover letter**. Your cover letter should address the position listed in the ad. Don't just attach your resume and let it fly. Take time to write a proper cover letter in your email.

- **Apply in a timely fashion**. For most employers, responses come in the first few days of posting an ad. If you wait a few days before responding, the position may already be filled.

- **Submit a resume**. A well-written resume describes your successes, skills, and experience. Make sure that yours is error-free and easy to read. Be certain to submit your resume following the guidelines in the listing.

- **Follow the directions.** Two of the most important qualities employers usually look for are attention to detail and the ability to follow directions. Many a job seeker has blown his chance simply by not paying attention to the instructions in the job posting. For example, a growing number of companies will not open email attachments. If they are asking for email submissions, they'll require your resume to be included in the body of your email. If a listing doesn't specify a preference, I would play it safe and include both.

Good luck with your job search, and don't give up. You never know what's going to show up on craigslist the next day!

 Warning 4U As with other areas of craigslist, be on the lookout for scams. Although the craigslist staff works hard to minimize the number of scams posted, some sneak by. Check out the **AVOIDING SCAMS & FRAUD** link at the top of any **jobs** category page to learn more.

Fill Your Social Calendar with the Personals

Are you looking for love, companionship, or just friends? Apparently, you're not alone. The **personals** section on craigslist is one of the busiest areas on the site. The **personals** section is a world unto itself, and it's not for the faint of heart. This section introduces you to the listings and how to search them safely.

Warning: Enter at Your Own Risk

Before I introduce you to the adult aspect of the **personals** section, I feel I should share a few warnings first. Unlike some of the other dating sites on the Internet, the craigslist **personals** section often seems to operate with an "anything goes" kind of attitude—literally. Listings in this section can be very graphic, both in text and visuals. With many other online dating sites, users pay a fee and rules of conduct are strongly enforced. In craigslist **personals**, there are some rules, which I'll go over shortly, but by and large you can expect to encounter a *lot* of adult content. Perhaps because listings are free and anonymous, posters are often brazen and uninhibited. If you're not expecting this the first time you peruse the listings, the content can be a bit shocking.

As mentioned in the craigslist terms of use, "craigslist does not control and is not responsible for content made available through the service, and […] by using the service, you may be exposed to content that is offensive, indecent, misleading, or otherwise objectionable." This definitely applies to the **personals** section, so consider yourself forewarned.

So on that note, here are the rules for this section:

1. You must be at least 18 years old to enter the **personals** section of craigslist.

2. You must understand that all the categories within the **personals** section may include adult content.

3. You agree to flag as "prohibited" anything illegal or which otherwise violates the craigslist terms of use.

4. You agree to report suspected exploitation of minors to the appropriate authorities.

5. By entering the **personals** section, you release craigslist from any liability that may arise from your use of the site.

Visit Chapter 12, "Listing in Personals," to learn about safe dating with craigslist. You can find more tips by clicking the **PERSONAL SAFETY TIPS** link on the main page.

Tip 4U Worried about children accessing craigslist's **personals** section? craigslist has implemented the Platform for Internet Content Selection (PICS) content-labeling system, a Web standard for helping parents and teachers to control what children see on the Internet. It works with content-control software to help filter out unwanted Web content. A good content-control application can really help keep kids safe online, and you can find more information about programs compatible with your computer on the Web.

Using an anonymous email address specifically for this section of the site is an extremely good idea. In fact, it would be foolish not to. As on any area of the Internet, you need to protect yourself. Although you've seen such information mentioned countless times before, a few commonsense tips can help you to navigate these choppy waters:

- Create a separate email account to respond to craigslist listings, and use an account that doesn't have your full name attached to it. Because this rule is so important, I'm mentioning it twice!

  - Don't give out personal information too quickly and never *ever* give out credit card numbers, Social Security numbers, or personal information of that type.

  - Make sure that you know what you're getting into and take it slowly. Research the person/people you're meeting, ask questions, check criminal records—whatever it takes to stay safe.

  - Trust your instincts, especially when your instincts sense danger or deception.

- If you find someone you trust enough to meet, choose a safe, very public spot. Consider bringing along a friend (safety in numbers, you know).

Don't worry about being picky. When it comes to meeting people online, many people agonize about turning off a potential dream date by being too specific or sounding too demanding or picky. Don't let your standards fall or become lax when it comes to online dating. As people often say, love typically happens when you least look for it, so if you're having trouble connecting through craigslist personals, consider jumping into the **activities**, **groups**, and **volunteers** categories in the **community** section to look for extracurricular activities to pursue. You never know who you might meet along the way.

Many people try to be open to a relationship with someone who lives outside a reasonable traveling distance or who is unfamiliar with the challenges of a long-distance relationship. I advise you to think long and hard before jumping into romance from afar. Love is grand if it's realistic, but difficult and stressful if you aren't prepared or have unrealistic expectations.

Online romance is always a tricky endeavor, but if you use common sense, screen the listings you respond to, and screen emails in response to any listings of yours, you should be okay. Remember, you're never obligated to answer anyone's email.

Personals Categories: Something for Everyone

The craigslist **personals** section operates a lot like the classified ads in your paper, grouping interests into nine different categories:

- **strictly platonic**
- **women seeking women**
- **women seeking men**
- **men seeking women**
- **men seeking men**
- **misc romance**
- **casual encounters**
- **missed connections**
- **rants and raves**

Most of the categories are self-explanatory although some are a bit vague. For example, the idea behind the **strictly platonic** category is friendship-building. Very often this category isn't really platonic. Terms like "open-minded" or "likes to try new things" can be subtle ways of indicating that the person is looking for more. If you're truly looking for friends, try searching the **events**, **groups**, **classes**, and **activities** categories in the **community** section.

The **misc romance** and **casual encounters** categories are pretty much open for anything. The **missed connections** category is more along the lines of missed opportunities. Say someone caught your eye, but you didn't have the courage to talk to that person and now you can't stop thinking about it. Go to **missed connections** and see if you caught his or her eye, too.

The **rants and raves** category is exactly what its name implies—a lot of ranting and raving about anything and everything, from sports to the opposite sex.

When searching through many of these categories, you can set a minimum and a maximum age range in the **Poster's Age** fields. You can also choose to view only ads with images, or search only the title text and not in the listings. Spend some time scanning through the listing titles in these sections to help you figure out what keywords you want to search for to narrow your results.

From Here...

Now you know your way around the <u>community</u>, <u>personals</u>, <u>jobs</u>, and <u>gigs</u> sections. In the next chapter, you'll learn how to navigate the <u>housing</u>, <u>services</u>, <u>for sale</u>, and <u>resumes</u> sections.

Win-Win Results in Listings

So far in Part III, we've covered how to respond to listings, pursue activities in the craigslist community, find a friend or date, and search for potential jobs. Are you ready for the rest of craigslist? This chapter polishes off the remaining sections.

If wheeling-and-dealing is your goal, the **housing**, **for sale**, and **services** sections should be just your thing. This chapter covers how to use the **housing** section on craigslist to find real estate properties, vacation rentals, apartments, and other housing situations. If you're looking for stuff rather than property, the **for sale** section is sure to tickle your fancy. Whether you're looking for furniture, a car, collectible items, farm equipment, or event tickets, you'll learn how to search through listings and find just what you want.

Perhaps you're looking for some help with painting the house, or you need a good plumber or maybe someone to repair your treasured vacuum cleaner? The craigslist **services** section is all about selling expertise and know-how. You'll learn how to search through services to find a dependable person to help you with your needs, or post your own services. This **services** section is also where you'll find product listings. Odd as it might seem, the **for sale** section is for private listings only. Regardless of whether they are selling a product or service, all businesses are supposed to list in the **services** section.

Finally, are you an employer looking for help? You'll find out how to scan through the <u>resumes</u> section of craigslist to find qualified people to fill whatever position you have open.

Find Your New Abode in Housing

Everyone needs shelter, even if it's just for a day. The craigslist <u>housing</u> section features a myriad of housing categories to meet your shelter needs. You'll find listings for homes, apartments, house swapping, vacation rentals, storage, even office and other commercial properties. Whether you're renting, buying, or swapping, craigslist is an excellent source for lodging selections. In this section, you'll learn your way around all the housing categories and how to use them to find a place to stay.

The <u>housing</u> section offers the following categories:

- <u>apts/housing</u>
- <u>rooms/shared</u>
- <u>sublets/temporary</u>
- <u>housing wanted</u>
- <u>housing swap</u>
- <u>vacation rentals</u>
- <u>parking/storage</u>
- <u>office/commercial</u>
- <u>real estate for sale</u>

The best way to search among the housing categories is to select the category you want to look through and then enter additional information into search boxes to narrow the results. For example, if you want to search a specific neighborhood, type in the name; if you're looking for a set amount of square footage, include it in the <u>search for:</u> field. Do you prefer new construction, a renovated home, woods or water nearby? Are you looking for something on the north side, south side, or downtown? All of these are keywords to use when searching for housing.

In all the craigslist categories, you can choose to search titles only, or only listings that include images. In addition to these ever-present check boxes, other search tools may appear, depending on what category you select. In **apts/housing**, the additional search tools include fields for setting a minimum and maximum dollar amount for rental prices, and a pop-up menu for choosing how many bedrooms you want (see Figure 15.1). You can also specify cats or dogs if you're looking for pet-friendly locales. You'll learn more about these special search settings in the sections to come.

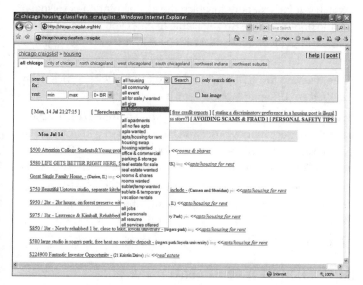

Figure 15.1
Use the search fields to narrow your search through the listings.

Tip 4U
If you're searching for apartments in New York City, the first page you see after clicking the **apts/housing** category is a page offering several ways to view apartment listings. You can choose to view all apartments, all no-fee apartments, by-owner apartments, or registration fee (a subscription-fee-based apartment location service).

Start your search with only a couple of terms to get broad results, and refine your search from there. Remember that people often refer to things differently. Depending on your location, ownership, and design, a single residence in multi-family housing could be called an apartment, a co-op, a flat, a unit, a condo, or a townhouse—and those are not all the possibilities.

When entering listings, people often misspell words, so if you aren't getting the results you want, play around with your search terms.

As with everything on the craigslist site, be wary of scams. Here are a few cautionary tips:

- **Meet the person who's selling/renting.** In the **housing** section, watch out for situations in which the person renting or selling a home or rental place isn't available to meet you in person. I can't state this point enough: deal with people you can meet in person!

- **Avoid wiring funds.** If you're asked to use any wire service, such as Western Union or MoneyGram, it's probably a scam.

- **Watch out for counterfeit checks.** If you attempt to cash a counterfeit check or money order, the bank will hold you responsible a few weeks later when the fake is found out. Be sure that the source and the financial institution issuing the check are credible.

- **Don't give out financial info.** Never give out your Social Security number, bank account numbers, or any other financial information.

- **Avoid escrow services.** These services are rife with scams.

Looking for Houses or Apartments to Rent

The listings in the **apts/housing** category include apartments to rent, homes to lease, lease-to-own offers, furnished apartments, townhouses, and the like. The majority of the listings are rentals. When you first display this category onscreen, the search tools include options for searching for a rental price range, number of bedrooms, and check boxes for choosing whether the lodging allows cats or dogs. Figure 15.2 shows a typical page of listings from the south Florida area, including Miami.

The best way to look through this category is to specify the location and the number of bedrooms you need. You can go on to specify a price range and add any additional keywords to further narrow your search. When you find a listing you want to reply to, simply click the appropriate email link and fire off a message with your questions or stating your interest. If the rental market is strong in the area you're searching, you may have to put some extra work into diligently checking the listings several times a day.

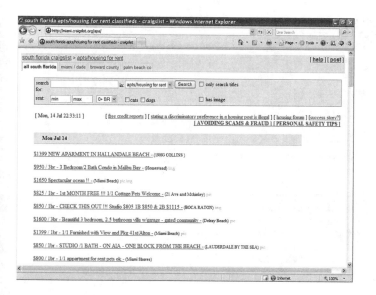

Figure 15.2
Use the **apts/housing** category to look for a place to rent.

Finding Rooms or Roommates

Are you looking for a roommate situation? The craigslist **rooms & shares** category (called **rooms/shared** on the craigslist homepage) is the place to search for shared living arrangements (see Figure 15.3). As with the apartment and housing rentals, you can set a minimum and maximum rental price range to conduct a search. You can also search for accommodations that allow cats or dogs. When comparing listings, be sure to take into consideration any stated utility costs.

When responding to a listing in this category, be sure to ask lots of pertinent questions, such as finding out about access to parking, kitchen, and laundry amenities; whether a deposit is expected; and so on. You should also be mindful of the importance of personalities in shared living situations. Factors like neatness expectations, personal hygiene (such as smokers versus nonsmokers), noise, schedules, and a lot of other little issues can affect the success of any living arrangement. Be sure to ask questions pertaining to these issues, especially when meeting the person face to face.

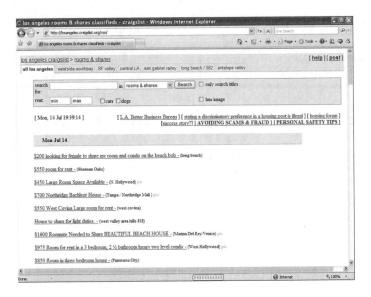

Figure 15.3
Use the **rooms & shares** category to look for a roommate.

Seeking Sublets or Temporary Spots

If you're looking for a short-term living situation, try the **sublets & temporary** category. Here, you'll find listings for rental and lease opportunities, furnished and unfurnished apartments, and homes. This category is ideal for anyone in between more permanent living arrangements. For example, you might be building a house, but you've already sold your last home and need somewhere to stay. Temporary housing might be just what you need. Or maybe you're in town for a short while for a work project and only need a small space until you're finished. Figure 15.4 shows an example of listings from the **sublets & temporary** category.

Sublets are residences rented out by tenants to a third party. This happens when tenants sign a lease and then for some reason can't stay the required amount of time, so they sublet the space to someone else for the duration of the lease. Some landlords allow this practice, others don't, so make sure that everything is cleared before entering into such arrangements.

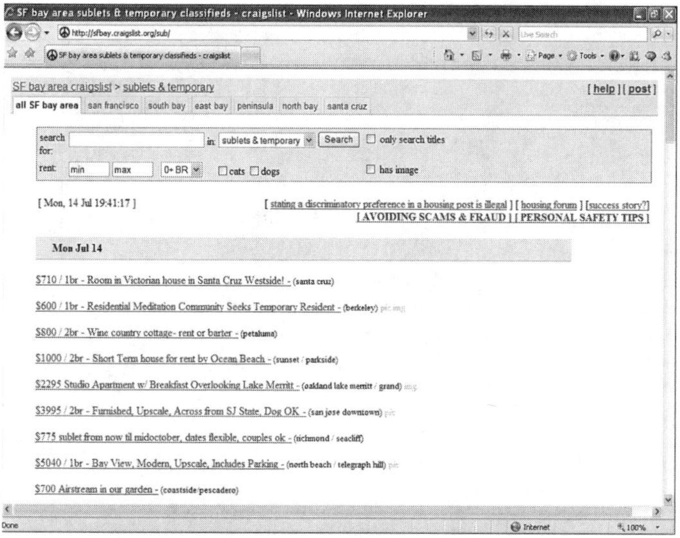

Figure 15.4
Use the **sublets & temporary** category to look for temporary housing.

When searching through this category, you can plug in the desired rental range and choose whether dogs or cats are allowed. When inquiring about a listing, be sure to find out the length of the short-term stay. Many listings mention this information up front; others may not.

Housing Wanted

The **housing wanted** category listings are for tenants, renters, or potential owners looking for housing situations for themselves. In other words, these are folks listing their needs to find shelter. If you're a property owner, apartment owner, or need someone to share living arrangements, you can find potential renters/sharers in this category. Among the search options you can specify are rental price range, number of bedrooms, and pet allowances. Figure 15.5 shows an example of listings from this category found in the Dallas area.

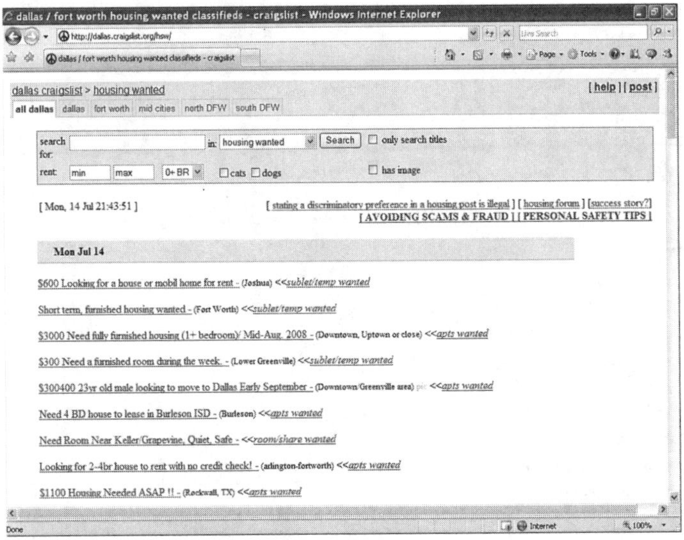

Figure 15.5
The <u>**housing wanted**</u> category is for people who are looking for a home.

Swapping Houses

The <u>**housing swap**</u> category is all about trading homes permanently or temporarily. For example, maybe you're looking for a week-long getaway on the other side of the country? Maybe it's cold where you live and you want a weekend in a sunny spot somewhere else. There just might be someone who'll swap locations with you for a while. Other listings in this category are looking for permanent swaps. Figure 15.6 shows an example of listings typically found in this category.

The listings in this category mention time frames, descriptions of the homes, and areas in which they're located. Pictures frequently are included. If you're looking for a swap, locate the city or area on craigslist, and then look for a listing suiting your time frame and travel needs. The nice thing about a temporary swap is that no real money is needed, other than expenses you'll incur traveling to and from the destination swap, and the food and activities required when you get there.

Figure 15.6
You can use the __housing swap__ category to swap houses for a vacation.

For permanent swaps, the listings in this category are generally from people wanting to move back to an area or who just got a new job in the region. House trading can also be useful for investors who want to transfer holdings from one area to another. Strangely enough, the properties don't have to be of equal value because cash or mortgages can cover the difference. The odds of finding a good swap, however, are slim. When two parties are swapping houses permanently, both deals should close simultaneously and should use the same title company at closing. It's not a good idea to swap a house with someone who owes more than the house is worth. Consult with legal help or a real estate expert for more information about this concept and to make sure that the swap is on the up-and-up.

Finding Vacation Rentals

Are you looking for a vacation getaway? Try shopping around craigslist's __vacation rentals__ category. Here, you'll find all kinds of abodes available for rental. For example, you may want to find a house or condo for a two-week stay in Florida, or maybe you're planning to visit family and need a bigger place to rest your head at night. Perhaps you're looking for a remote cabin for a fishing adventure or a more cosmopolitan spot in the middle of a bustling tourist area. Whether you're looking for something in your favorite holiday dream locale or just something near a specific destination, the vacation rentals category might just fit the bill. Figure 15.7 shows some sample listings from the Florida Keys area.

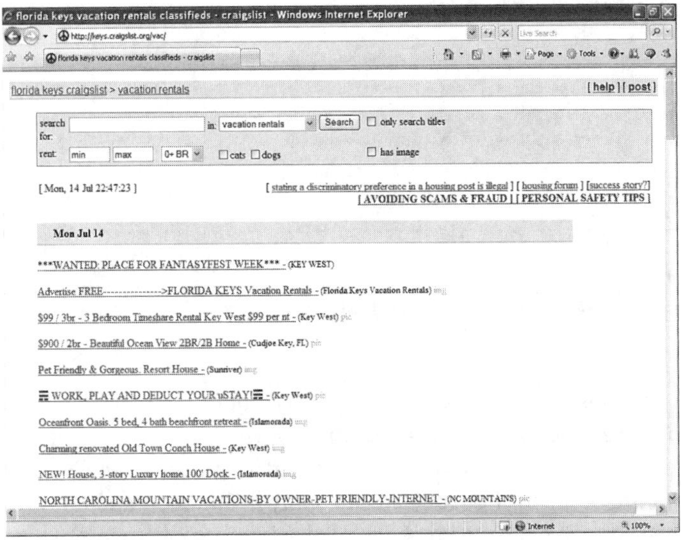

Figure 15.7
Find your next vacation getaway in the **vacation rentals** category.

When inquiring about vacation rentals, keep in mind that dealing directly with the owner of the property is much better than going through an agent. The owner knows the property well and can answer specific questions. Also remember that terms like *beachfront*, *beach view*, *ocean view*, *steps to beach*, and *beach accessibility* can mean very different things. With some places, the only access to the shore is through a crowded public beach, which may be far from the rental property. Beaches can also be located on bays instead of directly on the ocean, and waterfront views can mean canals or bays as well. You would be wise to ask specific questions to find out what's in store.

You should also inquire about amenities, such as parking, laundry, spa or pool use, linens and towels, cooking items and dishes, television and Internet access, and so on. If you're planning on bringing along pets, always ask if they're allowed. The same is true regarding smoking privileges.

Finally, be very clear about vacation time, reservations, deposits, and booking policies. Getting these items in writing is always good to protect all parties involved in the transaction.

Searching for Storage Space

Are you in desperate need of some storage space? Perhaps you need a large spot to store your boat or camper. Or maybe you have a garage full of possessions you need to store somewhere else for a while. You can search through the craigslist **parking & storage** category to find all kinds of storage options for all sizes of stuff. This category lists docking slips, warehouse space, self-storage facilities, storage containers, and more. When searching for storage space, you can specify a minimum and maximum rental rate. When inquiring about storage space, be sure to ask about deposits, monthly or yearly rental costs, security issues, utility costs, and the like. Figure 15.8 shows an example of storage listings from the San Diego area.

Looking for Commercial Space

If you're looking for office or warehouse space, try the **office & commercial** category in craigslist's housing area (see Figure 15.9). Here you'll find all kinds of buildings for commercial enterprises, from renting and leasing to buying. Whether you're looking for space to set up an executive office or an artist's studio, or a spot for a workshop or other labor-intensive pursuit, you'll find a myriad of options among the listings in this category.

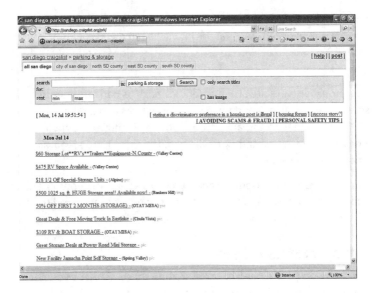

Figure 15.8
Use this category to look for storage space.

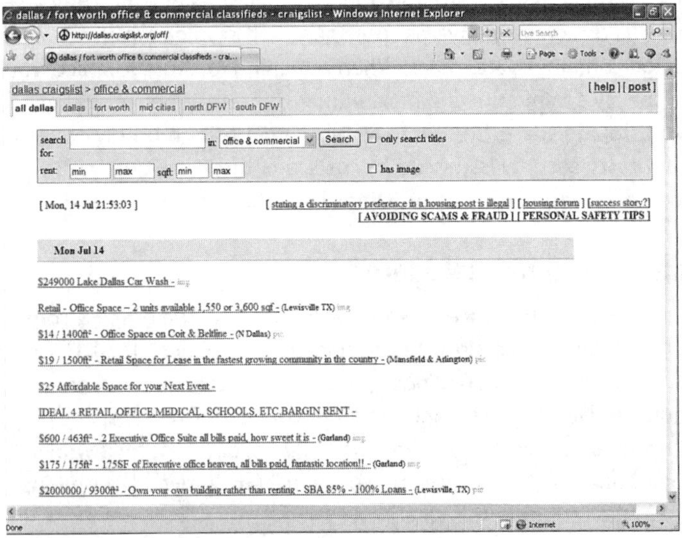

Figure 15.9
Use the **office & commercial** category to find commercial space.

When searching for a commercial property or space, start by choosing a city or area closest to the spot you want. If you don't see what you want, try expanding to another area close by. When replying to ads, don't delay; otherwise, you may end up losing the property that interests you. Be sure to respond as directed by the listing. Some ads include a phone number, others just an email address. Write down the listing's ID number so you can reference it in your response if you're calling. Because the listings are updated regularly, check back often to see what's been added.

Real Estate for Sale

The last category in housing is **real estate for sale**. This category lists houses for sale. It includes new construction, old homes, condos, duplexes, and more. Before you jump in and start looking, here are a few tips that can help your craigslist search prove more profitable:

- **Check your finances.** Take time to get your financial information in order, such as an updated credit report, an analysis of your financial situation (total income and expenses), important documents (tax returns, pay stubs), and so on.

- **Set a budget.** After determining whether your finances are in order, figure out what sort of budget you can afford and stick to it.

- **Mortgage preapproval.** Get preapproved for a mortgage. Doing so makes the whole process easier and helps you to know how much the lender approves for a home in your situation.

- **Determine a location.** Decide where you'll want to live, and do some homework to find out about the area you're looking into, average home prices, what sort of access you have to shopping, schools, public transportation, and so on.

- **List your wants and needs.** Make a list of things you're looking for in your next house, such as square footage, number of bedrooms and bathrooms, eat-in kitchen, single floor or multilevel, and garage. If you want to be really organized, list your wants and needs separately. This list can help you keep perspective as you look through various ads.

▥ **Note what you *don't* want.** Make a list of things you absolutely do not want, such as a noisy street location, stairs, limited backyard space, or a pool.

When you're armed with some crucial information up front, the search for a home will go much more smoothly. If you're looking to buy a house with some help from craigslist, start by searching the desired area or city. If you don't find many listings to suit your needs, try expanding the search to include outlying areas. Figure 15.10 shows an example of typical listings found in the **real estate for sale** category.

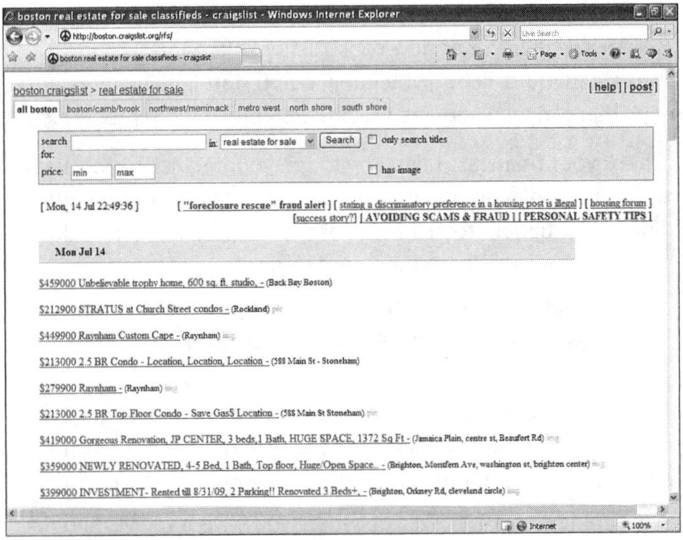

Figure 15.10
Use the **real estate for sale** category to find a house or condo to buy.

The **real estate for sale** category is a unique area of craigslist. Following the spirit of the site, all listings in this category must be about a particular property that is available. With that in mind, however, many real estate agents (rental and sales) advertise on craigslist using a house listed on the Multiple Listing Service (MLS) that isn't their listing. They do this looking for buyers/renters whom they can represent. Although this practice isn't horrible, it certainly is outside the spirit of craigslist. Also, it's good to know what you're getting into. One way to tell is that the agent will usually include some disclaimer that the information is from the MLS.

If the real estate terms in the listings baffle you, visit Chapter 7, "Listing in the Housing Section," to review a complete list of common real estate industry lingo.

When you're ready to make an inquiry about a listing, simply follow the instructions in the listing. Some ads ask you to respond using an email link; others might offer a phone number you can call. Be prepared to refer to the ad number if making a phone call, and let the person know where you saw the ad.

Let's Make a Deal in Merchandise

Are you looking for an item to buy or trade, or maybe you'd like to find something free? Check out the **for sale** section of craigslist for a huge selection of merchandise. Here, you can shop for everything from bikes and books to campers and cars. Just like the classified ads in the back of your local paper, the **for sale** section offers a wide variety of stuff you can buy locally, provided that you're willing to go and get it. There are 31 categories in this section of craigslist, and you can expect to find everything from the mundane to the obscure. Table 15.1 lists the categories and examples of what you can find within them.

Table 15.1   Categories of the for sale Section

Category	Description
barter	Trade something you don't want for something you do—anything from appliances and electronics to cars and trucks.
bikes	Bicycles, scooters, motorbikes, mountain bikes, and accessories.
boats	Canoes, rafts, yachts, motorboats, fishing boats, sailboats, and anything that floats.

Category	Description
books	Fiction, nonfiction, college textbooks, dictionaries, encyclopedias, magazines, vintage books, and anything related to printed media.
business	Business and commercial equipment, office furniture, and gazillions of business schemes.
computer	Computers and technical paraphernalia: laptops, towers, peripherals, printers, computer furniture, parts, cables, and software.
free	Items people just want to get rid of, such as furniture, remodeling debris, firewood, swing sets.
furniture	Tables, recliners, couches, chairs, mattresses, desks, bedroom sets, and cabinets.
general	A catchall category for items that don't necessarily fit into other categories or are listed in two or more places.
jewelry	Gemstones, diamonds, gold, silver, rings, earrings, necklaces, bracelets, watches, antique and costume jewelry.
material	Construction materials, fencing, flooring, shingles, reclaimed fireplace mantels, windows, and so on
rvs	Recreational vehicles of all kinds: campers, trailers, and motor homes.
sporting	All kinds of sporting and fitness equipment: treadmills, ping-pong tables, golf clubs, home gyms, rollerblades, punching bags, and more.
tickets	All kinds of event tickets: concerts, bands, plays, orchestras, races, headliners and entertainers, and sporting events.
tools	Saws, routers, welders, ladders, hoists, drill presses, jacks, and so on.
arts+crafts	Artistic endeavors of all kinds: paintings, prints, scrapbooking supplies, sewing machines, yarn, rubber stamps, quilts, and so on
auto parts	Axles, bumpers, tires, rims, doors, shells, engine and mechanical parts galore.
baby+kids	Kid's furniture, clothing, toys, play sets, high chairs, and baby paraphernalia.
cars+trucks	All kinds of cars and trucks, vintage, classic, modern, and new.
cds/dvd/vhs	Music, movies, and TV shows in all three media formats, classic to new releases.
clothes+acc	All kinds of clothing and accessories, coats, purses, scarves, hats, shoes, and so on
collectibles	Antiques, coins, stamps, dolls, toys, furniture, baskets, lunchboxes, and so on
electronics	Cell phones, iPods, BlackBerries, game consoles, CD players, TVs, cameras, digital camcorders, stereo equipment, projection TVs, and anything electronic.

Category	Description
farm+garden	Farm equipment, plows, turkeys, chickens, horses, plants, tractors, mowers, tillers, garden produce, and much more.
games+toys	Game consoles and games that go on them, computer games, air hockey tables, board games, radio-control boats, and children's toys.
garage sale	Listings of local garage and moving sales, including yard sales, tag sales, neighborhood sales, and estate sales.
household	Anything related to household items: refrigerators, stoves, washers and dryers, dishwashers, microwaves, grills, humidifiers, decorator items, air conditioners, furniture, dishes, and so on.
motorcycles	Everything related to motorcycles and scooters: parts, scooters, Harleys, Hondas, dirt bikes, seats, trailers, and so on
music instr	Pianos, guitars, keyboards, trombones, violins, amps, music stands, drum sets, saxophones, speaker systems, and more.
photo+video	Camcorders, cameras, lenses, darkroom equipment, photo printers, batteries, film, enlargers, underwater cases, and anything related to photography or videography.
wanted	Listings looking for specific kinds of items, such as furniture, computers, tickets, antiques, and so on

Whew! That's quite a list of categories. As you can imagine, each is filled with various listings from time to time, or sometimes all the time. Most of the categories are pretty self-explanatory. Some might involve listings in two or more places, but most are reasonably clear-cut. The only one to really watch out for is the **business** category, which seems to be a haven for all kinds of business schemes and moneymaking opportunities that are often just scams. These particular listings typically have links to take you elsewhere on the Web, so be warned.

When searching through items for sale, you can either select a specific category and search within it, or start with the **for sale** section link at the top of the category, go to the **for sale** search page, and enter relevant search terms to search all the categories. You can then begin narrowing from that point using more specific search terms. When conducting a search through the **for sale** items, you can specify a minimum and maximum price, as shown in Figure 15.11.

Limiting your search this way might help if you're shopping for cars, a new boat, or a game console system.

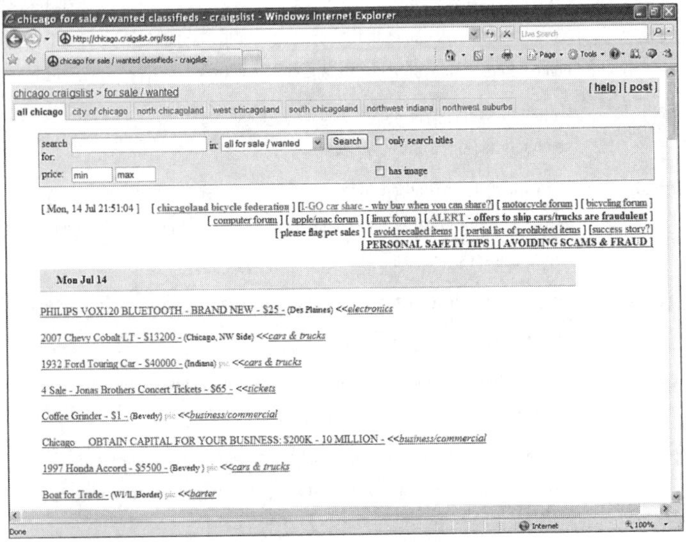

Figure 15.11
Use the search tools to help narrow your search results.

Depending on the ad, some listings allow you to call to inquire, whereas others simply provide an email link you can click. When you call, be sure to refer to the craigslist ad you're inquiring about. Some users run multiple (unrelated) listings, and they might not know which ad you're referring to if you don't tell them directly.

Here are some more tips to help after you think you've found the next bargain:

- As you search for items, make sure that you're searching areas and locales in which you're willing to drive to and view the item. For example, if the seller is an hour away, you may not want to drive that far to find out whether it's the item you want, especially if the price of the item is less than the cost of the gas you'll consume.

- The first person to respond usually has a better chance of getting the item, so be timely in your inquiries.

- When picking up an item, make sure that you've thought of everything. Do you have enough room in your vehicle to haul away the item, or do you need extra hands to help load it?

- Always show up with the agreed-upon amount of cash. Negotiating is okay unless the seller indicates the price is firm. It never hurts to ask.

- For your own safety, take along a friend when you're going to view an item. Safety in numbers, they say.

If you don't find what you want right away, keep on checking. The listings are updated regularly, and you never know what's going to pop up the next time you look.

Get It Done with Services

The **services** section is the place to go to search for all kinds of services, everything from accounting services to carpet cleaning to tree removal. Services generally center around someone's expertise or labor. There are 17 categories under **services**. Table 17.2 shows examples of what you can expect to find listed in each category.

Table 17.2   Categories of the services Section

Category	Description
beauty	Hairdressers and salons, makeup artists, tanning booths, bridal hair and makeup specialists, laser hair removal, manicures and pedicures, and anything related to the world of fashion and beauty.
computer	Certified technicians, custom website designers, programmers, computer repair, and related computer technology services.
creative	Artists offering services: photographers, graphic designers, talent scouts, wedding photographers and videographers, and so on
erotic	Adult entertainment and escorts.
event	Party and wedding planners, bands and musicians, DJs, bartenders and wait staff, personal chefs, children's party entertainers, and event suppliers.

Category	Description
financial	Accountants, financial advisors, insurance agents, stockbrokers, bookkeepers, and so on
legal	Legal services of all kinds: lawyers, divorce attorneys, tax attorneys, bankruptcy services, and so on.
lessons	Music lessons, golf lessons, tennis lessons, sewing lessons, tutors, personal trainers, language lessons, and more.
automotive	Mechanics, auto restorers, body work, and all other kinds of garage and car repair.
household	Pet sitting, organizers, cleaning services, heating and cooling experts, laundry services, carpet cleaners, and so on
labor/move	Movers, hauling and delivery, vehicle transportation, yard work, debris removal and other manual labor services.
skill'd trade	Painters, plumbers, electricians, carpenters, general contractors, carpet installers, chimney cleaning, flooring installers, piano tuners, and more.
real estate	Real estate agents, brokers, and property managers.
sm biz ads	Listings from small businesses of all kinds.
therapeutic	Massages, acupuncturists, hypnosis, counseling, and so on
travel/vac	Travel agents, vacation rentals, and deals.
write/ed/tr8	Writers, editors, copywriters, transcription services, resume writing, translators, grant writers, and so on (tr8 is short for "translate.")

Here again, most of the categories are fairly straightforward. You'd expect to find movers listed in the **labor/move** category or a hair-dresser advertising services in the **beauty** category. Figure 15.12 shows a sample of listings from the skilled trade category in Indianapolis.

Some of the categories are a bit more vague and often have a pot-pourri of listings. For example, the financial, legal, real estate, small business ads, and travel/vacation categories may include get-rich ideas, links to disreputable websites, and other scams. Just use caution when perusing these areas. There are often illegitimate businesses masquerading as real businesses in these areas.

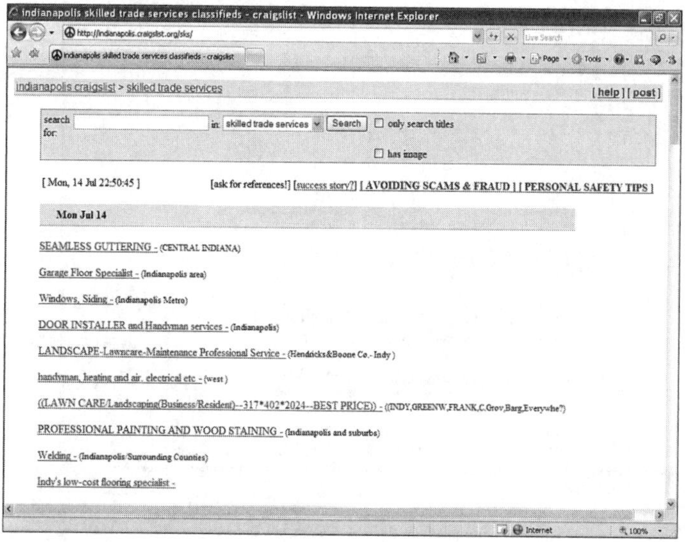

Figure 15.12
The **services** section of craigslist offers all kinds of services, from small business owners and contractors to large corporations.

One area that does necessitate its own separate discussion from the rest is the **erotic** category. One doesn't normally associate the word *erotic* with business, but you'll see why in a minute. When you attempt to enter the **erotic** services area, a warning screen appears, as shown in Figure 15.13, prompting you to assert that you're at least 18 years old to be able to continue. Of course, there's no bouncer at the door here at craigslist, so anyone can click right on through. The warning screen also tries to signify that human trafficking and exploitation of minors are not tolerated, but this category really relies on the craigslist community to report any such violations. In many respects, this category of craigslist (along with some of the **personals** areas) is the sordid underbelly of a generally well-intended community-reaching website.

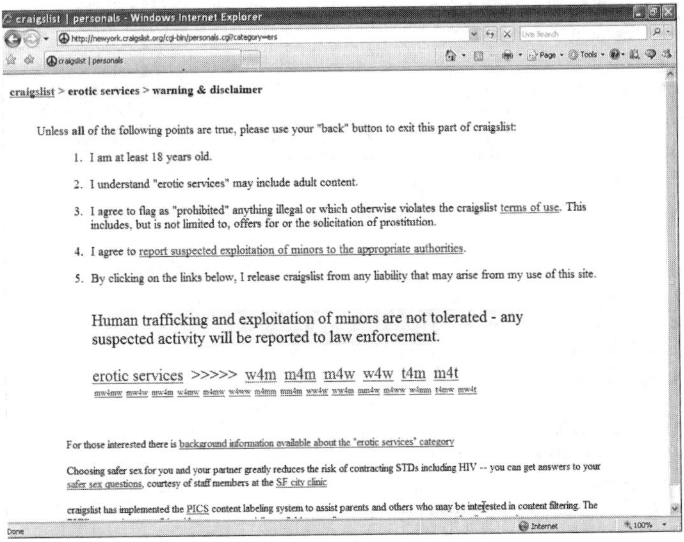

Figure 15.13
The warning screen that appears when you enter the **erotic** services category of the site.

Loosely billing itself as a category for adult entertainment, massage, and escort services, in some communities the **erotic** services category is mostly about prostitution and other interactions. Move very cautiously when considering responding to listings in the erotic category. Unless such behavior is legal in your state, you'd better have your lawyer's phone number handy when pursuing this area of craigslist. News reports sometimes describe police breaking up a prostitution ring on craigslist and throwing the participants and perpetrators in jail.

The listings found in this category of craigslist are predominantly prostitutes seeking clients for both "incalls" and "outcalls," which is code for "my place" or "yours" (or somewhere else). In fact, there's a lot of secret code here that only a "professional service provider" would really understand. For example, many of the listings actually mention the price of the service, but not in dollar amounts. Instead, an ad might advertise a girl for "crazy fun" for the bargain price of

200 roses/incall or 300 roses/outcall. A lot of these ads also show pictures, suggestive or graphic in nature. The vast majority of these pictures are NOT the person doing the listing, but borrowed from other better-lit sources.

A scant few of the listings even take time to present fine print that says something to the effect of "I am not soliciting, implying, offering, or selling anything. Any donations given are considered to be gifts for my time and modeling, and are not in any way to be considered as compensation for any actions that may or may not occur between two consenting adults." Such lawyerly terms and conditions probably come out of a previous run-in with law enforcement officials.

craigslist added the **erotic** category to the **services** section, in part, to help reduce the number of erotic listings that were showing up in the other **services** categories and in the **personals** section. Although this activity is extremely hard to track and verify, craigslist is making a concerted effort to address illegal activity listings throughout the various communities. Management openly and willingly cooperates with law enforcement agencies across the U.S. Users can continue to do their part by flagging questionable ads and not responding to any listings.

Fill That Job Opening in Resumes

The **resumes/job wanted** category is just what its name implies: an area to post your resume and sort of send up an "I'm for hire" flag to the craigslist community. Chapter 11, "Listing in Resumes," discusses the details of posting a resume in this area. If you're an employer looking for a good employee and you're not having any luck posting your ad in the regular **jobs** section, this area of craigslist might prove to be an excellent place to look. Figure 15.14 shows a sample page of resume listings from the Seattle area.

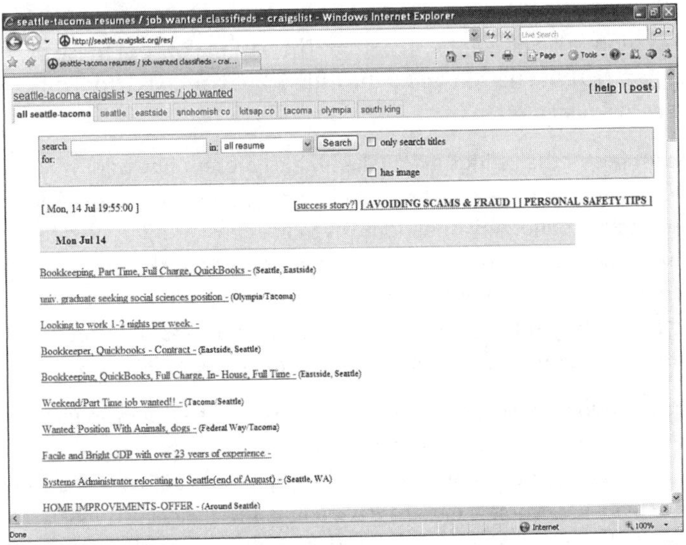

Figure 15.14
The **resumes** section of craigslist is the place where job seekers post their resumes for consideration.

When you're searching here, your best bet is to enter specific key-words pertaining to the type of job you need to fill or the types of skills you need, such as **computer**, **sales**, **advertising**, or job titles like **inventory management**, **payroll analyst**, or **interior designer**. When you find a potential applicant, you can fire off an email message describing the job position you have open and set up an interview. Because posters here are discouraged from including their names, addresses, and phone numbers to avoid scams and other misuse, you'll have to rely on email to make the first contact.

From Here...

In this chapter, you learned what's available in the **housing**, **for sale**, **services**, and **resumes** sections of the website. And if you started at the beginning, you now have the inside scoop on all of craigslist. If you haven't already, why don't you give craigslist a try? And if you have a question or a craigslist story to share, feel free to email me at c4e@craigslist4everyone.com!

Index

NUMBERS

24 Hours on craigslist, 28

4-1-9 scams, 53

A

abbreviations (personals section), 227-230

account settings page, 23

accounting+finance category (jobs section), 189

accounts
creating, 20-22
customizing settings, 23
handles, 33-35
passwords in, 22

acronyms (personals section), 227-230

Action (AIDA), listing creation, 87

activism (social). *See* volunteers category (community section)

activities category (community section), 255

activity partner section, 92

add a handle link, 33

admin/office category (jobs section), 189

ads
automated ads, 64
blocked ads, criteria for, 74-75
browsing, 245-246, 249
confirmation notices, 71
creating, 65, 70, 78-80, 85-88
DEA, 63
deleting, 76, 156
editing, 76
flagging links, 75
for sale section, 143-155
gigs section, writing for, 203-204
HTML formatting in, 73
jobs section, 65, 193-198, 201, 205-206, 268
layout of, 62-63
links, adding to, 73
office/commercial section (housing section), 136-137
personals section, writing for, 230-237, 241-242
pictures, 98
    adding to, 63, 67-69, 81-82, 88
    hosting, 73
previewing, 70, 156
prohibited items, 65, 74-75

real estate for sale category (housing section), 117-133

reposting, 88

responding to, 65, 156-157, 251-252

resumes, writing, 208-223

rules for, 64

services section
    automotive services category, 169-170
    beauty services category, 170-171
    computer services category, 171-172
    creative services category, 172-174
    erotic services category, 174
    event services category, 174
    financial services category, 175
    household services category, 176-177
    labor/move services category, 177
    legal services category, 178
    lessons category, 179-180
    marketing strategies, 164, 166-168
    offering free content, 168
    phone verification, 160, 163
    real estate services category, 180
    requirements for, 160
    skilled trade services category, 180-181
    small business ads (sm biz ads) category, 181-182
    therapeutic services category, 182-183
    travel/vacation services category, 183-184
    writing/editing/translating (write/ed/tr8) services category, 184-185
    troubleshooting, 73
    unsuccessful ad example, 78

adult category (gigs section), 204.
    See also See erotic category (services section)

Advance Fee scams, 53

AIDA (Attention, Interest, Desire, Action), 85-87, 128

Altos Research website, finding home sales data, 121

animals. *See* pets category

anonymous handles, displaying in forums, 36

antispyware software, 44

antivirus software, 44

apts/housing category (housing section), 134, 279-280

arch/engineering category (jobs section), 189

art/media/design category (jobs section), 190

artists
creative services ads, writing, 172-174
event services ads, writing, 174

artists category (community section), 100-101, 256-257, 263

arts+crafts category (for sale section), 142

asterisks (*), wildcard searches, 267

Attention (AIDA), listing creation, 85-86

auto parts category (for sale section), 142

automated posting, 64

automotive services category (services section), 169-170

avoid scams & fraud link, 27

AVOIDING SCAMS & FRAUD link, jobs category (community section), 272

B

baby+kids category (for sale section), 142, 151

backgrounds (photography techniques), 82

backups for security, 44

barter category (for sale section), 141, 150

beauty services category (services section), 170-171

BEST OF page, 28

best-of-craigslist link, 28

bikes category (for sale section), 141, 150

biotech/science category (jobs section), 190

blocked listings, criteria for, 74-75

boats category (for sale section), 141

books category (for sale section), 141, 150

bootleg items, selling on craigslists, 65

browsers (web), updating, 44

browsing categories, 245-246, 249

Buckmaster, Jim, 8, 109

business category (for sale section), 141

business/mgmt category (jobs section), 190

buyers

out-of-area buyer scams, 49-52

responding to, 156-157

C

calendar, 25

career listings, writing, 208, 214

accomplishments/successes, 215

anxiety, coping with, 209

contact information, 220

craigslist guidelines, 224

marketing strategies, 216

objectives, 221

power words list, 217-220

references, 223

research, 210-211

sample resume descriptions, 216

summaries, 222

web resources, 212-213

work histories, 222

carpooling. *See* rideshare category (community section)

cars+trucks category (for sale section), 142, 152

casual encounters category (personals section), 236-237

cds/dvd/vhs category (for sale section), 142, 152

childcare category (community section), 102-103, 257

ChoiceMail One spam filtering software, 47

City-Data.com website, selling real estate, 127

classes category (community section), 93-95, 266

classifieds

listings, creating, 25

navigation column (home page), accessing from, 24

post to classifieds link, 25

searching, 25

clothes+acc category (for sale section), 142

collectibles category (for sale section), 142

community home pages

accessing via sites page, 17

community menu, city links in, 19

discussion forums, 31-33, 36

navigation column

accessing classifieds from, 24

accessing event calendar from, 25

avoid scams & fraud link, 27

best-of-craigslist link, 28

craigslist factsheet link, 27

craigslist foundation link, 30

craigslist movie & dvd link, 28

defend net neutrality link, 30

community section

activities category, 255

activity partner category, 92

artists category, 256-257, 263

childcare category, 257

classes category, 93-95, 266

events category, 93-95, 261

general category, 258

groups category, 93, 96, 259

local news category, 263

lost+found category, 98-99, 262

musicians category, 263. *See also* gigs section

pets category, 260

politics category, 264

rideshare category, 105-107, 264

searches in, 253-254

volunteers category, 107-108, 265

community menu (home page), city links in, 19

community name link, 36

computer category

for sale section, 141, 151

gigs section, 204

computer services category (services section), 171-172

confirmation notices (listings), 71

contact information in listings, 88

contacts, responding to, 156-157

controlled substances (drugs), selling on craigslist, 65

counterfeit items, selling on craigslist, 65

cover letters (job listings), responding to, 271

craigslist

development of, 8-9, 13

eBay's lawsuit against, 11

expansion of, 9-11

factsheet link, 27

help, finding, 41-42

movie & dvd link, 28

newspaper industry, effects on, 14

terms of use website, 42

yearly revenues, 11

Craigslist Foundation, 15-16, 30

creative category (gigs section), 204

creative services category (services section), 172-174

crew category (gigs section), 204

current events, 104-105

customer service category (jobs section), 190

D

data backups for security, 44

date listings page, finding event information, 25

dating (online). *See* personals section

DEA (disposable email addresses), 46, 63

defend net neutrality link, 30

deleting

listings, 156

posts, 76

descriptions

for sale ads, writing for, 148-149

HTML in, 149

Desire (AIDA), listing creation, 86

discussion forums

accessing, 31

creating, 40

customizing settings, 34

handles, 33-36

help, finding, 41-42

hidden forums, accessing, 32-33

posts (messages), 36-40

threads (messages), 36

trolls, 36

Domania website, finding home sales data, 121

domestic category (gigs section), 204

drugs (medication), selling on craigslist, 65

dvds

cds/dvd/vhs category (for sale section), 142, 152

craigslist movie & dvd link, 28

E

eBay's lawsuit against craigslist, 11

editing services, write/ed/tr8 services category (services section), 184-185

education category (jobs section), 190

electronics category (for sale section), 142

email

addresses, craigslist account creation, 20

confirmation email messages, craigslist account creation, 22

confirmation notices, 71

DEA, 46, 63
personals category (community section), 273
security, 45-46
virtual email services, 46
email me all new replies to this thread check box (preview pane), 37
Emailias virtual email service, 46
erotic services category (services section), 174, 297-299
ETC category (jobs section), 192
event category (gigs section), 204
event services category (services section), 174
events (calendar), 25
events category (community section), 93-95, 261

F

factsheet link (craigslist), 27
farm+garden category (for sale section), 142, 152
Federal Trade Commission website, 127
fees, job postings, 198
filtering spam, 44, 47
financial services category (services section), 175
FindLegalForms.com website, 115
firewalls, 43
focus (photography techniques), 82
food/bev/hospitality category (jobs section), 190
for sale section, 140, 277
ads
    deleting, 156
    descriptions, 148-149
    planning, 143-145
    previewing, 156
    responding to, 156-157
    submission guidelines, 157
    titles, 147
    writing, 153-155
arts+crafts category, 142
auto parts category, 142
baby+kids category, 142, 151
barter category, 141, 150
bikes category, 141, 150
boats category, 141
books category, 141, 150
business category, 141
cars+trucks category, 142, 152
categories of, 291-293
cds/dvd/vhs category, 142, 152
clothes+acc category, 142

collectibles category, 142
computer category, 141, 151
electronics category, 142
farm+garden category, 142, 152
free category, 141
furniture category, 141, 151
games+toys category, 142
garage sale category, 142, 152
general category, 141
household category, 142
jewelry category, 141, 151
material category, 141
motorcycles category, 142
music instr category, 142
photo+video category, 142
RVs category, 141
searches in, 293
sporting category, 141
tickets category, 141
tools category, 142
wanted category, 143
foreign languages, translating. *See* write/ed/tr8 services category (services section)
formatting listings via HTML, 73
ForSaleByOwner.com website, 115
forums
    accessing, 31
    creating, 40
    customizing settings, 34
    handles, 33-36
    help, finding, 41-42
    hidden forums, accessing, 32-33
    posts (messages), 36-40
    threads (messages), 36
    trolls, 36
fraud/scam protection, 27, 280
free category (for sale section), 141
Free Press Action Fund website, 30
friends, making. *See* strictly platonic category (personals section)
FSBO.com website, 115
furniture category (for sale section), 141, 151

G

games+toys category (for sale section), 142
garage sale category (for sale section), 142, 152
general category, 104-105
    community section, 258
    for sale section, 141
general labor category (jobs section), 190

gigs section, 203-204, 270. *See also* musicians category (community section)
Global Creative Leadership Summit, 15
Gmail email service, 47
government category (jobs section), 190
groups section, 93, 96, 259
guidelines (submissions)
    for sale ads, 157
    job postings, 197

H

handles
    accounts, adding to, 33
    anonymous handles, displaying in forums, 36
    rules for, 35
    unregistered handles, displaying in forums, 36
help, finding, 41-42
hidden forums, accessing, 32-33
home page
    accessing via site page, 17
    community menu, city links in, 19
    discussion forums, 31-33, 36
    navigation column
        accessing classifieds from, 24-25
        avoid scams & fraud link, 27
        best-of-craigslist link, 28
        craigslist factsheet link, 27
        craigslist foundation link, 30
        craigslist movie & dvd link, 28
        defend net neutrality link, 30
household category (for sale section), 142
household services category (services section), 176-177
housing section
    apts/housing category, 134, 279-280
    categories of, 278
    housing swap category, 284
    housing wanted category, 283
    office/commercial category, 135-137, 287
    parking/storage category, 137, 287
    real estate for sale category, 114-133, 289-291
    rooms/shared category, 134, 281
    searches, 278
    security tips, 280
    sublets/temporary category, 134, 282-283
    vacation rentals category, 134, 285-286

HTML (Hypertext Markup Language)
ad descriptions, 149
listings, formatting, 73
message posts, adding pictures to, 40
human resources category (jobs section), 190
humor in listings, 98

I

illegal activities, posting on craigslist, 65
images
listings
adding to, 63, 67-69, 81-82, 88, 98
hosting for, 73
message posts, adding to, 40
photography techniques, 82-84
real estate listings, 133
Interest (AIDA), listing creation, 86
Internet
defend net neutrality link, 30
security
antispyware software, 44
antivirus software, 44
backups, 44
browser updates, 44
email, 45-46
firewalls, 43
personals section, 55-57
safe transactions, 54
scams, 49-53
sharing personal information, 48
spam filtering, 44, 47
wireless networks, 44
Internet engineers category (jobs section), 190

J

jewelry category (for sale section), 141, 151
job listings, writing, 65, 208, 214
accomplishments/successes, 215
anxiety, coping with, 209
contact information, 220
craigslist guidelines, 224
marketing strategies, 216
objectives, 221
power words list, 217-220
references, 223
research, 210-211
sample resume descriptions, 216
summaries, 222
web resources, 212-213
work histories, 222

jobs section, 267
accounting+finance category, 189
admin/office category, 189
ads
responding to, 205-206
writing, 193-198, 201
arch/engineering category, 189
art/media/design category, 190
AVOIDING SCAMS & FRAUD link, 272
biotech/science category, 190
business/mgmt category, 190
categories in, 268-269
customer service category, 190
education category, 190
ETC category, 192
food/bev/hospitality category, 190
general labor category, 190
government category, 190
human resources category, 190
internet engineers category, 190
legal/paralegal category, 190
manufacturing category, 190
marketing/pr/ad category, 191
medical/health category, 191
nonprofit sector category, 191
real estate category, 191
responding to listings, 271
resumes section, 278
retail/wholesale category, 191
sales/biz dev category, 191
salon/spa/fitness category, 191
search tips, 267-268
security category, 191
skilled trade/craft category, 191
software/qa/dba category, 191
systems/network category, 191
technical support category, 191
transport category, 192
tv/film/video category, 192
web resources, 188
web/info design category, 192
writing/editing category, 192

K - L

keywords, writing ads for jobs section, 195
kids. *See* childcare category

labor category (gigs section), 204
labor/move services category (services section), 177
lagging links, blocked/prohibited listings, 75
languages, translating. *See* write/ed/tr8 services category (services section)
legal services category (services section), 178

legal/paralegal category (jobs section), 190
lessons category (services section), 100, 179-180
lighting (photography techniques), 84
links
listings, adding to, 73
message posts, displaying in, 40
listings
automated listings, 64
blocked listings, criteria for, 74-75
browsing, 245-246, 249
community section
activities category, 255
artists category, 256-257, 263
childcare category, 257
classes category, 93-95, 266
events category, 261
for sale category, 277, 291-293
general category, 258
gigs category, 267, 270
groups category, 259
housing category, 277-281, 285-291
housing swap category, 284
housing wanted category, 283
jobs category, 267-269, 272, 278
local news category, 263
lost+found category, 262
musicians category, 263
personals category, 272-276
pets category, 260
politics category, 264
responding to listings, 271
resumes/job wanted category, 299
rideshare category, 264
searches in, 253-254
services section, 277, 295-299
sublets & temporary category, 282-283
viewing recent listings, 254
volunteers category, 265
confirmation notices, 71
creating, 25, 65, 70, 78-80, 85-88
DEA, 63
deleting, 76, 156
editing, 76
flagging links, 75
for sale section, 143-155
gigs section, writing for, 203-204
HTML formatting in, 73
humor in, 98
jobs section, 65, 193-198, 201, 205-206
layout of, 62-63
links, adding to, 73
office/commercial section (housing section), 136-137

personals section, writing for, 230-237, 241-242

pictures, 98
  adding to, 63, 67-69, 81-82, 88
  hosting, 73
  previewing, 70, 156
  prohibited items, 65, 74-75
  real estate for sale category (housing section), 117-133
  reposting, 88
  responding to, 65, 156-157, 251-252
resumes, writing, 208-223
rules for, 64
services section
  automotive services category, 169-170
  beauty services category, 170-171
  computer services category, 171-172
  creative services category, 172-174
  erotic services category, 174
  event services category, 174
  financial services category, 175
  household services category, 176-177
  labor/move services category, 177
  legal services category, 178
  lessons category, 179-180
  marketing strategies, 164-168
  offering free content, 168
  phone verification, 160, 163
  real estate services category, 180
  requirements for, 160
  skilled trade services category, 180-181
  small business ads (sm biz ads) category, 181-182
  therapeutic services category, 182-183
  travel/vacation services category, 183-184
  writing/editing/translating (write/ed/tr8) services category, 184-185
troubleshooting, 73
unsuccessful ad example, 78
local news category (community section), 104-105, 263
lost+found category (community section), 98-99, 262
LTR (long-term relationships), 237

M

MailWasher Pro spam filtering software, 47
manufacturing category (jobs section), 190

marketing
  activity partner section, 92
  artists category, 100-101
  childcare category, 102-103
  classes category, 93-95, 266
  events section, 93, 95
  groups section, 93, 96
  job listings, writing, 216
  lessons category (services section), 100
  musicians category, 100-101
  real estate listings, 127
  research, 79-80, 85
  services section strategies, 164-168
  strategies for, 96-98
marketing/pr/ad category (jobs section), 191
material category (for sale section), 141
medical/health category (jobs section), 191
medication, selling on craigslist, 65
message posts, 36
  editing responses to, 37
  links, displaying, 40
  notifying responses to, 37
  pictures, adding to, 40
  previewing responses to, 37
  replying to, 37-39
message threads, 36
message forums, 37
Mindjet MindManager website, researching job listings, 210
misc romance category (personals section), 236
missed connections category (personals section), 239
missing items. *See* lost+found section
MLM (multilevel marketing), 65
motorcycles category (for sale section), 142
movies
  24 Hours on craigslist, 28
  cds/dvd/vhs category (for sale section), 142, 152
  craigslist movie & dvd link, 28
multiple pictures (photography techniques), 84
music instr category (for sale section), 142
musicians category (community section), 100-101, 172-174, 263. *See also* gigs section

N

navigation column (home page)
  avoid scams & fraud link, 27
  best-of-craigslist link, 28
  classifieds, accessing from, 24
  craigslist factsheet link, 27
  craigslist foundation link, 30
  craigslist movie & dvd link, 28
  defend net neutrality link, 30
  event calendar, accessing from, 25
net neutrality, 30
networking
  activity partner category, 92
  artists category, 100-101
  childcare category, 102-103
  classes category, 93-95, 266
  events category, 93, 95
  groups category, 93, 96
  lessons category (services section), 100
  musicians category, 100-101
  rideshare category, 105-107
  strategies for, 96-98
  volunteers category (community section), 107-108
new password page (Account Log In page), 22
NewAssignment.net website, 15
Newmark, Craig
  biography of, 12
  blog of, 14
  craigslist development, 8, 11-13
  Craigslist Foundation, 15-16
  email address of, 14
  Global Creative Leadership Summit, 15
  NewAssignment.net website, 15
  One Million Voices website, 15
  social activism, 15-16
news
  general category, 104-105
  local news category, 104-105
  politics category, 104-105
newspaper industry, craigslist's effects on, 14
Nigerian 4-1-9 scams, 53
notifying responses to message posts, 37
nonprofit sector category (jobs section), 191

O - P

office/commercial category (housing section), 135-137, 287
One Million Voices website, 15

online relationships. *See* personals section

out-of-area buyer scams, 49-52

overpayment scams, 53

Owners.com website, 115

parental control, personals category (community section), 273

parenting. *See* childcare category

parking & storage category (housing category, community section), 287

parking/storage category (housing section), 137

passwords, craigslist account creation, 22

payments, overpayment scams, 53

personal information in listings, 48, 88

personals section, 225-226, 272-274
  abbreviations/acronyms/slang list, 227-230
  ads, writing, 230-237, 241-242
  casual encounters category, 236-237
  categories of, 275-276
  misc romance category, 236
  missed connections category, 239
  parental control in, 273
  PERSONAL SAFETY TIPS link, 273
  PICS labeling system, 273
  rants and raves category, 240
  security, 55-57
  strictly platonic category, 238

pets category (community section), 108-111, 260

pets, selling on craigslist, 65

phone verification, service section ads, 160, 163

photo+video category (for sale section), 142

PICS (Platform for Internet Content Selection) content-labeling system, 273

pictures
  listings
    adding to, 63, 67-69, 81-82, 88, 98
    hosting for, 73
  message posts, adding to, 40
  photography techniques
    backgrounds, 82
    focus, 82
    lighting, 84
    multiple pictures, 84
    zoom, 82
  real estate listings, 133

politics category (community section), 104-105, 264

post to classifieds link, 25

posting agents, 64

Posting Description field, 155

Posting Title field, 147

postings. *See* ads; listings

posts (messages), 36
  editing responses to, 37
  humor in, 98
  links, displaying in, 40
  notifying responses to, 37
  pictures in, 40, 98
  previewing responses to, 37
  replying to, 37-39

preview pane, email me all new replies to this thread check box, 37

previewing
  listings, 70, 156
  responses to message posts, 37

prohibited items, selling on craigslist, 65, 74-75

promotions
  activity partner section, 92
  artists category, 100-101
  childcare category, 102-103
  classes category, 93-95, 266
  events section, 93-95
  groups section, 93, 96
  lessons category (services section), 100
  musicians category, 100-101
  real estate listings, 127
  strategies for, 96-98
  volunteers category (community section), 107-108

Q - R

rants and raves category (personals section), 240

real estate category (jobs section), 191

real estate for sale category (housing section), 114, 289-291
  listing creation
    AIDA, 128
    common industry terms, 122-126
    contact information, 132
    determining goals, 121
    financial terms, 130
    home features checklist, 117-120
    market research, 120-121
    marketing strategies, 127
    pictures, 133
    writing copy, 128-131
    writing titles, 132-133
  real estate agents and, 116

real estate services category (services section), 180

Realtor.com website, 127

RealtyTimes.com website, 127

relationships (online). *See* personals section

reply to this post link, 37

reposting listings, 88

research (market), listing creation, 79, 85

resumes section, 278, 299-300
  listings, responding to, 271
  listings, writing, 208, 214-217
    accomplishments/successes, 215
    contact information, 220
    coping with anxiety, 209
    craigslist guidelines, 224
    marketing strategies, 216
    objectives, 221
    power words list, 217-220
    references, 223
    research, 210-211
    sample resume descriptions, 216
    summaries, 222
    web resources, 212-213
    work histories, 222

retail/wholesale category (jobs section), 191

rideshare category (community section), 105-107, 264

rooms & shares category (housing category, community section), 281

rooms/shared section (housing section), 134

RVs category (for sale section), 141

S

sales/biz dev category (jobs section), 191

salon/spa/fitness category (jobs section), 191

scam/fraud protection, housing category (community section), 280

scams
  Advance Fee scams, 53
  avoid scams & fraud link, 27
  Nigerian 4-1-9 scams, 53
  out-of-area buyer scams, 49-52
  overpayment scams, 53

searches
  classifieds, 25
  community section, 253-254
  events, 261
  for sale category (community section), 293
  help, finding, 41-42

housing category (community section), 278

jobs category (community section), 267

musicians, 263

rideshares, 265

sublets & temporry category (housing category, community section), 283

wildcard searches (*), 267

security
antispyware software, 44
antivirus software, 44
avoid scams & fraud link, 27
backups, 44
browser updates, 44
email, 45-46
firewalls, 43
housing category (community section), 280
personal information, sharing, 48
personals section, 55-57
safe transactions, rules for, 54
scams, 49-53
spam, filtering, 44, 47
wireless networks, 44

security category (jobs section), 191

seminars, promoting. *See* events section

services section, 277
automotive services category, 169-170
beauty services category, 170-171
categories of, 295-296
computer services category, 171-172
creative services category, 172-174
erotic services category, 174, 297-299
event services category, 174
financial services category, 175
household services category, 176-177
labor/move services category, 177
legal services category, 178
lessons category, 100, 179-180
listings, writing, 160, 163-168
real estate services category, 180
skilled trade services category, 180-181
small business ads (sm biz ads) category, 181-182
therapeutic services category, 182-183
travel/vacation services category, 183-184
writing/editing/translating (write/ed/tr8) services category, 184-185

ShieldedMail virtual email service, 46

sites page, accessing, 17-19

skilled trade services category (services section), 180-181

skilled trade/craft category (jobs section), 191

Skype website, selling real estate, 132

slang (personals section), 227-230

small business ads (sm biz ads) category (services section), 181-182

social activism. *See* volunteers category (community section)

Socrates.com website, real estate sales forms, 115

software/qa/dba category (jobs section), 191

spam, filtering, 44, 47

specifics, adding in listings, 80

sporting category (for sale section), 141

strictly platonic category (personals section), 238

sublets & temporary category (housing category, community section), 282-283

sublets/temporary section (housing section), 134

submission guidelines
for sale ads, 157
job postings, 197

Submit New Handle option (handle forum screen, 33

swapping houses. *See* housing swap category (housing category, community section)

systems/network category (jobs section), 191

T

talent category (gigs section), 204

technical support category (jobs section), 191

terms of use website, 22, 42

therapeutic services category (services section), 182-183

threads (messages), 36

tickets category (for sale section), 141

titles, writing for sale ads, 147

tools category (for sale section), 142

transaction safety, rules for, 54

translating services, write/ed/tr8 services category (services section), 184-185

transport category (jobs section), 192

travel/vacation services category (services section), 183-184

trolls (forums), 36

troubleshooting listing creation process, 73

tv/film/video category (jobs section), 192

U - V

unregistered handles, displaying in forums, 36

unsuccessful listings, example of, 78

updating browsers, 44

USP (unique selling propositions), service section ad marketing strategies, 165

vacation rentals section (housing section), 134, 285-286

vacations, travel/vacation services category (services section), 183-184

virtual email services, 46

volunteers category (community section), 15-16, 107-108, 265

vqME AntiSpam spam filtering software, 47

W

wanted category (for sale section), 143

weapons, selling on craigslist, 65

web/info design category (jobs section), 192

wildcard searches (*), 267

wireless network security, 44

writing category (gigs section), 204

writing/editing category (jobs section), 192

writing/editing/translating (write/ed/tr8) services category (services section), 184-185

X - Y - Z

Yahoo Pipes website, precise web searches, 268

Yahoo! Mail Plus email service, 47

Zillow.com website, 121

ZoEmail email service, 47

zoom (photography techniques), 82

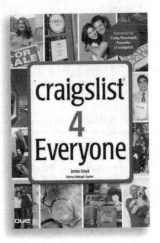

FREE Online Edition

Your purchase of **craigslist® 4 Everyone** includes access to a free online edition for 45 days through the Safari Books Online subscription service. Nearly every Que book is available online through Safari Books Online, along with more than 5,000 other technical books and videos from publishers such as Addison-Wesley Professional, Cisco Press, Exam Cram, IBM Press, O'Reilly, Prentice Hall, and Sams.

SAFARI BOOKS ONLINE allows you to search for a specific answer, cut and paste code, download chapters, and stay current with emerging technologies.

Activate your FREE Online Edition at www.informit.com/safarifree

> **STEP 1:** Enter the coupon code: QSR2-TTKP-CTZY-9EPW-WS1F.

> **STEP 2:** New Safari users, complete the brief registration form. Safari subscribers, just log in.

If you have difficulty registering on Safari or accessing the online edition, please e-mail customer-service@safaribooksonline.com

Safari.
Books Online

Addison Wesley | Adobe Press | ALPHA | Cisco Press | FT Press | IBM Press. | lynda.com | Microsoft Press | New Riders

O'REILLY | Peachpit Press | PRENTICE HALL | que | SAMS | sas | WILEY